Practical Composition

PRACTICAL COMPOSITION

Exercises for the English Classroom from Working Instructors

Edited by RUSSELL BRICKEY,
LAURA L. BEADLING *and*
EVELYN MARTENS

McFarland & Company, Inc., Publishers
Jefferson, North Carolina

LIBRARY OF CONGRESS CATALOGUING-IN-PUBLICATION DATA

Practical composition : exercises for the English classroom from
working instructors / edited by Russell Brickey, Laura L. Beadling
and Evelyn Martens.
p.   cm.
Includes index.

ISBN 978-0-7864-7696-1 (softcover : acid free paper) ∞
ISBN 978-1-4766-1547-9 (ebook)

1. English language—Composition and exercises—Study and teaching
(Secondary)   2. English language—Rhetoric—Study and teaching (Higher)
I. Brickey, Russell.   II. Beadling, Laura L., 1973–   III. Martens,
Evelyn, 1959–

LB1631.P667 2014   428.0071'2—dc23   2014020468

BRITISH LIBRARY CATALOGUING DATA ARE AVAILABLE

On the cover: open book with hand (buchachon/iStock/Thinkstock)

Printed in the United States of America

McFarland & Company, Inc., Publishers
Box 611, Jefferson, North Carolina 28640
www.mcfarlandpub.com

Table of Contents

Bibliography and Citation Style

Idea and Thesis Generation

Language Usage and Grammar

Organization

Visual Rhetoric

Preface

Practical Composition is a compilation of writing exercises and in-class activities collected from professors, graduate students, and lecturers from colleges and universities across the United States. We hope that these hands-on exercises will be of use to instructors from high school writing teachers and first-time teaching assistants to experienced writing professors looking for ways to enhance their courses. *Practical Composition*'s step-by-step instructions are meant to guide teachers through class discussions and exercises on a variety of topics ranging from invention, argumentation, formatting, thesis development, and organization, to rhetorical situation, visual rhetoric, peer review, and revision. This book is not a "reader," which there are plenty of already, or a "guidebook" designed as a reference resource for grammar and citation; rather, *Practical Composition* is intended as a collection of individual lessons, readings, assignment sheets, discussions, and worksheets tested by instructors in their own classrooms. Instructors can either follow the procedures as they appear on the page, or can take inspiration and revamp exercises to fit their own pedagogical objectives.

While most entries are designed to be delivered as stand-alone exercises and usually fill a standard 50-minute class, instructors will find that some exercises can be expanded to cover multiple class periods and even provide homework assignments. In some instances, participating authors have provided the broader framework for their exercises, and we hope that these might offer ideas for structuring larger segments of class-time or even suggest overall approaches to syllabus design. One strength of *Practical Composition* is that it offers readers a wide sampling of ideas from which to pick and choose. We hope instructors will be able to use what they find to complement what they already do well, and we hope the collection will also offer suggestions for new pedagogies.

Initially, *Practical Composition* was conceived of as an aid to graduate teaching assistants, particularly those in their first few years as instructors. For anyone who first stepped into the freshman composition classroom (possibly only a couple of months away from being an undergraduate), the onus of producing a worthwhile, workable plan for each and every class day was a nerve-wracking experience. *Practical Composition* can help new instructors expand their repertoire by offering accessible instructions in plain English accompanied by worksheets, assignment sheets, and suggested readings. We hope that such instructors—whether in their first year as a high school teacher, a graduate instructor, or even a professor on the tenure track—will find something to ease the strain of preparation.

As work on the project progressed, it become apparent that many of our experienced colleagues were also enthusiastic about the idea of a collection of classroom-tested composition exercises. In fact, we editors have already used ideas, exercises, and whole assignments from the collection as it was being compiled. It is worth noting that the teaching of English, particularly if it is done well, is a learning process for the student and for the teacher. In this regard, *Practical Composition* offers instructors a chance to see what other English professionals are doing in the classroom and constitutes a dialogue of sorts among a variety of people who share the important common interest of teaching.

How to Use This Book

Practical Composition is divided into ten sections:

- Argumentation, Research and Analysis
- Audience and Mode
- Bibliography and Citation Style
- Idea and Thesis Generation
- Language Usage and Grammar
- Organization
- Peer Review
- Revision
- Writing Process and Paraphrase
- Visual Rhetoric

Designating and classifying the entries in *Practical Composition* was not as easy as it would at first appear. Very often, the creativity of our contributors meant that an exercise, assignment, or discussion covered multiple writing issues and techniques. Thus, the editors have tried to indicate where entries can be applied to more than one learning objective as indicated by its placement within the table of contents.

Whenever possible, to make finding what you are looking for easier, exercises are accompanied by

- An **Abstract**,
- An approximate time **Duration** meant to help instructors plan class time accordingly,
- A description of **Materials** and **Preparation** needed (when applicable),
- A breakdown of the classroom **Procedure** laid out step-by-step,
- A **Rationale,** which describes the learning outcomes behind the exercise,
- And a section detailing any **Potential Problems** that an instructor might encounter in the classroom.
- Additional **Readings, Assignment Sheets** and **Exercise Worksheets**. Instructors can adapt these readings, assignments and worksheets to their classroom needs. In some instances, contributors have provided us with essay style **Discussions** of their materials.

Entries are meant to be read quickly so that instructors can scan each listing and decide on-the-spot if what they are reading is pertinent to their class. And since student learning is often predicated upon matching learning styles with particular kinds of classroom experiences, the editors have attempted to indicate where entries cover multiple subjects not necessarily associated with its designation within the table of contents—an exercise on revision might also teach citation style or a peer review may also teach aspects of visual rhetoric or organization; whenever possible, we have pointed out these nuances. Finally, entries are also meant to be used as sources of inspiration: the editors encourage instructors to take lesson plans, prompts, ideas, bits and pieces, chunks, and snippets from exercises and revamp, recombine, and reinvent what they read on these pages.

Teaching writing is of course both challenging and rewarding in a variety of ways. Deciding on a pedagogical approach can be challenging, especially if an instructor is teaching more than one section of writing. This book seeks to reenergize writing teachers by reinvigorating actual classroom practice. While we can often get stuck behind our own classroom and office doors, this book is an attempt to bring our pedagogy into a communal space where a range of instructors can learn from and inspire one another.

Argumentation, Research and Analysis

Generating "Because" Statements
Using the Conjunction to Reason Through Arguments

• Becky Adnot-Haynes •

Abstract: Students learn to use the subordinating conjunction "because" to reason through an argumentative statement.

Duration: 30 minutes

Preparation: I often use this activity after we have discussed persuasive writing, or after I have introduced an argument essay assignment. It dovetails nicely with a discussion of reasoning and evidence and how these concepts are used in persuasive writing. This exercise accompanies any form of argument essay or persuasive writing.

Procedure: First, I discuss with the class why it is important to include "because" statements in their writing. (See handout / script below.)

Second, I review example "because" statements (likewise, see below).

Third, I ask students to come up with their own "because" statements for the examples below. (Note: this exercise works with the given examples, but it is even more effective if the instructor develops his or her own sample topics, since they will be more relevant and familiar to his or her students and the subject matter they are studying.)

Rationale: The main goal of this exercise is to emphasize to students the importance of supporting their claims with reasoning and evidence—too often I see students make claims without explaining or supporting them.

Potential Problems: It is important to discuss with students the difference between evidence and reasoning—that is, just because they think that they've provided a valid reason for an argument doesn't mean they've actually done so. However, I find that this exercise is a useful springboard into that discussion.

WORKSHEET

Coming up with a "because" statement is a vital step in finding reasoning for your argument, an important part of developing a persuasive essay.

Example

Restaurants should have to post calorie counts on their menus because...

... If people are more aware of what they're eating, they'll make healthier choices.

... It will encourage customers to learn more about nutrition in general, not just when they visit restaurants.

... It's unethical to imply that some menu items (such as salads) are healthy when really they aren't.

... Nutritional facts are posted on items in grocery stores, so why shouldn't this information also be available for restaurant foods?

On Your Own

Come up with two or more "because" statements for the following arguments.

1. Playing violent video games has/does not have a harmful influence on teenage boys.
2. Looking at fashion magazines does/does not have a harmful influence on teenage girls.
3. The school year for grades one through 12 should/should not be lengthened to 11 months.

Finding That Weak Link
Supporting an Argument Exercise
• Laura L. Beadling •

Abstract: Designed to be executed with an argumentative paper, students highlight their own thesis statements; partners then comment on what they expect from the paper, what they see as the author's position, and highlight claims and evidence. Finally, partners record their reaction to the paper.

This exercise can also be used as a form of peer review.

Duration: 50 minutes

Preparation: Computer classroom (note: can also be done using various colored highlighters)

Procedure: I ask the students to bring up their argument paper on their computer. Then I ask them to bold their thesis statement.

Next, I have students stand up and switch seats. When everyone is at a computer with someone else's paper in front of them, I ask them to first read the introduction and thesis statement carefully.

Using the comment feature on Word, I ask them to write a comment to the writer explaining what they expect the paper to cover, what position they see the author taking, what the introduction and thesis set readers up to expect in terms of the argument, and any other relevant thesis information for the specific paper being worked on (e.g., the advertising analysis paper they complete requires that the thesis statement indicate which visual elements of the ad will be analyzed, so I ask them to comment on that specific issue in this part of the exercise).

I also ask that each reader identify him or herself as sympathetic to, hostile toward, or uninformed about the writer's argument.

After everyone has commented on the thesis, I ask them to read the paper slowly and carefully. While reading, I ask them to use Word to highlight in yellow all the author's claims and highlight in green all the supporting evidence and examples the author offers for those claims.

Finally, I ask each commenter to write a note to the author at the bottom of the document giving their reaction to the paper. I ask them to specifically write about their position in relation to the argument being made. If students identified as sympathetic to the author's argument, I ask them to write about what additional reasons or evidence might they suggest the author include. If readers identified as hostile to the argument being made, I ask them to identify specific places in the paper where the reader had objections to the argument or evidence. I also ask that hostile readers articulate their counter-claims or objections to the argument as a whole so that the author of the paper can identify opposition that he or she should address in the paper to make it more convincing to hostile readers. Finally, if the commenters identified as uniformed about the argument, I ask them to specifically address where the author needed to include more explanation, history, or background information so that an uninformed reader can follow the argument being made.

If I have enough time, I will sometimes ask students to switch computers one more time. Then, the new commenter can offer additional thoughts on the thesis, highlight any claims or evidence the first commentator might have missed, and write another reaction to the argument.

I finish the class by having the students return to their own computer and look over the highlighting and comments. One of the things that should result from this exercise is that students should have an obvious visual guide to where their paper has problems. If there is a lot of yellow and little green, they might need to go back and include more evidence and perhaps break up the claims into more paragraphs. If there isn't very much yellow, they need to include more reasons and claims concerning their argument. If there is more than one or two bits of yellow per paragraph, they might need to revise the paragraph structure. Either in class if we have time or as homework, I ask them to make a plan for revision by writing notes to themselves concerning where they can see their argument lacks enough evidence, revising the thesis, or other changes or issues raised by the readers.

Rationale: This exercise offers both an easy-to-see visual representation of the paper's claims as well as a chance to hear from sympathetic, hostile, and uninformed readers about specific parts of their paper that are convincing and those that need more work in order to be persuasive.

—⁂—

Meat Eaters' Manifesto
Research and Argue the Politics of Consumption
• Russell Brickey •

Abstract: Pretending that a vastly superior alien race has conquered the Earth, students must justify the practice of killing and eating animals, first by writing their initial beliefs about meat consumption and then by bolstering (or abandoning) those beliefs through research.

Duration: One ten-minute explanation of assignment followed by up to three 50-minute class periods

- First class: Explanation of assignment (approximately 10 minutes)
- Second class: The "debate" section of the exercise
- Third class: In-class computer research day
- Optional fourth class: Student presentation of research (can be assigned as written homework)

Preparation: Instructors should probably be prepared to discuss the following:

- Basic nutrition, particularly the sources of protein and the role of protein in the human body
- Factory farming
- Basic economy of meat consumption
- Ecological factors of factory farming
- The politics of People for the Ethical Treatment of Animals (P.E.T.A.)
- Why fruits and vegetables do not feel pain (these are essentially seeds with no central nervous system)

Editor's Note: Many of these subjects are covered on the Internet; below are a sampling of websites (key words provided):

("online library articles about vegetarian and vegan diets dr. furman")
   http://www.drfuhrman.com/library/article5.aspx
("UN urges global move to meat and dairy-free diet the guardian")
   http://www.theguardian.com/environment/2010/jun/02/un-report-meat-free-diet
("Is going vegetarian really better for you? The pros and cons of meatless eating miller NY daily news")
   http://www.nydailynews.com/life-style/health/vegetarian-diet-better-article-1.1253
   309#ixzz2ff6P4IeX
("How to get protein on a vegetarian diet about.com")
   http://vegetarian.about.com/od/healthnutrition/tp/protein.htm
("How healthy are vegan diets? david katz")
   http://www.oprah.com/health/the-benefits-and-dangers-of-a-vegan-diet-advice-from-dr-katz
("Vegetarianism and the environment: the need for sustainable diets umurj")
   http://umurj.org/feature-articles/vegetarianism-and-the-environment/

Materials: Optional: overhead projection; a computer classroom for student research.

Procedure: I usually begin argumentative units with this exercise as a method of illustrating what we think we know versus the facts, and the problem of examining our beliefs. Most students, I have found, believe that meat is a necessary component of our diet, that not eating meat will result in a "protein deficiency," and that the practice of factory farming is basically humane. Instructors should be prepared for some vigorous debate from students.

First Class Period—Assigning the Argument

At the end of the first class period, I give students the following prompt:

One day all the radios, TVs, iPhones, iPods, and computers everywhere in the world broadcast the same message: *"We are a vastly superior race from the planet Vega. We have taken over the Earth and are outlawing any activity that is cruel or violent toward any sentient being."*

I explain that the Vegans land at the U.N., that their technology is so vastly superior to ours that resistance is futile, and that there is no place on the planet that is not under their control. In addition, the Vegans are hyper intelligent and eminently logical, so any appeals to emotion are likely to be met with indifference.

Upshot: Whatever petitions we take before the Vegans must be based on fact and reason.

The Vegans peacefully outlaw a great many horrible practices that (almost) all of us agree we could live without: murder, war, robbery, drug cartels, genocide, etc.

- *Note:* Students will sometimes get a bit too literal here and ask derailing questions such as "How can they outlaw war without shooting laser beams at our tanks?" or "How could they possibly watch every criminal everywhere in the world?" and the like.
- I remind students that, firstly, this is an academic exercise and not a science fiction movie (so don't get too caught up in the particulars of the scenario), and/or, secondly, that the Vegans are so advanced that they can simply stop the terrorists and criminals with benevolent all-seeing super robots.

I then explain that, in addition to the things we all wish would go away, the Vegans also banish the killing of animals simply to provide sustenance—such a practice is cruel and violent to a sentient living being. Cows and chickens, while they may never run for president or cure cancer, do feel fear and pain; killing them will virtually always cause fear and pain and it is necessarily violent. Therefore, killing animals is outlawed. Likewise, the generally cruel practices of factory farming are also outlawed.

Upshot: Humans can no longer kill animals simply to eat them. The practices of meat consumption as we know them are over.

"Obviously," I tell the students, "a lot of people are upset over this development."

- *Note:* Students are generally curious about the scenario up to this point, but the sudden plot-twist can mute their enthusiasm—they intuit what's coming.

Prompt: Now, having learned about their magnificent reasoning and rhetorical skills, the Meat Industry Council has asked the students to argue for the right of humans to consume meat.

Their task, I tell students, is to put together a fact-based manifesto or petition to take before the Vegan High Council that factually and logically argues a basic human right: the right to eat meat.

Students are to come back in the next class period with reasons why meat consumption is necessary to humanity.

They are *not* to do research for this first class period, but simply to brainstorm ideas.

Second Class Period—The Debate

Almost without variation, student responses fall along these lines:

1. We *have* to eat meat because our body needs the protein (almost always the first out of the gate).

2. There are so many cows and chickens that, if we didn't kill them, they would take over the planet (almost always the second out of the gate).

3. Farmers are good people and deserve to make a living (particularly if you are teaching in an agricultural section of the country).

4. Meat consumption is a tradition (or, sometimes, an aspect of religion).

5. Meat is so "tasty" humans will go "insane" if they don't eat meat.

6. Since animals are not as intelligent as humans, we can do anything we want to them.

7. What are we going to do with the lions and tigers and bears (oh my)? Are they not allowed to eat meat also?

8. How do we know that fruits and vegetables don't feel fear and pain?

The Vegans, I respond, are almost certain to respond to reasons 2 through 5 with the same answer: *"Simply being inconvenient to humans is not a sufficient reason to kill something. In other words, just because it is good for you does not mean it is right or good for the world."*

2. Farm animals may, in fact, thunder across the landscape, but since they have a right to live on the planet just as humans do, you cannot kill a sentient animal simply because you don't want it in your backyard; besides, humans bred these animals in vast numbers the first place.

3. Farmers may be good people, but again, just because something is good for humans does not mean we can circumvent the laws against cruelty and violence toward a sentient being; animals have rights too in this new Vegan world.

4. Tradition is fine, but once again, that alone does not mean that cruelty and violence is justified; humans cannot be cruel and violent simply because they've always been cruel and violent.

5. Ditto the above: "tasty" is not solid logical reasoning.

The point is that students usually conflate their own personal interests (in this case, the interests of the species) with a basic *right* or *need*. I also ask students what other things have humans always done that we could do without (rape, torture, murder, etc.)—these are all "traditions" in the loosest sense of the word; does that alone make them right?

The weakness of reason 6 should automatically be obvious: *"Who says that superior intelligence means humans can do whatever they want to less-intelligent animals?"*

- I remind students that they are speaking to vastly advanced super-beings with truly superior intelligences and technologies—are we sure we want to argue that differences in intelligence merits an anything-goes-mentality on the part of the superior-being?

Reason 7 is equally obvious: *"This debate is about the role of humans in the world, not carnivorous animals. No one said anything about them."*

- I point out to students that this is a typical Strawman argument—arguing something that the original debater did not posit.
- I also pose a rhetorical question to students: "The challenge assumes that we are the

same kind of being as a tiger, but in what ways are we different?" (Hint: we do not really live in "nature," as would a predator [even in a zoo], and we have a broader diet than a tiger or lion would and are thus not bound to meat consumption.)

And finally, reason 8: I ask students, "Do we really think an apple feels pain when we eat it?" (Hint: If students insist "we don't know if an apple feels pain," I will ask the class, "What does an organism need to feel pain on this planet?" Obviously, this is a central nervous system.)

Very occasionally, a student has an original idea about why humans should eat meat (one student actually and triumphantly suggested that "Chickens would eat humans if they could!"), but almost always student reasoning falls along the eight lines of reasoning above.

After this original foray into the subject, I tell students they have "discovered" only one *need* that any reasonable being would have to acknowledge: Reason #1, the necessity of protein in the human diet.

Now, the task is to come back to the Vegan High Council with the *facts* concerning protein consumption.

I usually end the class with a discussion about the differences between kinds of web pages (government and academic versus blogs and industry ".org" sites).

Also, this is a good moment to introduce the concepts of ethos, pathos and logos, and/or syllogisms and enthymemes.

Third Class Period—Computer Classroom Research

In the second class I have students research the dietary necessities of humans. The main question is *Is meat the only way that humans can get protein in their diets?*

I tell students that this is a great opportunity to decide whether or not a source is objective or has an agenda.

- Is the Meat Industry Council really an objective source?
- For that matter, is P.E.T.A.? (note: students will find all sorts of misinformation on P.E.T.A.—instructors may need to arbitrate what students find on the subject).

I usually reiterate that students must be careful about their sources, and I point out that we are often too ready to believe web pages that tell us what we want to hear.

- *Upshot:* There are multiple sources of protein for the human body, humans (Americans in particular) actually consume unhealthy amounts of protein and meat in general, and, in any event, there are many sources of protein in legumes and vegetable sources.

I usually assign a short writing assignment associated with the manifesto which can be done during class time.

Optional Fourth Class Period—The Results

Finally, I spend part or all of a fourth class period discussing what students found, looking at and evaluating the web pages, articles, etc., and discussing the problems of confronting our strongly held beliefs.

I do ask students if there is a "compromise" that can be made, namely, could we wait for animals to die naturally and then consume them? This is often met with the usual objections ("That would take too long," "The cost of meat would go way up," "You'd have to be there just at the right time or the animal would rot," or "It would not taste as good"). I grant students all these things, yet, I suggest, wouldn't this be better than simply abandoning meat altogether? Nevertheless, this is a great moment to introduce compromise and concession in an argument.

Instructors do have the option of turning this into a group writing project and having students actually construct "Manifestos."

Potential Problems: This exercise does have the potential to be a minefield and a humorous approach is the best.

Be prepared for students to get somewhat hostile to the argument; some students will actually get angry (people like to eat meat). Instructors can mitigate negative student responses by reminding students that this is only an academic exercise (not to mention a ridiculous imaginary scenario) and that students are not being proselytized to—they need not actually switch to a vegetarian lifestyle, simply examine their beliefs.

Likewise, instructors will need to debate with entire classrooms; on the occasion when I have had vegetarians in the classroom, they are usually silent in a classroom of carnivorous classmates.

Another problem is that, given the constraints of the basic argument, students are backed into a corner and find it difficult to justify something most of them assume is a natural practice.

Students will sometimes cling to fairly dubious and biased Web sources—anti–P.E.T.A. blogs, industry web pages, or pseudo-medical sites that sell dietary supplements; these will often make claims about the "dangers" of vegetarian lifestyles, which warrant further examination.

—ɯ—

Analyzing Creative Sources
Moving from Emotional Response to Critical Analysis
• Rita D. Costello *and* William Lusk Coppage •

Abstract: Students learn the process of close reading by identifying and analyzing their own responses to a distinctive work of art and then apply this process of analysis onto more extensive subjects.

Duration: 50 minutes

Follow up exercises are homework.

Materials: Overhead projection

Preparation: Instructors should be familiar with the following concept: An "emotional response" describes the initial reaction one has to a work. One can have an emotional response to both fictional and nonfictional sources or to three-dimensional objects (architectural features or paintings) and situations (such as being asked to write a research paper). Although this exercise is about creative sources—e.g., paintings, poems, and songs—the skills here can be applied elsewhere as well; it is useful to point out parallels or to repeat the steps with a non-creative source/object to illustrate this for students. I make it clear to students that, in the context of these discussions, there is no such thing as "a wrong emotional response."

Procedure: Painting is preferred because it is static and can be projected during the exercise. I suggest Salvador Dalí's *Crucifixion (Corpus Hypercubus)* housed in the Metropolitan Museum of Art in New York City.

1. Ask students to call out responses to the painting and make note of one or two of the responses. A potential response for the Dalí painting is "I feel cold and lonely ... maybe even isolated from the rest of the world."

2. Before moving on, talk about emotional responses in general. An emotional response may be positive or negative (or even both simultaneously); however, it is important to realize that a negative emotional response does not mean that one dislikes the work. If a negative response is the artist's goal, then it is actually likely that one appreciates the work. I explain to students that creative sources frequently illuminate complex issues. In this case, a negative response is ideal because Dalí's painting seems to imply a worldview bereft of the comfort often associated with the Christian religion.

3. Highlight one or two of the responses and prompt students to identify what elements of the image created them. Ask students questions such as: "Michael said the painting makes him feel 'cold and lonely,' what can you see in the painting that might explain why he has those feelings when looking at this?" It may be necessary to lead the first response, so it is good to have multiple student responses for use at this point.

Looking at the elements that cause emotional responses provides a common language among people who may have different responses or interpretations. The next step for discussion above might look like this: "The space between the blocks and between all the other elements in the painting are what make me feel cold and lonely; also, the perspective of continuing distance in the background seems to go on forever and is empty, which is why I feel isolated, like the distance between the blocks and between the people also applies to the whole world and all of time."

4. Sometimes simply observing elements that cause emotional responses will actually provide analysis, even if students are unaware that they are doing a "close reading" of an aesthetic object; nevertheless, in my experience, students need to be prompted to make sense of their impressions, and instructor guidance is required. Talk to students about determining a purpose for the creative source and for the response. Ask students to call out ideas about what the painter's purpose or message was with the painting (or, in other words, reasons the painter would want to generate the feelings being focused on in the emotional response.)

5. Responses should be shaped using common language and terminology. Also, talk about removing the unnecessary first person from this stage (in other words, making the personal emotional response into an audience's emotional response). Again, for example: "Dalí's *Crucifixion (Corpus Hypercubus)* illustrates a distance from religious culture by conveying a cold and lonely crucifixion that uses separated blocks to form the cross. However, what makes the painting most powerful is the empty background perspective that continues out infinitely behind the cross implying that the loneliness and isolation are not simply a point in time or a particular incident, but forever and everywhere."

6. Make parallels to other lengthier sources—such as movies, short stories, and so on—in order to analyze an emotional response that is not static. If a writer has several responses, either sequentially or simultaneously, or identifies many elements that contribute the emotional response, it is best to list them all and then look for patterns. If one is looking at a painting, there may be only one emotional response; however, if one is reading a short story or watching a movie, there may be many emotional responses and reasons for those responses. After looking for patterns and similarities, a writer uses these to determine a purpose for the creative source and communicate that to the reader using the common language of elements in the work.

7. Talk about the purposes of using creative sources—i.e., with a complete analysis, creative sources are often the best way to provide examples of cultural responses to an issue or complexities that tie together the issues of individual scholarly sources.

8. Reiterate that this is actually the same process we go through with non-fiction sources; we are just less likely to be aware of each step when dealing with non-fiction sources and more likely to get stuck on the first/emotional step when dealing with creative sources.

Additional Author's Notes: Students will do well with the exercise as long as they see the purpose of what they are doing. However, it is always a good idea to have a ready set of examples for each stage just in case student contributions do not take an anticipated direction. A painting is easiest, but the exercise works well with most any visual image.

"Patriotism"
Four Definition Exercises
• Rita D. Costello •

Abstract: Students debate the meaning of the word "patriotism" by working through the following three exercises: (1) contrasting abstract and concrete words, (2) increasingly narrowing a single definition, (3) defining through differentiation, and (4) identifying a definition's flaws.

Preparation: Have five to 10 words ready for students to define before beginning the first day of teaching definition, but allow students and student interests to contribute when possible.

Suggested Reading: Stephen L. Carter's "The Insufficiency of Honesty" (use author and title as key words) www.csun.edu/~hfmgt001/honesty.doc.

Procedure: For this exercise (and for my other "definition" exercises contained in *Practical Composition*) I introduce the idea of "definition" by asking students to define *patriotism*. This discussion is meant to shock students a little bit.

First, I have students define *patriotism* aloud, and then I point out to them that by the definitions they inevitably provide, the Nazis are a far better example of patriotism than the students themselves are. Typically, this leads to a flurry of redefining because students want the word *patriotism* to maintain the positive connotations they associate with the word.

After finishing, or after stopping the discussion if the discussion gets too heated, I then have students analyze their own definition process.

Defining the Abstract (Exercise 1)

Before lecturing on definition, I have students take out a piece of paper and pen/pencil. I give them two sets of words, one at a time. In each set, the first word is concrete and the second word is abstract (such as photo frame/artistic; garden glove/success).

After the first set of definitions are written, I have students read their definitions out loud and we talk about why the definitions for the first word are all almost the same and the definitions of the second word have so much variety.

We do a second set for emphasis and further discussion.

Usually, I begin recording pieces of each definition for the last word on the board and begin lecture by having students argue out the pieces toward creating a common definition for a sample thesis statement.

Either as part of this last step or directly following this last step, I introduce the concepts of connotation and denotation (sometimes these words get defined for the students during our initial discussion of the first set of words, but even if it does, I find it helpful to follow up on the board/overhead).

Two examples that usually cement an understanding of denotative versus connotative meaning in students are mother/mom/ma/mommy and house/home. With each set, the denotative meaning is the same, but the connotations may be radically different. The goal is that by the end of this lesson students recognize that in order to write an interesting and purposeful definition, the word should be abstract and the focus more on the connotative than the denotative meaning.

Writing a Definition Thesis Statement (Exercise 2)

This exercise can be done in class, but it works just as well as a handout for homework.

Having a strong thesis statement in a definition essay can help to keep the essay from being unintentionally focused on the denotative meaning. The following is a thesis template; it is not the form a final thesis would take, but what is written in the blanks provides the material needed to have an argumentative thesis statement.

The worksheet follows.

Rationale: While these exercises break down elements of definition for teachers and students, they should also specifically:

- allow teachers to address concrete versus abstract words (and why abstract words are best for definition essays);
- introduce and explain the concept of denotative versus connotative meaning;
- provide a way to reach an argumentative thesis statement in the definition mode;
- practice definition through differentiation, and identify flawed definition claims.

WORKSHEETS

Exercise 2

1. Most people believe that *patriotism* means _____,
but really, patriotism is _____
_____.

- Now, to turn this into a potential thesis, eliminate everything up to and including "but really" and reword for clarity: _____
_____.

2. Most people believe that *comedy* means _____,
but really, comedy is _____
_____.

- Again, eliminate everything up to and including "but really" and reword for clarity and detail: _____
_____.

This structure for creating a definition thesis statement should work whether you are attempting to expand a definition or argue against the existing definition.

Definition Through Differentiation (Exercise 3)

Often we define through differentiation; that is, we look at two very similar words and expand or change the definition of one of those words by contrasting it to the other. Look at these word pairs and define one of the words by explaining how it is different from the other word:

Pair 1: Truth/Honesty _____
_____
_____
_____

Pair 2: Freedom/Independence _____
_____
_____
_____

Pair 3: Creative/Artistic _____
_____
_____
_____
_____

Identifying Flaws in Definition (Exercise 4)

There are pitfalls one must watch out for when writing an extended definition, such as the Circular Reasoning fallacy (defining something by restating the same thing in different words); this includes defining one abstract term with another equally abstract term. An additional problem involves switching from defining to telling what something includes or how to identify it instead of what it *is*. One more frequent issue is beginning with a noun and defining it as a verb (or vice versa). Beware of phrases such as "is when" or "is where," which are often signs of a problem. Below are several definition sentences; pick the best one and attempt to determine what prevents the others from being strong definitions:

- *Patriotism* is when one loves his or her country.
- *Patriotism* means behaving in a patriotic manner
- *Patriotism* means making decisions in the best interests of one's country
- In order to have *patriotism*, one must vote.
- *Patriotism* means blind loyalty to nationalism.
- *Patriotism* is where one supports his or her country's decisions no matter whether he or she agrees with them or not.

An Essay That Bridges Narrative with Research

• Christine Cucciarre •

Abstract: This is assigned as the second essay of the semester. It provides a bridge between students' first narrative essay (where they react to one source with some narrative intertwined) and the final researched paper of the semester where they don't use any narrative.

In the following essay prompt, students are required to confront a topic that they may not have thought about as a young adult. It forces them to take a personal issue (one that they care about) and research it as a scholar would. The student must take an intellectual and objective leap into ways to approach a topic that are very different than the ways he or she may have thought about it before.

This assignment is useful for the composition classroom because it takes elements of narrative and research and blends them in a way students often think cannot be done. The difficulty is getting students to see the many avenues of research for a personal topic. Brainstorming with other students and with their instructor is a key component to this assignment; that brainstorming usually generates so many ideas that students also begin to see the value of talking to others about their paper ideas.

This exercise also has a narrative component.

ASSIGNMENT SHEET

Length: At least four full pages, but no more than five

Draft 1 Due: _____

(to Peer Team and instructor)

Peer Letters Due: _____ (two hard copies of each)

Draft 2 Due: _____ by _____
Final Draft Due: _____ emailed to _____ by _____

This essay should be an argument on a topic of your choice, but you are to write an essay about the moment that you realized a long-held belief was not true. This paper idea is based off of the imitation exercise you did on Langston Hughes's essay, "Salvation." This is an open-ended paper that needs to explore why you believed what you believed. What perpetuated the belief? Who perpetuated the belief? How do beliefs like this become "fact" or "lore?" (This is the arena in which you might get sources to support your ideas.)

Given that this essay is four to five pages, you should not stay in your narrative too long (no more than one page) because I want you to use research to explore the reasons behind the belief (personal, social and cultural). You are essentially trying to persuade your audience to understand the belief itself, what made it believable, and how you held on to it for so long. If Langston Hughes were to write this paper, he would start with his narrative and continue by perhaps finding sources that discuss congregational pressures in church, faith issues that explore "being saved," conflicting religious beliefs, etc. He might write about the church helping hold families together and/or how religious deception can challenge faith. He might argue that the belief is important even if it isn't true. In short, you will do research on your topic and find sources that are talking about the issues that might have contributed to this belief or its revelation.

Pick a belief/topic that is interesting to you (and your audience), complex, and manageable. Make certain that your paper also considers alternative viewpoints. For instance, if your revelation was that Santa Claus is not real, consider your parents' reasons for perpetuating the lie. Consider how you might perpetuate it yourself one day. Advocate for others who might argue that the lie, deception, or lore is the better alternative than the truth or reality of the issue.

Unlike your first essay, this paper is more research heavy. The short narrative is a way to frame the research topic. This essay is meant to be a bridge from Essay #1 to your Researched Paper.

Please employ rhetorical concepts and strategies that we've studied and discussed this semester. I want to see what you've learned about writing and rhetoric manifested in this and the last paper. The paper must have *only three sources* (no more, no less); choose and use them wisely. And the paper must be in MLA format with a Works Cited page.

Investigative Research Essay
Exploring Local Issues
• Melissa Dennihy •

Abstract: In an essay that asks writers to solve a local "real world" problem, students are introduced to research, analysis, and citation style. Discussion and assignment sheet follow. **This assignment also involves citation.**

Materials: Handouts, enough for each student

Preparation: Instructors should be familiar with UC Berkeley's website "Evaluating Web Pages: Techniques to Apply & Questions to Ask" (use title as keywords) http://www.lib.berkeley.edu/TeachingLib/Guides/Internet/Evaluate.html

Discussion: The investigative paper assignment, a "mini" research essay that asks students to investigate (and ultimately try to grapple with and improve upon) a local issue or problem that is of concern to them, is a useful assignment for building argumentative, critical, and analytical thinking skills; introducing students to basic approaches to different types of research; and encouraging students to consider connections between the composition classroom and the "real world." Depending on the overall goals or requirements of a given composition course, this assignment works well as either the penultimate or ultimate assignment in a Composition I class.

In composition courses that are expected to culminate in a formal academic research paper, this research assignment—which does *not* require the use of academic/scholarly sources—works well as the penultimate essay of the semester. It gives students a chance to familiarize themselves with the process of choosing a narrow and focused research topic, and looking for and assessing sources for that topic, before plunging into the work of doing scholarly research for a final course paper, which usually involves the more daunting tasks of finding and using academic journals/articles, book-length academic studies, etc. In a more basic composition course, where the focus of all paper assignments is primarily on thesis, evidence, and argument, rather than on conducting a course that culminates in a final academic research project, this assignment works well as the final paper assignment of the semester. It asks students to demonstrate that they can effectively utilize several different types of sources and forms of evidence to support their argument, while also asking students to move beyond the information provided by sources in order to develop their own original suggestion or solution for improving the problem they have researched. While not a formal academic research assignment, this type of paper can also introduce students in any kind of composition course to critical elements of the research process—including using MLA format and writing a Works Cited page—which will prove useful to them in a variety of courses across the disciplines once they leave the Composition I classroom.

One of the weaknesses of this assignment, which is that it does not require the use of academic sources or book-length studies in order to conduct the research, is also one of the great strengths of the assignment. By introducing students to a variety of different types of potential research sources (newspapers, radio broadcasts, televised news reports, personal interviews, images and advertisements seen around the neighborhood in which they live, etc.), and by requiring the use of at least one print and one non-print source, this assignment encourages both a creative approach to the research process and the use of a diverse range of sources to support an argument. Another potential weakness of the assignment, which is that it lends itself easily to the (mis)use of online sources, is, again, also a potential strength of the assignment, in that it allows a moment of opportunity for participants in the course to have an open and honest discussion about both the potentialities *and* the limitations of online sources—a conversation many students may not ever get to have in any other class. Allowing for a more open-ended and creative approach to research, while also encouraging students to learn how to carefully and critically assess the validity and usefulness of any sources they find, is a great way to teach responsible use of *all* types of sources—print and non-print, web and non-web.

That said, one important and practical tip for making this assignment work is to have a well-considered and careful plan for how to discuss the use of online sources with students. The use of Internet sources for classroom research is often a difficult topic to "teach," as some students will see the web as a free-for-all, with anything posted anywhere as "fair game" for use in a research assignment, while others will see the web as a terrifying mass of mostly useless information, something that's sure to get them accused of plagiarism or inadequate research if they use it to write a paper. One of the instructor's goals for this assignment should be to encourage all students to have a more balanced, critical, even-handed approach to using the web for academic work. A good start toward reaching that goal is to have a discussion which will help students to come up with some real, concrete techniques for evaluating web sources. One particularly valuable resource that I use in order to begin this discussion is UC Berkeley's guide to evaluating web pages; thankfully, as the web becomes ever more present in our lives, similar guides and checklists continue to become available from other universities and writing labs across the country.

Finally, making this assignment work requires, perhaps, a bit more effort than usual on the part of the instructor. Students may, at least at first, shy away from a project that asks them to use non-traditional sources, such as people in their own neighborhood, and to research non-traditional topics, such as local problems that impact their own lives directly but may seem "small" or "insignificant" in the larger scheme of composition textbook debates. Because of this, instructors may need to do a little extra research of their own to figure out what exactly is going on in the area in order to help students in selecting appropriate topics, and, from there, to also help them find appropriate sources and resources for investigating those topics. The more knowledge the instructor has about the neighborhoods and communities in which the students may conduct research, the more the instructor will be able to assist in the research process. The added advantage is that, in the process, the instructor also learns more about the everyday lives of his or her students outside of the classroom—information which can be surprisingly valuable in helping us, as teachers, to re-think what we do in the classroom, why we do it, and how it connects to the "real world" in which our students live outside of the academy.

- -

ASSIGNMENT SHEET

Due Dates

Topic/Two Sources: [one month prior to final due date]
Drafts Due: [two weeks prior to final due date]
Final Due Date: [TBD based on individual course]

Assignment

Four page investigative research essay; three to five sources
    This essay asks you to research a *current* and *local* issue or problem of concern to you—something going on in the *immediate* area where you live, work, or attend school—and to use your analytical and argumentative skills to assess the nature and extent of that problem and to propose a *recommendation* or *solution* for addressing or improving that problem. In addition to drawing upon the skills you worked to develop in previous papers, including utilizing evi-

dence to understand and support a position, this essay also adds the additional challenge of asking you to develop your own original and unique recommendation, solution, or proposal for how to improve upon the problem or issue you have investigated.

Use of Sources

This assignment is intended to introduce you to basic research (including finding and utilizing sources, using MLA format, and developing a proper Works Cited page) while also encouraging you to utilize a diverse and creative range of sources in seeking to investigate your issue and develop your argument. The specific requirements for source use are as follows:

At least one of your sources must be a *print* source (newspaper, magazine article, newsletter, etc.) that is covering or has recently covered this problem or issue. A good place to start is by looking at major accredited journalistic publications (such as the *New York Times* or *The Wall Street Journal*); however, major newspapers aren't your only options—you might also look at local ethnic or religious newspapers (such as *Our Time Press* or *The Jewish Week*), borough and neighborhood newspapers (such as the *Brooklyn Daily Eagle* or *The Queens Courier*), school newspapers, newsletters published by local organizations, etc. Furthermore, print sources may also include those printed materials we encounter constantly in our everyday lives, but often don't think of as "sources" for a paper—advertisements, billboards, photographs, subway posters, etc. Be creative and feel free to make use of the world around you to help you research!

At least one of your sources must be a *non-print* source. Non-print sources may include, among other things, a speech or lecture, a radio or television broadcast, a documentary film, or an interview which you conduct with a relevant individual. Interviews can be conducted both in person or via email (we will discuss how to go about this in more detail in the coming weeks); interviewees might include experts on the topic (for example, an MTA employee who can explain the financial reasons behind service cuts on city subways) as well as "ordinary" people who might provide different perspectives on that same problem (for example, individuals in your neighborhood who ride the subway daily and can speak to how service changes impact their commute, work life, family life, etc.).

The most important thing is that the sources you choose provide you with the necessary knowledge and information you will need to develop a persuasive and well-reasoned solution or recommendation for the problem, while also allowing you to explore and consider this problem from a variety of different angles and perspectives.

Please document your sources in proper MLA format throughout your essay and include a bibliography with all necessary publication/citation information.

Your essay should:

- Provide an analysis of the nature, extent, and possible or probable cause(s) of the problem
- Demonstrate to readers why this problem is particularly pressing or urgent
- Develop a knowledgeable, well-informed, and persuasive argument about how to best improve or resolve this problem

Note: It is required that the issue you choose is a local and current one—an issue that recently occurred or is occurring in the general area in which you currently live/work/attend school. There are several reasons why I think that researching a local issue is a particularly interesting and productive activity:

- When someone writes about an issue that directly impacts his or her life or the lives of the people he or she is surrounded by, this writer tends to be more interested and invested in the subject. Having a stake in the subject you are writing about is likely to produce writing that is more impassioned and informed—writing that will convince readers that this issue is important and that your solution is a smart, insightful, and effective one.

- Writing about a local issue gives you the opportunity to use your own knowledge about the area—its people, its history, its culture, its geography, etc.—as well as your own experiences as a resident of that area to strengthen your argument and to provide your readers with an "insider's" insight. Although it is crucial that you do the necessary research for the paper, your own perspective can also be an extremely valuable contribution to your argument.

- Although it may be hard to remember this at times when we are working in the composition classroom, writing does not exist in a "void"—and neither do writers. In fact, writers have a responsibility to their community; not only should they listen to and consider the views of others, but they should also consider using their own writing as a tool for social change. For this assignment, you are highly encouraged to send in your paper (or an appropriate selection from your paper) to a relevant official or publication (depending on the topic of your paper, this might include university presidents or school administrators, local government representatives, the head of a local business or organization, or the editor or editorial board of a local newspaper or publication). If you receive a response from your chosen official, or if any portion of your paper is published in a local publication, your grade for the assignment will be raised by two-thirds (for example, from a B– to a B+). More importantly, you'll get the chance to see your written work "move beyond" the composition classroom and out into the "real world"—an important opportunity and gratifying experience for any writer!

Have fun and good luck!

Argument Analysis and Evaluation Essay
• Martin J. Fashbaugh •

Abstract: The following essay assignment is one I gave for Composition II, a class that focuses on analysis, research, and argumentation.

The first major assignment of the semester is intended to help students gain an appreciation of the many rhetorical tools at a rhetorician's or artist's disposal.

By sensitizing them to the various strategies they employ, students are likely to be more conscious of the choices they make when writing their argumentative-research essays during the latter half of the semester.

Assignment Sheet

During the first few weeks of the semester, we will be watching Michael Moore's *Sicko* and reading essays about the health care system in the United States. We will also be reading about the elements of argument and learning how to identify and disassemble these elements in the arguments that we have read. For the first major paper, you will select from *Sicko*, Joseph A. Califano's "America Has the Best Care System in the World," David R. Francis's "Market Models Do Not Apply to America's Current Crisis," Judi King's "Health Insurance and 'Personal Responsibility': Shifting the Bill from the Employer to the Worker," George D. Lundberg's "Insurance Companies Limit Necessary Medical Care," or an essay of your choosing, found on the library's website. If you choose the last option, please see me in advance.

For this essay, you will be analyzing the elements of argument (the claim, warrants/underlying assumptions, evidence, etc.) at work in the essay or film, the audience being addressed, and the rhetorical appeals being used (ethos, logos, pathos). In addition, you will need to evaluate how effectively or ineffectively you feel the argument proves its claim, persuades its audience, etc.

The Introduction should consist of a brief summary of the main claim that the author or filmmaker is making, his or her intended audience, and a thesis statement that addresses the rhetorical appeals being used and how effective the author or filmmaker is in using these appeals to persuade you to accept or at least appreciate the argument's validity.

In the body, you will be analyzing how the author/filmmaker conveys his or her message and evaluate the rhetorical strengths of these methods.

The conclusion should summarize what you think is effective and ineffective about the argument and end with a thoughtful comment that puts everything into context.

Points to Remember

Thesis Statement: Should be clear, have a solid argument that is proved throughout the paper, and should appear very early (usually in the first paragraph).

Works Cited: Should appear as the last page of the paper and follow MLA guidelines. If you are writing on an essay, the paper should also include proper in-text citations whenever points from the essay are referenced.

Length: Three to four pages, not including the Works Cited

Argumentation and Logical Fallacies
Headlines as Inductive and Deductive Examples
• J.D. Isip •

Abstract: Students use headlines as a starting point to construct deductive and inductive statements and then apply ethos, pathos, and logos (and a variety of other argument tactics) to their statements.

This exercise also deals with evaluation of the media.

Duration: One to two 50-minute classes

Preparation: Instructors should be prepared to discuss the following terms:

- Inductive and deductive reasoning
- Ethos, Pathos, Logos
- Argumentative concepts and terminology (see exercise)

Materials: A handout comprised of logical fallacies. There are plenty of these online, too (just be sure the definitions to whatever link you provide are close to your own definitions)

Suggested Resources: I usually have my students watch *Fox News* and *MSNBC*, one show on each. There are plenty of other avenues you can take, but I chose the political one.

Procedure: Introduce the terms *inductive reasoning* and *deductive reasoning*

Very briefly give an example of each (there's also the very popular "Person A says X, Person B says Y, etc." set up, but this can confuse students, so I tend to stick with solid examples).

I usually have CNN on the overhead, but you can also pass out magazines, newspapers, etc.—anything that is going to give students a variety of topics.

Have the class, in groups, construct some *inductive* and *deductive* statements about any articles that interest them. Remember, they really only need to read the headline; they don't need a ton of information to make a statement.

Introduce Aristotle's types of appeal (*ethos, pathos, logos*). Most of my students are familiar with these terms, so it is a good time to let students share from their past experience.

Give students examples of each type of appeal and allow for the class to offer their own examples. Be sure to save *logos* as the last appeal you talk about as it will lead nicely into logical fallacies.

I usually ask my students, "Of these appeals, which do you think you would put the most faith in. That is, which would you *trust* most?" They always (always!) say *logos*.

Remind them of how "logical" inductive and deductive reasoning seemed. Then introduce them to a few logical fallacies.

You can choose your favorites, but I like Bandwagon, Red Herring, Straw Man, Ad Hominem, Begging the Question, Poisoning the Well, and, of course, Slippery Slope.

Students get a real kick out of seeing how these work, so make sure that you let them try their hand at creating some logical fallacies—whether they do it in a short homework assignment or a creative essay (details below).

Rationale: The point of the exercise is to show them how to make "bad arguments," which is, at least to me, much easier than showing them how to make good arguments. Once I eliminate all of these bad argument tactics from their repertoire, I find that their arguments naturally become more fact based.

The Bad Argument Essay

Rather than assigning a traditional argument essay where a student establishes an argument and supports the argument with research, I ask my students to create an essay that employs as many logical fallacies as possible in arguing for or against a normally "taboo" topic like gay marriage, abortion, legalizing marijuana, the existence of God, etc. I want them to feel like they are allowed to write about whatever it is that concerns them. I find we make subjects taboo because we have settled them in our own heads, but these things do concern our students

By creating "bad arguments" for these subjects, I avoid the potential debates and/or preaching. Also, by constructing some of the very same bad arguments they may hear and even believe, my hope is that my students can begin to sniff these things out and question their own assumptions

On a personal note, this assignment is one of the most gratifying for me to read. It is usually quite funny, and, more importantly, I see my students relish the opportunity to use these *tricks*. A couple of times I have felt the need to allow them to share their papers in class because they were just so excited about their master works of bad arguments.

Potential Problems: If you get caught up over-explaining the types of reasoning or Aristotle's appeals, you can lose the class. Simply saying the name "Aristotle" can cause eyes to glaze over (sadly), so it is important to move through this exercise at a brisk pace and keep from talking.

Also, the Bad Argument essay can work well with less controversial topics. For high school teachers, I would certainly keep the taboo taboo.

—⚏—

Assignment Sheet
Literacy Analysis Assignment
• Tessa Mellas •

Assignment Context

Because our ability to use language is so important to the way we interact with the world, we have all had a lot of instruction in how to use language effectively. Some of these experiences have been positive ones that empower us. Others have been negative, leading us to feel incompetent and souring our relationship with certain forms of communication. All of our literacy experiences combined, especially our formative ones, have influenced our current attitudes and beliefs about reading, writing, and language use and our self-identity as language users, and will continue to influence them in the future as we encounter new writing tasks in both professional and personal situations. These literacy experiences will have a large effect on whether we succeed or fail or even participate in certain forms of reading and writing at all. If our past literacy experiences dictate so much of our life, doesn't it make sense to analyze the control they exert over us and to redefine literacy on our own terms to take it back? That's this essay's goal.

Assignment Description

In a four to six page analytical narrative essay, you will reflect on a few of your most important literacy experiences. You will explain how they influenced your current attitudes and beliefs about reading, writing, and communication, how they influenced your self-identity as a language user, and how they have shaped your current literacy practices. Readings and class discussions will allow you to reconsider what literacy is in order to problematize, reconsider, expand, and rewrite your personal definition of literacy. In the essay, you will redefine literacy on your own terms and will use your new definition to explain how your analysis of your past literacy experiences has allowed you to reconsider your current and future literacy practices in order to take ownership of them.

Key Concepts: discourse community, rhetorical situation, literacy, literacy ritual, self-sponsored literacy practices, private versus public literacies, narrative, analysis.

Assignment Format: Your essay needs to be four to six pages long (1,000 words minimum), double spaced (no extra spaces between lines). Use Times New Roman 12 point font and include your word count in the header (not heading) of the first page. Use MLA style for formatting and documentation. This essay needs to include at least 1,000 words of text, but feel free to use your creativity to include more than just text if it makes sense for your essay.

Proper Documentation: Please remember to properly cite any information or ideas that are not or were not originally your own. Use MLA style of documentation.

Special Issue

Collaborative Writing and Editing to Produce an Academic Journal

• Lauren Matus •

Abstract: As a group, students work as an editorial team to produce a series of academic style "articles" on the same theme (one article from each individual student) and then all collaborate on an introductory "editorial"; the concept is that students are publishing a "Special Issue" of an academic journal.

This exercise also teaches organization.
Duration: Usually eight weeks
Materials: Overhead projection and Internet access
Examples for students:

- A Magazine Cover
- An Editorial
- Individual Thematic Articles

Suggested Reading: Merchant, Guy, and Victoria Carrington, "Literacy and Identity, " Special Issue of *Literacy 43*(2): 63–64, http://onlinelibrary.wiley.com/doi/10.1111/j.1741-4369.2009.00524.x/full (keywords "merchant Carrington literacy and identity 2009").

Procedure:

First Unit of the Exercise

First, students debate within the "research threads" from course themes or topics and conduct research.

The next step is for the team to decide what theme they would like to explore and what kinds of articles they will write. For example, one team looked at Conspiracy Theories and applied an analytic framework to four common conspiracy theories—the JFK assassination, the moon landing, 9/11 and the New World Order. Similarly, another team applied an analytic framework to cult films and each team member assessed whether or not films could be defined as cult films according to their framework. Yet another team of education students wrote their themed articles on the topic of alternative schooling—charter schools, homeschooling, etc.

Students are then asked to draft a short rationale for their Special Issue—what is the overarching theme? Is it a topical theme, or is it a theoretical theme? Why is this an interesting topic of study? Why is a Special Issue on this theme necessary?

During workshops, individual members research his or her own topic, but are in constant collaboration with the team.

Students can submit multiple drafts, and I always schedule team conferences to check progress along the way.

Second Unit of the Exercise

The last two steps of the project are drafting the editorial and designing the cover.

The editorial is a full collaborative effort where all team members must contribute to the final product. I show students examples, like the one in the *Suggested Reading*, to help guide them through the process. Likewise, the cover design is an opportunity to employ visual rhetoric and be creative; all team members must contribute.

Potential Problems: Some teams need a little hand-holding, but because of the collaboration students usually learn from each other. I have only had to give a small push when momentum was lost.

—⁂—

Narrowing the Argument
Finding a "Researchable" Topic
• Lauren Matus •

Abstract: In this broadly outlined classroom approach, students are taught to move from broadly defined research topics to more specific research questions. Students are taught the difference between "umbrella questions" (broadly defined concepts) and "target questions" (specific ideas).

This exercise has elements of visual rhetoric associated with it.

Duration: This exercise can take several weeks because of the amount of research that is involved.

Procedure: When given an argument assignment, many students go to a website to peruse a list of topics such as abortion, corporal punishment, drug legalization, etc. However, these types of topics are easily plagiarized and do not require students to synthesize information from different kinds of sources to develop a unique argument. I dissuade my students from using topics in their comfort zone and instead ask them to develop a unique argument in a new content area.

I begin by showing students the following images:

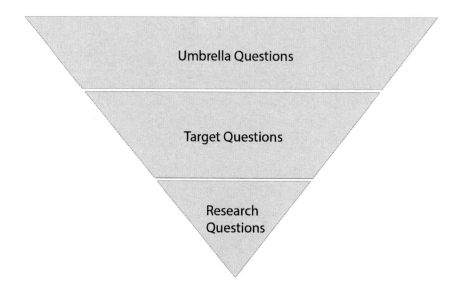

Umbrella questions are broad-scope questions that ask a general question about a particular topic. I suggest beginning with the basic WH-Questions: Who, What, Where, When, Why and How?

Students conduct research to try to contextualize some of these broad-scope umbrella questions. They have to explore different kinds of sources and see what kind of information exists. Chances are they will not find exact answers, and more than likely they will discover that their topic is much too large.

Once students realize that their umbrella questions are much too broad, I ask them to develop target questions based on their research. Target questions seek to narrow the scope of the paper. Target questions use the information students uncovered through research to begin "breaking apart" a large concept into smaller, more manageable parts.

After narrowing the scope by developing target questions, I ask students to develop a "tight" research question. The better the research question, the better the final argument and the easier it is to write the paper. The research question should not be frontloaded with any assumptions and should be phrased in such a way that a yes or no answer suffices. For example, beginning questions with "do" or "does" limits the answers significantly.

Rationale: Specifically, this exercise was developed to accompany argument papers. This exercise helps students narrow their focus to find a researchable topic, and also teaches them about the research process. Typically, I will also use the Toulmin Model as a productive tool to help students build their argument.

Potential Problems: The main issue that I have faced is that students tend to revert to what they know, and it takes some pushing back on my part to encourage their exploration into new topics. Often I will hear, "There isn't anything to argue here." So, working with students in workshops or during individual conferences is very important to the success of this project.

—∿—

Underlining the Plot
Using Movie Clips to Teach Analysis
• Alexandra Oxner •

Abstract: Students watch a short video (author recommends a movie trailer) in class, write a short analysis of one scene from the video, and exchange these with a partner; students are then asked to indicate where the writers actually performed an analysis and where they merely provided plot summary.

Editor's note: This is the second of three exercises in a series designed to teach revision (see also "Oxner and Bouier: Genre Bending" and "Oxner: Making Connections"); each exercise can be used as a standalone or as part of the sequence.

This exercise has elements of visual rhetoric associated with it and employs peer review.

Duration: 30 to 50 minutes

Materials: Overhead projection and Internet access

Preparation: Watch the video you will use before class and take notes. You probably know how to analyze cultural texts more effectively than your students. They might need you to help engage them in discussion.

Procedure: I have taught summary versus analysis with movie clips, music videos, commercials, etc. But my students absolutely love when I teach analysis with current *movie trailers*.

Watch a movie trailer in class.

Have students complete a three-to-five-minute free-write. Their task is to analyze one scene from the trailer.

Have your students pass their analysis to another student. Each student will then read the classmate's response and underline anything that they think is merely summarization.

Students pass back their papers. Give them a few minutes to read their classmate's response. In this way, students will get to test out their own writing skills, and they will also have the opportunity to try distinguishing between "summary" and "analysis" in the work of others.

Now play through the trailer again. This time, pause whenever you find a moment worth analyzing with your students. Each time you pause the trailer, try to engage the class in discussion. Ask students to share their free-write responses, or ask them specific questions.

Example—Django Unchained *Trailer*

At 0:26, Christoph Waltz's character appears on screen. What does it mean that he has a European accent in the South? What might his mode of transportation symbolize? (He is a dentist and his vehicle features a large tooth. We know this film discusses slavery, and we understand that Waltz's character is anti-slavery. What does it mean that he extracts rotten, decayed things for a living?)

Examine the language. (Waltz says "inventory," "specimen," and "acquire.")

After the first slave trader has been shot (0:50), the music changes. It shifts from Johnny Cash (traditionally considered a southern/country artist) to a song which incorporates funk/hip-hop elements. Examine Django's character after the shift occurs (he throws off his blanket, revealing scars and muscles).

At 1:00, Django rides into a town on horseback. His head goes directly through a noose hanging from one of the buildings. Waltz's neck is spared. What does this mean?

At 2:09, Django shoots one of the "Brittle Brothers." The man has a piece of paper taped to his chest. If you look closely, it is a page from *The Bible*. What might this mean?

At 2:17, a man asks Django about his name. The white actor is Franco Nero, the actor who played Django in the 1966 version of the film. Why might Quentin Tarantino have included the actor from the spaghetti western version of the film?

You could easily analyze this movie trailer for an entire class period. Choosing an up-to-date trailer is best since students are typically looking forward to seeing the film if it is a big release. (I also recently taught this lesson plan with the trailers for *Les Misérables*, *World War Z,* and *Pacific Rim.*)

Rationale: This exercise aims to teach students how to distinguish between summary and analysis. This lesson works especially well when taught in conjunction with an analytical paper, such as a rhetorical analysis. This exercise also gets students to think critically about cultural issues such as social class discrepancies, racial tensions, gender relations, etc.

A Trip to McDonald's

An Introduction to Basic Research and Argument

• Dana Washington •

Abstract: In this complicated, extended assignment, students are broken into groups and use nutritional information available on the McDonald's website to research the most and least healthy meal choices based on a number of common categories (age, gender, etc.); students then construct an argument based upon the reliable source material

This exercise also deals with the evaluation of websites.

Preparation: Instructors should be familiar with and be able to direct students to the following websites:

McDonald's nutrition information:

(key words "mcdonald's nutrition facts for popular menu items pdf")
http://nutrition.mcdonalds.com/getnutrition/nutritionfacts.pdf

Mayo Clinic nutrition information:

(key words "mayo clinic nutrition facts")
   www.mayoclinic.com/health/nutrition-facts/NU00293

U.S. government dietary guidelines:

(key words "usda gov publications dietary guidelines appendices 2010")
   www.cnpp.usda.gov/Publications/DietaryGuidelines/2010/PolicyDoc/Appendices.
   pdf

Materials: The author used information on "tray liners" taken from McDonald's restaurants.
   Assignment sheets, one each for each group of students.

Discussion: When it's time to move students from writing about what they know to finding and using unfamiliar information to construct an argument, students may come to class resigned to a boring repetition of what they've already learned in high school or worse, afraid that they don't know enough to even begin to handle the material at the college level. To reduce the fear and resistance, I used a familiar real-world situation to which the students could relate and turned it into an intersecting set of interactive group activities. This exercise can work equally well as a transition to a course in research and argument at the end of a developmental or expository writing course, or as an introduction to research and argument near the beginning of a more advanced course.

First Class

I began by setting the stage based on the calendar. The first time I tried this exercise was near the end of a pre-composition course in the fall semester, so the upcoming holidays were very much on the minds of the students, who had previously been told to bring their laptops or other Internet-connection devices to class for the next three sessions. To begin the exercise, I told them that we were going to spend the next three class days (50-minutes each) planning what they were or were not going to eat at McDonald's while they were doing their holiday shopping.

Although most of the students were tired, this statement immediately grabbed their attention.

Any other seasonally relevant outing (going to the "big game" next weekend, going home to go out with family or friends, any upcoming event or break in which most will participate) can be used to arouse interest in the activity.

I then briefly described their objectives: to plan the healthiest and least healthy breakfast, lunch or supper, or afternoon snack (beverage plus snack *or* dessert). This automatically created the need for six groups, two for each category. Students began making eye contact with their regular group members at this point; they sensed fun.

Once the students moved into their groups, I gave each group one of the six assignment sheets, which provided the meal parameter for the group and outlined exactly what was to happen each day in class. The assignments listed in the course management system between class periods directed the students to finish up any portion of each day's work that hadn't been completed in class, which generally required some sort of communication among group members between class sessions. Students could work via cell phone, e-mail, on-line chat in the course management system, Facebook, or face-to-face, depending on group preferences. I also distributed tray liners, which McDonald's workers had given to me upon request (figure no more than six to eight will be handed over in any given visit—but the coffee's not bad) and directed the students' attention to the back listings of nutritional information about most of the menu items available.

To make the list more complete, I told them they could go to the McDonald's website: <http://nutrition.mcdonalds.com/getnutrition/nutritionfacts.pdf >.

Throughout, I was waiting for the questions to begin. As the students began looking over the nutrition information, one asked, "So how do we know what's healthy and what's not?" I asked for class input, and soon the class concluded that "healthy" and "unhealthy" couldn't be defined simply on the basis of any one of the factors they all already knew about: calories, fat, cholesterol, and sodium. "So how do we decide?" was finally asked, and my reply was that they'd need to figure that out. To help with that, I told them, they could use information on daily requirements and limits for major nutrients—but they'd need to use reliable information.

That opening allowed me to introduce the concept of reliable sources. The nutritional information from McDonald's was assumed to be reliable because the company would get into trouble with the government and watchdog groups if it lied about such critical information. Where could we find reliable information about good nutrition? After some discussion, we agreed that government and medical sources would likely be the most reliable. At that point, I referred the students to a now-visible resource I'd entered in the course management system: McDonald's nutrition information,

- plus links to the Mayo Clinic's
  (http://www.mayoclinic.com/health/nutrition-facts/NU00293)
- and the U.S. government's
  (http://www.cnpp.usda.gov/Publications/DietaryGuidelines/2010/PolicyDoc/Appendices.pdf)

guidelines for what should or should not be eaten by males and females of different ages.

After reminding the groups that they'd need to account for differences in age and gender in their groups, I suggested a few ways to informally attribute their sources ("According to McDonald's nutrition guidelines"). My final directions advised them to be realistic, keeping in mind such ideas that although a 20-calorie side salad without dressing might theoretically sound like a healthy snack, no exhausted holiday shopper would be revived by it and anyone who suggested it would not be taken seriously. After similarly warning against other extremes in quantity or unrealistic combinations (no ordering of every dessert on the menu, plus multiple whipped-cream-filled beverages and claiming they're unhealthy—what reasonable person could argue with that?), I let the research and discussions begin.

This was the point when I knew that the idea for the assignment—triggered by reading the back of one of those tray liners and thinking I didn't want to order anything except coffee ever again—was going to work. Although I was doing my usual circulating among groups to answer questions or to encourage the students to figure out answers, I was not encountering any off-task activities. The students were fully engaged because they had a reason to be learning what they were learning—and they wanted to help each other stay healthy and enjoy their holiday shopping and fast food breaks. They also wanted to give the best and most convincing presentations to the rest of the class. I could hear the group pride as they anticipated being recognized for giving good advice.

Second Class

At the beginning of the second class period, with much of the research completed and organized, I explain that in order to persuade the rest of the class that their advice was good, they'd need to apply the principles of argument. At this point, I pass around sheets of blank unlined paper, enough for each student to take one. I usually introduce argument as a basic three-part process using a three-column pre-writing sheet, with the columns labeled *reasons for*, *reasons against*, and *rebuttals*, aka *arguments/assertions*, *counterarguments*, and *refutations*. I then explain that a valid argument must express an opinion with which a reasonable person could disagree and offer some examples which the students must label as arguable or inarguable opinions—or inherently inarguable facts.

For this exercise, I asked the students to fold their sheets or use a line to divide them into three columns and label them, then present an example of how this pre-writing system works, using a general topic that is relevant to the entire class (possibilities: why course materials should or should not be offered online in face-to-face courses; parking fees on campus; special quiet hours in dorms before exams; the need for _____ on campus). The students quickly see how the counterarguments must logically relate to the arguments, and the refutations to the counterarguments.

As I circulated to help the groups construct their arguments, I learned quite a lot—sometimes to my horror. "Here's our argument against this drink," said one student to the group, then to me, "Did you know that this one drink has all the calories an 18-year-old woman is allowed for a whole day?!" I had not known that, nor had I known about a meat-based sandwich that provided all the fat a young man or woman would need for two to three days. I did not have to feign surprise, nor did I have to keep the students on task; what they were finding was not merely horrifying or interesting, but also relevant and important—and they knew it. Towards the end of this class session, I taught the basics of constructing an argumentative thesis and suggested that each group plan who would write which paragraph of their short essay's body for that night's assignment.

On day three, after a brief lesson on the elements needed in each part, the groups wrote the introductory and concluding paragraphs to their arguments together and planned their presentations. Many of these were amusing, especially those written by groups assigned to design the most unhealthy options. All of the groups were prepared to defend their choices against accusations of being unrealistic, and the chatter before and after the presentations related to what they would or would not be eating when they went to McDonald's over the break.

As the students became more comfortable locating and reading the data they needed to construct their arguments, I noticed that they were also helping each other become more comfortable applying and synthesizing the information. Although most of the groups asked me at least a couple of questions as I moved around the room, I also overheard a great deal of pride of ownership as the students figured out for themselves the meaning of what they were discovering.

For me, the most important aspect of this assignment, beyond meeting the learning objectives for the sessions and course, was the excitement in the room as the students enjoyed the feeling of empowerment that comes from figuring out how something works. For me, that's the embodiment of genuine learning, and it's an experience that is offered to only a fortunate few in educational settings. Learning was once satisfying for all of those students (think of what pre-schoolers can do and how curious and eager to learn they are); for many, going to school seemed to have squelched the curiosity, the sense of achievement, and the joy of learning. The social motivations built into the activities (the well-documented desire of college students to communicate with each other, the desire to help others, the desire to stay healthy and look it, and the desire to make a good impression) not only helped the students connect with the material, but made me feel like a more effective teacher.

Sample assignment sheets follow.

— · — · — · — · — · — · — · — · — · — · — · — · — · — · — · — · — · —

ASSIGNMENT SHEET

Day 1

Plan the most unhealthy beverage and snack and beverage and dessert combinations you could order at McDonald's. This should not be a meal, but the sort of snack you might stop for in the middle of an afternoon of holiday shopping. Use the online resources listed under Week 14 to find the information you need.

Explain the ways in which these are unhealthy. Prewrite a list. Use the online resources listed under Week 14 to find the information you need. This will be the most time-consuming part of this activity.

When you have consulted a source for your information, use informal attribution to cite it:

According to McDonald's nutrition chart...
In the Mayo Clinic's guidelines for a healthy diet...
In the U.S. government chart showing daily recommended intake for...

and similar ways of indicating where you found your information.

If you need additional information, go to http://www.usa.gov/ and type in a keyword or phrase.

Day 2

Draw three columns (two lines) on a sheet of paper.

In the first column (label it "Arguments For"), list your three best reasons for not eating this meal.

In the second column (label it "Arguments Against/Counterarguments"), come up with two or three reasons someone might give for ordering it (be specific; assume that person could choose something else, but really wants *this*).

In the third column (label it "Refutations"/Reasons We're Right), come up with a response to each counterargument.

Use these three columns, either going down or across, to construct an outline of a short paper showing reasons for, reasons against, and refutations.

Write an argumentative thesis for this document.

Day 3

Write an introduction and a conclusion to this short, argumentative paper.

Audience and Mode

Essay Exam Exercise
Practicing Taking an In-Class Test
• Laura L. Beadling •

Abstract: Students are prepped by the instructor with strategies and practice taking in-class essay exams.

Duration: The exercise alone takes one 50-minute class period. If the instructor chooses to make the essay exam a graded assignment, it can be done in two or three class days.

Preparation: The instructor must come up with three to five essay-style questions related to the composition class.

Examples I have used in the past include "From which assignment did you learn the most about writing to a specific audience," "What is the most important revision strategy you learned this semester and how did you apply it to one of your essays," and "Which essay taught you the most about the importance of organization."

This exercise works well at the end of the term to prepare students for in-class essay exams and to practice strategies for writing under time pressure.

Procedure: I spend the first half of the class period going over some common essay exam words and what they mean. For instance, we talk about the difference between writing an essay that "compares and contrasts" with one that "analyzes or defines." The words I go over include: "definition," "discussion," "description," "analysis," "causation," "comparison/contrast," "explain," "summarize," "illustrate," and "evaluate."

I also go over some strategies for approaching essay exams. I stress the need to read the instructions carefully and make a plan for how the student will use the time. We talk about prioritizing questions and making a plan for using the allotted time. Then, I show several examples of essay questions, and we discuss the importance of reading the question closely and writing an essay that addresses the question fully.

Finally, I tell my students that the subtext of every essay exam question is "demonstrate your mastery of this material. Be specific and concrete in your answer while calling on plenty of details and information. Think through your answer and make sure your thoughts are organized before you start writing." I make sure to tell them not to simply regurgitate everything they know, but instead craft a specific answer to the question being posed.

I stress to the students that these are not questions they will have to study for (no doubt they already have plenty of other exams that they are stressing out about!) and that they will not be graded on the content of the answer but instead on the process and the form. I tell them that they will be graded on how well they craft a specific essay, with a thesis and sufficient supporting evidence for a thesis that answers the question being asked. I also tell them that I will be looking for some prewriting, whatever form that might take, and annotations on the essay questions themselves (underlining of key words, jotting ideas down, etc.).

The Actual Exam (see Assignment Sheet): I have my students answer one essay question from a selection of questions. Generally, to give them the experience of a timed exam, I give them either 15 or 20 minutes to plan, write, and proofread their essay.

I then have them flip their paper over and write a brief reflection on how the exam went for them; did they experience difficulty in constructing a thesis, finishing in the allotted time, or coming up with specific and concrete supporting evidence?

Additional Author's Notes: If this is simply a learning exercise, I will often have the students exchange papers and give comments on their partner's essay, having them underline the thesis and the concrete and specific evidence.

If this is the final graded assignment of the semester, I grade them (they usually don't take that long to grade since the point of the assignment is not necessarily the content of the answer but the form and process) and then offer them the option to try it again if they aren't happy with their grade. I believe that it is beneficial to give them another try to master the form and process since this is a composition class in which revision and process have been stressed.

Potential Problems: Some students do not do well on this exercise, even though it is not about getting a specific "right" answer. Some do not finish in the allotted time. Even if they don't finish, I believe that they have learned something valuable from the exercise in that they know that this is a problem area for them and that they will have to be extra careful in actual timed essay exams they may face in other classes. This is also why I offer a rewrite in which they can try it again, answering a different question. If they were not able to finish on time, they need to practice.

Because this is a timed exercise, you should also make sure that you have a plan in place for any student with a documented disability that requires extra time on timed assignments or a quiet place for exams. This requires some extra thought, especially if you are using only part of a class period (as I do) and have plans for before and after the exercise.

ASSIGNMENT SHEET

The timed essay exam is a writing situation all college students will probably face at least once. Because this writing situation is so different from others we have worked on this semester, we will practice this during the final week of class and during finals week. The essay exam will be evaluated less on content and more on the planning, formatting, and execution of the answer.

The document you will produce:

- Must be completed within a timed situation (20 minutes)
- Must respond to the question in an interesting and relevant manner
- Must have a thesis statement within the first three sentences that accurately summarizes what the answer will cover
- Must use specific and concrete examples, details, and evidence
- Must have at least two paragraphs that support the thesis statement
- Must be accompanied by a page of planning

For instance, an IGNORE response to the question, "What effects result from a poorly planned interview for the Compare/Contrast through Interview Paper?" might look like this (although this certainly isn't the only possible A answer):

A poorly planned interview can negatively affect the paragraph development and the dominant impression of the Compare Contrast through Interview paper (CCI). If the interview that the student conducts for the CCI paper isn't well planned, the questions might be too simple or not get enough relevant material to incorporate into the paper. This can result in paragraphs that are insufficiently developed. For instance, if the student only asks one question about the interviewee's childhood but that turns out to be something that s/he wants to write about in the paper, then it will be difficult to generate enough material to fully develop the paragraph. This can result in an imbalance where the paper has too much material on the student and not very much at all about the interviewee. This was true of my rough draft in which I had only asked one question about my interviewee's relationships with her siblings. I decided to write about sibling relationships in my paper, though, so I didn't have nearly enough material on my interviewee.

This can also result in a weak dominant impression. First of all, if there isn't much information or quotes gained from the interview, it will be hard for the student to even form a concrete and specific dominant impression. This can lead to general or vague dominant impressions like "friendly" or "nice" that are difficult to make concrete or specific. This can also result in the student having a difficult time including enough quotes, details, and examples in the paper to create the dominant impression throughout the paper. I know this happened to me and I had to conduct two shorter follow up interviews in order to do the revisions of the paper and create a good dominant impression that was both specific and supported in my paper.

—⟨⟨⟨—

What People Are Seeing

A Lesson on Composing for Diverse Audiences

• Christina Boyles •

Abstract: Students write letters describing the exact same object to "formal" (ex. employer) and "informal" (ex. family member) audiences. Students then read their letters aloud to the class.

Duration: Writing: 15–20 minutes. Presentation: 10 minutes. Discussion: five to 15 minutes.

Preparation: Prepare one notecard for each group of three or four students in your class.

On each card, list two audiences to whom your students should write. Make sure that one of the audiences is "formal," such as a police officer or an employer, and that one is "informal," such as a child or a close friend.

Before completing this activity, I also go over the rhetorical situation so that my students are familiar with the fundamental elements of composition. Though there are various versions of the rhetorical situation, I tend to stick to the TRACE model—Text, Reader, Author, Constraints, Exigence—for its ease of use.

Editor's Note: Explanations of the "TRACE model" are readily available online (keywords "TRACE model Text Reader Author Constraints Exigence").

Suggested Reading: Before assigning this activity, my students complete two readings.

- The first is an excerpt from Kurt Vonnegut, Jr.'s *Breakfast of Champions*, which is written to aliens,
- The second is an excerpt from Truman Capote's *In Cold Blood*, which is written to popular audiences.

These two readings provide strong models for students and help them to see how audience shapes writing.

Procedure: After we have completed the readings listed above, I ask my students to divide into groups of three or four.

I give each group a note card with two specific audiences listed on it.

- For example, students may get a card that says "grandparents and aliens," "professor and family dog," or "political official and baby."
- Notice that in each of these pairings there is one "formal" audience member and one "informal or creative" audience member—structuring the cards in this way ensures that students will need to address two very different audiences.

Then I ask my students to write a letter to each audience *describing the exact same object*. When students describe the same object in two vastly different ways, they are more able to recognize the ways in which audience shapes their writing.

Once students have completed both letters, I ask each group to read their letters aloud. Afterwards, I ask them the following questions:

- Why did I have you write about the same object for two different audiences?
- What did we learn from this exercise?
- How can we apply what we learned here to future assignments?

Author's Note—Connection to Future Assignments: This assignment prepares students for the explanation essay. While the "two letters" assignment is a good foundation for explanation essays in a broad sense, it also assists them with my particular essay prompt in which they need to profile a person or place from their hometown. Often, these essays have three potential audiences: the members of the community, a historical society, or a family member or members. Having students consider audience, therefore, aids them in the composition of their explanation essays.

Potential Problems: Since this assignment is fairly simple and requires little preparation, there tend to be few issues, if any, when I assign it in class. One possible issue is that students may not be familiar with writing letters; if this is the case, then they can write e-mails to these audiences instead.

—m—

Code Switching
Appropriate Language, Situation, and Email Etiquette
• Rita D. Costello •

Abstract: Students discuss proper email etiquette by reviewing an "inappropriate mock email" and then rewriting it appropriately for three different audiences.

Duration: One 50-minute class period, but may take two class periods depending on how expanded steps 1 to 5 are; step 6 is the only part that might not fit into a single class period. In a TR (or 75-minute class), the entirety of steps 1 to 6 can fit in a single class period even if steps 1–5 are significantly expanded.

Materials: Overhead projection, smartboards, or chalkboards

Preparation: Start with a ridiculously inappropriate mock email from a student to a teacher. I suggest rewriting a new one each semester, at least until there are a few to rotate.

Procedure: Either project or write the email in the front of the class; this works best as a large group rather than individual work. Here is an example:

> *dude! i got so drunk last night i woke up covered in puke in someone else's apartment. i don't even know where i am or how to get to school from here, so i definitely won't be in class today. LOL! i hope i didn't miss anything important, but can u send me notes on what we did in class? my email is bongwater69@gmail.com. i'll be there ThirstDay. hope this doesn't hurt my grade!!!!*
>
> *Greg*
>
> *p.s. can you also tell me how many absences i have now?*

2. Provide some sort of email etiquette guidelines. These may be individual handouts; however, there are also plenty of guidelines available online that may be simultaneously projected if you are in a smart classroom. At our school, we publish ours in a guidebook for the composition classes, so I can just ask students to turn to that page in their books.

3. Let students laugh and make fun of the email for awhile before continuing. (For teachers with experience, this can also be a place to read aloud a few real-life examples). Once the class settles a bit, go through the email etiquette guidelines with the mock email to see where it falls short. Keep the tone humorous during this portion if possible.

4. Ask students to take out a piece of paper and write their names on it, then ask a few introductory questions, such as:

- What is your personal email address?
- What does this address say about your personality?
- What would a professor think about you/your personality if you used this email address?
- Would you be embarrassed to have an instructor think this?
- Why or why not?

5. After the surface questions, ask students to rewrite the email in an appropriate way for an email to an instructor using the email etiquette guidelines. Ask a few (or all) students to read aloud their revised emails.

6. I like to repeat this exercise almost exactly (during the same class period if possible,

or soon following if not possible) using an introductory paragraph for an essay. The sample paragraph should be in first person and about a controversial issue. The variations I ask for during the written part are that I ask students to rewrite in three ways:

I.   if telling this information to friends in a bar/restaurant,
II. if telling this information to an elderly close relative, and
III. if telling this information to a scholarly audience that they have to convince to trust them in order to convince readers of some point or purpose.

Additional Author's Notes: While step 6 could be left off (if one wants to deal only with email etiquette), I highly recommend including it, because it is one of the few times that what is said about academic writing before any formal assignment is given can really stick with students. It is also a useful exercise to refer back to throughout the semester whenever students have trouble with audience-aware language. Some students may feel a little embarrassed during the course of the lesson due to self reflection on past emails; thus, it is important to keep the tone light rather than critical.

Rationale: Especially early in college, students tend not to think of implications or assumptions made about them based on their actions or speech. This exercise helps tremendously and also reduces the ridiculousness of the emails instructors tend to get from students. It also helps to link the idea of communication with a purpose to the idea of essay writing, as well as the idea that code-switching is not just an academic situation but a constant one.

WORKSHEET

Students should follow proper email etiquette when communicating with instructors as opposed to the more causal style used with friends. Adhere to the following guidelines for every email sent to an instructor, not just those teaching English. Whether intentional or not, teachers judge the seriousness and intelligence of a student by what they see in the emails they receive.

1. Include a subject line with a clear but brief description of the content or purpose of the message (i.e., "Question about Essay 2").

2. Include proper salutations such as "Dear" or "Hello." The instructor's title such as Dr., Professor, or Mr./Ms. should be included. The appropriate title is on the course syllabus. If in doubt, use Professor. (Miss or Mrs. is never appropriate unless the instructor has specifically requested one of those titles be used.)

3. Be clear and direct without being wordy. Clear, short messages are often responded to faster than longer ones.

4. If absent, do not ask questions such as, "Did I miss anything important?" Important work occurs in every class. Instructors cannot recreate the experience for absent students.

5. When signing the email, include a name, course and section number. Most instructors teach several sections of the same class in one semester. If the instructor cannot identify what class the student is in, he or she might not be able to respond.

6. Proofread for typos, spelling, and grammar. Do not use "text language" such as u, btw, lol, etc. Use capital letters where appropriate.

7. Be patient. Wait a minimum of 24 hours before expecting a response. No response should be expected until Monday for messages sent on Friday or over the weekend.

8. Do not send instructors chain letters, jokes, inspirational stories, or other forwards.

—⚟—

Letter to My Body
An Exercise in Poetry
• Gerardo Del Guercio •

Abstract: In "Letter to My Body," each student will be asked to prepare, in the form of a poem, a letter to one of their body parts (e.g.: "Letter to My Shoulders"). Students may work in groups or individually. Brainstorming can be done either in class or as homework.

This exercise works well for teaching figurative language.

Duration: Each round takes about 10 to 20 minutes. Each student plays one round.

Materials: No special materials are required, although students may opt to use a computer, overhead projector, or spot light.

Suggested Reading: Watcyn-Jones, Peter, ed. *Top Class Activities: 50 Fun Games and Activities by Top ELT Writers, Book 1* (London: Penguin, 1999).

Preparation: The editors suggest prepping the class by reading and explicating several different kinds of poetry and discussing the typical elements of poetry.

Procedure: Task students with writing a letter with two twists to it: it must be in the form of a poem, and it must be addressed to a body part.

Begin by having students brainstorm

- Metaphors for the body part and its relationship to the rest of the body
- Descriptive details about the part, the body as a whole, or the writer's self-image
- Five details about themselves
- How political/social/environmental issues shape body image

Students can work together in groups, or this section of the exercise can be assigned as homework.

Once the student has completed their text, they will read the poem to the class. The class is free to ask questions once the reading is done. Oral presentations should take about two to three minutes.

Variations: Ask students to prepare a poem of three lines or more that describes one of their body parts. The text could be Haiku, lyric, rhyming couplet, free verse, etc. The pupil can even present a parody of a text (e.g.: Shakespeare's Sonnet 14). It is the student's choice.

Ask students to explain the metaphor(s) they are going to use and then render themselves in that metaphor.

Additional Author's Notes—Script for In-Class Scenario:

If the Assignment Is an In-Class One (Scenario One): Hi, class. Today we are going to present our poems. I want you to take 10 to 20 minutes to write a letter to one of your body parts. The letter will be in the form of a poem. You can use whatever poetic form you like or you can even combine conventions. The poem cannot be banal, though. What I mean is that there has to be a metaphor. I want you to define the metaphor you are using and then render yourself in that metaphor. Can you define what a metaphor is? If the answer is no, I will define metaphor: a metaphor is a comparison without using "like" or "as." I do not mean that you cannot use similes in your poem (Define simile: a comparison using "like" or "as"). You will also need a thesis statement.

If the Assignment Is a Take-Home (Scenario Two): Hello, class. Today we are going to present our poems. You can take a few minutes to rehearse, prepare, and make any last second changes.

Additional Notes to the Instructor: Always explain in scenario one whether the assignment is take-home or in-class.

Although the focus is on composition, the assignment can also help improve the student's oral communication and public speaking skills.

Tally Phase: The professor will allot grades based on sentence structure, variety, style, grace, and speech. Please note that teachers are free to use other criteria to grade the presentations.

Rationale: The activity will help to build and refine the student's ability to brainstorm, argue, describe, and compare and contrast. The class is asked to use figurative language (e.g.: metaphor, simile, pun, etc). The exercise will also help students to create thesis statements, rebut arguments, and manage their time.

Potential Problems: Shyness is a common problem. Just remind the student to give a big smile and to make good eye contact. The professor is asked to stand at the back of the class while listening to the evaluations. Teachers should smile and not look at a note pad when writing comments. In doing so, the presenters will be more comfortable presenting their topic. The trick is to bond with the class.

From Written to Oral
Using a Venn Diagram to Teach Modality
• Josh Herron •

Abstract: This exercise asks students to work in pairs to develop a Venn diagram exploring the similarities and differences between written and oral presentations followed by a whole-class, instructor-led discussion of the various elements. Students will complete both written and oral presentations or will be required to adapt a presentation in one form to the other.

This exercise has elements of visual rhetoric.
Duration: 25 to 35 minutes.
Preparation: Prepare a Venn diagram that already compares and contrasts written and oral presentations and prepare reasons for your list and strategies for students as they adapt one medium to another.

(Optional) Prepare a mini-lecture on oral and written culture along with the shifts and importance of both in rhetorical and communication studies throughout time.

Additionally, see the "In-Class Activities" section below.

Editor's Note: A Venn diagram is fairly familiar to most people, even if the proper name is not. Essentially, a Venn diagram consists of interlocking graphics—usually circles—which visually illustrate commonalities between different things. A quick Google search will provide numerous examples.

Procedure: This is the opportunity for an instructor to offer explanations of strategies for and similarities/differences between written and oral presentations as various elements of each are discussed.

A sample compare and contrast of oral and written presentations is below, although students often are fantastic in noting elements that an instructor may forget.

Oral: Audience location; nervousness/anxiety of speaker; memory of speaker and audience

Written: Time and space difference of audience and speaker; editing and revising after completion

Both: Essential pattern of organization; need to cite sources; an audience and context to consider

In-Class Activities: Introduce students to the assignment for which you are preparing them, e.g., a persuasive speech based on their argument essay.

(Optional) Hold a brief mini-lecture / discussion on written and oral culture.

Pair students and have them brainstorm and create a Venn diagram that compares and contrasts oral presentations and written essays. Allow them 5–8 minutes on this activity. Students may have questions about what particular aspects you're comparing and contrasting, but allow them to go in any direction at this point.

Draw a large Venn diagram on the board. Call students' attention back to the board and ask students for labels to put on the diagram.

Check your prepared diagram to see if there are important similarities or differences that weren't mentioned that you want to emphasize.

Instructors may wish to elaborate on each similarity and difference as it appears or may want to take them as a whole after the diagram is complete.

Rationale: Many composition courses include oral presentations. Rather than have students see writing and speaking as separate acts, this exercise emphasizes the inherent connections between written and oral assignments as well as looks at the requirements needed to adapt one to another. Including discussion of oral culture and written culture can also add an interesting background to this exercise of practical strategy.

This activity is typically used when preparing students to present an oral presentation that may or may not be based on a written assignment they have previously completed. The assignment could also be used as part of discussions on multimodal composition.

Potential Problems: A Venn diagram can come across as oversimplified; however, for two forms of presentation that are so intricately connected but rarely explicitly discussed as such, the diagram provides a nice visual aid as well as an opportunity for discussion to prepare students for presenting in both formats.

—◊—

Using Twitter in the Composition Class

Writing Collaboratively Through Digital Technology

• Josh Herron •

Abstract: Using Twitter technology, this exercise suggests an overall approach for collaborative writing—it is not a specific assignment per se but a method for students to work together on text generation. This exercise requires a good working knowledge of Twitter and the ability to design an account for students to use.

Materials: Student access to a computer or mobile device with Internet capabilities; classroom computer and projector with Internet access

Author's Note: Many consider technology to be an integral part of the composition classroom in the 21st century, specifically interaction and analysis using digital media. Twitter is an efficient and easy-to-use method for students to compose and collaborate in a digital environment. Students will have access to this service on their computers, smart phones, and tablets, so it can be a mobile learning experience.

This activity can be used in almost any unit or module in the composition classroom. It works especially well when discussing multimodal composition, digital culture, media studies, or other directly related topics as it offers direct experience with these topics.

Intentionality is an important element in the use of digital media as Jennifer Swartz reminds in the *Kairos* article "MySpace, Facebook, and Multimodal Literacy": "We have to make sure our use of multimedia is not simply technology for technology's sake." Thus, it is necessary to underscore the intentional nature of this assignment and the learning objectives.

Preparation: Writing prompts that can be texted to students using Twitter.

Instructors may want to consult Twitter how-to guides to see how others have explained this service and its terminology to help you explain it clearly to students.

Create a course profile on Twitter. Even if you already have a personal account, a course profile eliminates unnecessary privacy issues and awkwardness for you or your students. You can use this profile to post questions for response, retweet students' responses, and post course announcements.

Find a hashtag that is short enough not to take up too many characters, easy to remember, and not used on Twitter already. This can be a bit difficult, but a common course hashtag includes the course number and section, e.g., #ENG102A.

Determine

- requirements for the number of tweets (will vary),
- the number of replies to other course members (necessary to ensure collaboration),
- the length of the exercise,
- a date and a methodology for counting the number of tweets,
- and a system to keep track of students' tweets and interactions.

Create an assignment sheet that explains the exercise and these requirements.

By requiring students to use the hashtag, you can easily find them by searching for the hashtag, but this must be done within the two-week timeframe that Twitter keeps these searchable. Using a spreadsheet is a simple and efficient method of keeping track.

Create a way for students to view how many tweets they have so that they can double-check and keep track without constantly asking the instructor or having any surprises. Using a shareable document such as a Google Docs spreadsheet is an efficient method.

Develop questions as the unit or semester progresses that relate to course topics and allow for students to reply to one another, building on each other's responses.

Procedure:

First Day of Exercise

Below is a sample purpose statement for the exercise (can be included in the assignment sheet or guidelines) that can help students understand the nature of the activity:

Why Twitter?

We're using Twitter to help us be intentional about our communication in new media. Twitter—and social media in general—is a unique rhetorical space that deserves more than just passive attention. We'll make use of this new media form as a method of collaborative learning and sharing, and we'll also do a bit of rhetorical analysis of the medium itself.

Familiarize students with how to navigate and use Twitter and make explicit the connection of the exercise to the course material. While this is an important first step for those unfamiliar with Twitter, you'll find that most students already have a working knowledge of the service. The emphasis on intentionality of the exercise on this first day is also important.

Explain the requirements and assignment guidelines. Discuss the importance of the course profile and hashtag. If a projector is available, show students the course profile and Twitter interface, including how to set up an account. It is important to remind students to make their profile public so that you and others can see their tweets.

(Optional) Allow students time in class to create an account and/or follow the course profile. This allows for students to ask questions on the spot.

Students may want to create an account just for the course if they already have one and don't want you or other students to stumble on it or if they don't wish to make their accounts public.

Subsequent Class Days During the Unit or Semester

Typically at the beginning or end of class, you'll want to remind students if you have posted a new response question and if you have a time limit for them to respond. It is a good idea to have more questions so that students do not feel they have to respond to each one to meet your requirements.

Incorporate the assignment into the class intentionally. This doesn't have to be every class, but using students' tweets to spur classroom discussion or allowing students to tweet a response during class are great ways to integrate the project into the class rather than being viewed as a separate task.

Potential Problems: While most students find this activity creative and somewhat "cool," there will be students who report their dislike of the intersecting of their social worlds and academic worlds. This, however, is a good opportunity to discuss this problematic binary. Some students will be resistant to using this technology, so having an alternative assignment available for them is key. For the instructor, tallying and recording tweets can become time-consuming, but setting up an efficient system right away helps with this. Do remember, however, that Twitter only keeps hashtags searchable for about two weeks, so you'll want to search within that timeframe.

—∿—

Narrative Structure of Storytelling
Using Freytag's Triangle to Teach Audience
• J.D. Isip •

Abstract: Using the essentials of narration (scene, dialogue, character), students create a scene which they then share with the class; students then respond to a "boring" paragraph written by the instructor to learn audience awareness.

This exercise also teaches writing process and creative writing techniques.

Duration: Two 50-minute class periods

Materials: A diagram of Freytag's Triangle (readily available online) using overhead projection, a white board or chalk board, or a handout

A chalk or white board is plenty, but being able to set up the dialogue in a Word document is very helpful

Preparation: Before we get started on a narrative essay in my classes, I try to make sure that my students have some "basics of storytelling" down. This tends to make the entire assignment more enjoyable as they start flexing their new found "creative writing" skills while still meeting the requirements of a standard narrative essay (though I encourage teachers to think outside of the box when it comes to the narrative—one can only read so many stories about graduation).

Suggested Reading: The exercise does not call for readings, but I find that reading a short one act play in conjunction with this exercise is helpful. *Sure Thing* by David Ives is a favorite of mine (though, I admit, it is a bit dated), but I have also used *Fat Pig* by Neil LaBute. The more contemporary the better. You want dialogue that sounds natural, so probably not the time to break out Shakespeare.

Procedure: Briefly, I show my students a very basic diagram of Freytag's Triangle (there are dozens online—look them up before taking the time to make your own, particularly if you are not good with graphics). I find that most students have come across this before, so it is a great opportunity to have them speak up and share from their previous experiences.

I overlap the terms provided by Freytag with essay terms:

- *Exposition*—This happens in the introduction and it includes the hook, background, and the thesis
- *Rising Action*—This happens in the first few supporting or body paragraphs; the characters are being introduced, the scene is being set, the reader knows what the problem or conflict is
- *Climax*—I like for students to believe that every narrative (even the one about graduation) needs a climax, some pivotal point where something changes; *change* is some-

thing I stress for my students' narratives. I tell them, "If nothing changes, why should I care?"

- *Falling Action*—This is optional for my students. I stress that if there were other characters (a best friend, a coach, etc.) who were introduced, it is nice to follow up and let the reader know what happened to them. However, I let them decide if doing so will take away from their overall narrative drive. If it is too much, they may just skip to the dénouement (and *do* use that word—they love it!)
- *Dénouement*—This, of course, is our *"So what? Moment"* and I ask my students to think about when they are watching a movie and get to the end; they want to know "what that movie was about" or "why it was worth watching." They need resolution and so does their reader.

This seems like a lengthy talk, but it really only takes about 10 to 15 minutes and it shouldn't take much longer. The idea is for them to start thinking of a narrative in stage or cinematic terms, getting them out of feeling like they have to write *Moby Dick*.

Description: Setting the Scene

Our first in-class exercise has to do with setting a scene.

1. Ask the class to give you the name of three to four locations (i.e., Hawaii, heaven, the gym, etc.). Write these on the board.

2. List some adjectives and phrases we associated with these locations across from the locations listed. Be sure to leave a few inches of space between the lists and the names (you'll be drawing lines between them)

3. Then ask the class to write a scene in one of the locations using words from the list of another location (i.e., using "the gym" words/phrases for "heaven")

4. Have them share or build an example on the board

Students know what an adjective is and usually have some idea of how to describe things. This is meant to get them to think outside of the usual vocabulary. The hope is that you will get something better than "I was excited" and "I could not believe it" and all the rest of that. We keep building...

Dialogue: Letting "Characters" Tell the Story

I find that setting up dialogue is almost completely foreign to most of my students. Depending on how well your students "get it," this is where you may need to give yourself another class period. This talk can take five minutes or it can take up to 15 minutes. Either way, I feel like it is important for students to know how to use dialogue.

1. Draw a page on the board or open a Word document on the projector. Demonstrate to the class that each new speaker gets a new paragraph/an indent:

a. This construction works for me (the point is to illustrate as many variables in dialogue as you can—notice all of the ways I have here, including absent dialogue tags):
      He said, "I don't know."

"But you like her, right?" his friend suggested.

"I guess," he was writing something down.

"So call her!"

He just kept writing, pretending not to hear.

2. Now have them create two characters to inhabit that "place" they created with the description portion of the exercise. These characters should have a conversation of at least five lines.

3. Have them share with their group. These are often very funny, and you can even encourage them to be outrageous (tasteful, of course, but outrageous). My students ask if their characters can curse. I respond by asking if real people curse (of course, I teach college students).

4. Have each group decide on one member's dialogue to share with the class.

While my class is writing and sharing, I am constructing a very boring paragraph on the board that is standard narrative stuff (i.e., "I was very nervous the night before the big game. I felt like I was going to die. I could not sleep.... Blah, blah, blah"). Make it as bland as possible.

1. Ask the class to take this paragraph and make it happen in a dialogue between two characters. This can work very well as a group exercise, or the class can all construct together on the board.

2. Be sure to offer some suggestions for situations—maybe friends are talking, teammates, parents, etc.

3. Ask the class which they would rather read, the dialogue or the paragraph.

I like to wrap up by asking my students what they have learned about description, dialogue, and storytelling. Then I give them their narrative essay assignment with a plea on the top: *"Please do not bore me."*

They think this is hilarious. I am pretty sure it is the height of sin in some pedagogical circles, but I want to make sure my students are conscious of their audience, that they do not write in a purely self-serving manner.

Potential Problems: I wouldn't necessarily call it a problem, but I do get students who want to write dialogue into their other essays (because they catch on to how much space it takes on a page).

You *can* potentially take too long "explaining" any one of the steps of this. Don't. This is a great exercise to let the students help one another figure things out. They all know what a good story sounds like, even if they don't use words like dialogue, description, and dénouement. They catch on pretty quick and, as much as I love to talk about this stuff, I have to force myself to shut up because they tend to like to write this stuff. In one of my student's words, "I feel like a real author, Professor Isip."

Class Database Project
Extended Project on Writing Presentations
• Denise Landrum-Geyer •

Abstract: In this extended project, small groups of students work collaboratively to design extensive presentations on some aspect of writing and/or grammar.

Duration: First three-and-a-half weeks of the semester

Preparation: Students should be aware of the concepts in Freytag's Triangle.

Procedure: Using the worksheet (included after "Procedure"), we go over the basic description of the project the first day of the assignment sequence, and once students get into groups, I ask them to look over each section together to make sure everything is clear to them. We also return to this over the course of the assignment sequence if any major questions arise.

I use the assignment sheet (following), which I call the "Class Database Project," as the first major project in my Composition I class. I start with the project for three main reasons: firstly, I've found that group projects early in the semester help create a sense of community; secondly, it can keep some students engaged who might otherwise disappear; and thirdly, since we discuss the rhetorical triangle from day one, this project makes the concept concrete for students (they see and know their audience, they're given a specific purpose, and they have to think about how they're presenting themselves along with their information). In addition, I end my Composition I class with a multimodal project, and I feel beginning with a multimodal-based assignment introduces the concept early in the semester.

This sequence usually takes the first three and a half weeks of the semester, during which time students get into groups, choose topics, and are assigned a final presentation date. The topics come from the students, as they list two or three writing and/or grammar-related questions they have on the first day. I tally the most common concerns, and this becomes the list of potential topics. I've also had students in computer classrooms present different technologies or software programs as options for multimodal assignments, too.

The class readings and discussion focus on thinking about rhetorical situations (audience and purpose primarily), writing concisely, MLA citation style, and visual rhetoric and design concerns for multimedia projects. This assignment does require some special attention to citation and plagiarism concerns, as some students don't think they need to cite where example sentences or exercises came from, which can lead to interesting discussions about what we cite and why we cite it. I also curate a list of resources students can turn to for more information, including their textbook (we use *Writing Matters* by Rebecca Moore Howard), the Purdue OWL, and a list of other grammar/writing resources I've collected over the years.

At least two full class periods are devoted to in-class work on presentations, though most groups still meet outside of class. I try to find a computer lab for at least part of the assignment sequence, as I like to offer students plenty of workshop time. At the end of these three and a half weeks, students go through a peer response session for their handout and multimedia presentation, and they then turn in their rough drafts to me for feedback. Since students present their projects to the class, they sign up in advance for dates throughout the semester, and the presentations run about two-thirds of the way through the semester.

I try to sequence the presentations to coincide with the other assignments we're working on: students are usually working on more traditional writing assignments (personal essay, review essay, rhetorical analysis) when the final presentations are presented to the class. There is usually one presentation per class period, and the presentation is at the very beginning of class, followed by a short period of time in which the rest of the class anonymously fills out the rubric. When giving comments (anonymously), students must list at least two things the group did well and two suggestions for improvement. I then collect and tally the rubrics, type up the student comments, add my own comments and rubric, read through each group member's memo, and return the comments to them. I keep the original rubrics that their classmates filled out in my office, and groups are allowed to review the rubrics if they wish.

As I stated above, this project can create a sense of community in the class, but the downside to that is if a student disappears from class, the rest of the group has to pick up the slack. I've tried to avoid that scenario by having the group create rough drafts in the beginning of the semester: that way, at least the group has a rough draft to work with, but if the student who disappears had volunteered to be the main speaker, then other group members have to take over the work.

I think these presentations allow students to feel more invested in the class and to understand what it means to "teach": students often comment on how hard it is to effectively teach their classmates, and I think it gives them a different perspective on the classroom. What's more, many students comment on how they feel that they understand a concept better because they had to know it well enough to teach it, and they are considered the class experts on their topic. Also, I find that the students give great feedback to their classmates, and that feedback gets better as the semester progresses; often, I don't have any personal comments to add, as the student comments cover everything. Of course, there are students who don't take the commenting seriously and give everyone a perfect score, but much more often, students deliberate while filling out the rubrics and think hard about what they want to say. It's also a positive experience when presentations set a high bar for the rest of the class and give students ideas to incorporate into their own work; the other side of that, of course, is how to deal with early-semester presentations setting a low standard, which can be difficult to recover from in a class.

This is a detailed assignment and typing up comments from multiple students can seem time-consuming, but I think the pedagogical benefits are important and the work time isn't as intensive once a routine is established.

ASSIGNMENT SHEET

Part One: Project Description

What

This first sequence project is a little different than most English class assignments. I am asking you to become a class "expert" (along with one or two of your classmates) in one writing- or grammar-related area. In order to share your English and writing-related knowledge with the rest of the class, and to avoid listening to me go on and on about topics you might be familiar with already, you will be developing a class "database," which we will turn to over the course of the semester. In groups of two or three, you will create a handout and multimedia presentation (PowerPoint, Prezi, Keynote, video, etc.) about a specific English-related topic (either a grammatical concept or some other writing-related topic). Your group will then present your handout/presentation and what you learned about your concept, sharing the information your group has developed with your classmates and me.

Who

There will be approximately two to three people in each group. Each group will have four tasks: create a handout that explains and defines your group's concept for your classmates; create a short multimedia presentation that complements your handout and explains your concept to your classmates quickly and clearly (the method of presentation is up to you—you could create a PowerPoint presentation, a short video, a skit, or talk through your handout); include an in-class activity for the class to make sure your classmates understand your concept; and present the handout/presentation to the rest of the class at some point during the semester.

You will sign up for groups on [date here], and we will spend the first few weeks of class developing these projects before presentations will begin.

How

I will leave the division of work up to each group, though I will say many groups choose to divide into sub-groups (multimedia presentation, handout, class activity, group spokesperson) in order to cover all bases. Regardless of how you divide the work, all members of your group will be expected to be familiar with your topic. Each group will be responsible for creating a handout and presentation as a resource for your classmates to return to over the semester, which I will post on the "class database" section of the class website. You will have plenty of time to develop a comprehensive, clear handout and presentation, and you will be able to get feedback on your project from your classmates and me before your final class presentation.

In addition to creating a handout, your group will be expected to present your information to the rest of the class. I suggest dividing the presentation into two parts: a five- to seven-minute presentation of the subject, and a seven- to 10-minute activity that helps your classmates understand the material more fully.

Your job is to introduce the subject to the class: introduce any necessary definitions, show us how the subject works in writing and/or reading, and provide examples of the subject (if, for example, you are presenting on the rhetorical triangle, use an example text to talk us through the components). You should also make an effort to connect your presentation to other topics we've discussed in class, including whatever writing project we might be working on at the time. You could also consider including a list of resources (such as books, websites, or chapters in our class textbook) that are relevant to your presentation subject. If you decide to quote from any other texts, you must use proper MLA citation to do so, which we will address in class (see the MLA section of our textbook or the "MLA Formatting Guide" on the *Purdue OWL* website for specific examples of MLA citation formatting).

Part Two: Grading Explanation

(I talk through the basic breakdown of the grading the first day of the assignment sequence, and the rubric is on the class website from day one, but we repeatedly come back to the grading explanation to make sure students understand the rubric as well as their responsibilities, especially when it comes to the writer's memos.)

Project

These presentations account for 100 points of your grade. You will have time during class to work on these presentations and develop a group work schedule, but you will probably need to work with your group-mates outside of class time, too. I also suggest each group schedule a conference with me outside of class to discuss your ideas and concerns about your project. In addition, you will participate in a peer response session and turn in your project drafts to me for feedback before you present your project to the class.

If a group member fails to complete his or her part of the presentation, or continuously slacks off, please let me know as soon as possible so that I can grade that person accordingly.

Your project will be graded using a rubric that we will discuss in class: because you are presenting your work to your classmates, who will be using the information over the course of the semester, your classmates will assess your work with me. Your grade will be calculated as follows: my score counts for 50 percent of the grade, and the average score your classmates give your group will account for the other 50 percent. These grades will be assessed after you present your project to the class and turn in your writer's memo this semester.

Writer's Memo

This project is an exercise in collaboration and team writing, which means your group will need to make sure work is evenly distributed. I will also ask each group member to compose and turn in a short writer's memo (at least 200 words long, double-spaced) in which you describe the work you contributed to the group project, reflect on the highlights and lowlights of your group's work process, and evaluate how the rest of your group-mates contributed to the project. This writer's memo will be confidential between you and I, and it will give you a chance to be honest and candid with me about this project. Memos will be turned in the day your group presents the final draft of your project in class.

So ... what about this "writer's memo" thing? The writer's memo is a chance for each of you to talk to me about your project before I read your draft. For this project, I'm asking you to talk through both your responsibilities and the responsibilities of your group member(s) (so each member of the group should write their own memo). The memo should include the following sections (the questions are to get you thinking; you don't have to answer all of them):

1. **Your Part:** What work have you contributed to this project? (Did you create the handout or PP? Were you the designated speaker? Did you work on the definition section of the handout and presentation?)

2. **The Process:** How has the work gone so far? What's gone well? What hasn't gone so well? Did your group's plan change significantly between the rough draft and your final presentation? Is there any specific part of the project you'd like me to focus on for feedback?

3. **Your Group Members:** Describe the responsibilities each group member has taken on for this project. What strengths did each member bring to the project? As a whole, do you feel your group worked collaboratively to finish the project? Why or why not?

4. **Is there anything else you'd like me to know about your project?** If so, now's the time to tell me. If not, no need to include this final part.

This is informal writing between you and me, but I do want you to use complete sentences and formal spelling. Even though it's informal, it should still be professional: the memo should be in MLA format (page number in top right corner; your name, my name, class name, date in top left corner; 11 or 12 point font, readable type, black, double-spaced). See Ch. 21: "Formatting a Paper in MLA Style" in our textbook for an example of what that looks like.

Rubric

Category	A	B	C	D
Presentation	Group has prepared a presentation that complements the handout clearly.	Group prepared a presentation that seems related to the handout most of the time.	The presentation is underdeveloped or there is little connection to the handout.	The group failed to create a presentation in addition to the handout or created a confusing, unclear presentation.
Content	Group includes all required parts of the assignment (presentation, handout, and activity).	Group includes 2 of the 3 required parts of the assignment (presentation, handout, and activity), but doesn't explain each section individually.	Group includes 1 of the 3 required parts of the assignment (presentation, handout, and activity).	Group doesn't address any of the required parts of the assignment.
Stays on Topic	Stays on topic all (100 percent) of the time.	Stays on topic most (90–99 percent) of the time.	Stays on topic some (75 percent–89 percent) of the time.	It was hard to tell what the topic was.
Handout	Group creates an easy-to-follow, thorough handout that is a useful introduction to the subject.	Group creates a thorough handout that is mostly helpful, but occasionally difficult to understand.	Group creates a handout that relates to the technology but is not useful or missing important information.	Group does not create a handout.
Spelling and Punctuation	There are no spelling/grammatical or MLA missteps in the handout or presentation.	There are minor spelling/grammar (misplaced commas, missing words, etc.) or MLA issues in the project.	There are major spelling/grammar (fragments, comma splices, run-ons) or MLA issues in the project.	The spelling and grammar issues are so severe that it is difficult or impossible to understand OR there is no MLA works cited list.

Part Three: Logistics & Tips to Consider

(I usually go over these once the students have formed groups and chosen topics, but before they are too far into drafting.)

This project is both an exercise in team writing as well as an exercise in writing to inform or teach. Your audience is your classmates and me, and you should assume that the majority of us are unfamiliar with the subject.

With these considerations in mind, I have the following suggestions:

- While this is a team project, it is likely that you will want to divide the work into smaller sections.
- You can do this in a few different ways: one or two people in the group can focus on creating the handout while the other people focus on the presentation of information to the rest of the class.
- Logically, the information you present in class should "match up" with the information you write, so this approach will require a lot of communication between group members.

Another option is to give each group member a subsection of the handout to write; each person could then present their specific subsection to the class. Again, communication between group members will be crucial to make sure that everybody's work complements the other work done in the group.

I leave the decisions as to how to divide the work up to the group. There is no minimum length requirement for the handouts, though concise, to-the-point writing is usually important in this genre. Ultimately, each group needs to decide the most effective way to get the information to the class.

When writing, think about all of the how-to guides or tutorials you've ever read: most guides use short, concise sentences with a focus on strong, active verbs. Depending on the subject, you might use short lists rather than complete sentences and paragraphs to convey information. You should also focus on giving your audience the most important information about your topic; remember, this is an introduction, not a complete guide to your topic.

This is a writing class, not a public speaking class, so we won't be too hard on those of you speaking to the class.

Delivery does matter, though, so please keep the following tips in mind:

- Speak loudly, clearly, and slowly when presenting.
- Be sure to practice the presentation a few times before you speak to the class.
- This can be informal (no need to dress up in fancy clothes), but still professional—take the presentation seriously and do your best to teach the class about your concept.
- You won't teach them everything; instead, you're introducing them to your topic and sharing some basic information with them.
- Most of all, think of this as a friendly exchange between colleagues—your classmates will be presenting to you, too, and I have to get up in front of you all every day, so I understand having nerves; we want to give you the best grade possible, but you do have to give us a reason to give you that grade. Smile, and—gasp—maybe even have a little fun!

As with any project, if you are unsure about anything, talk to me as soon as possible.

—ɯ—

The Art of Incorporating Sources and Discussion of "Slant" in Writing

• Debra Rudder Lohe •

Abstract: Following worksheet prompts, students select quotations and rewrite them for three separate audiences; students then read these aloud and discuss how the choice of audience "slants" the writing.

This exercise also teaches issues of plagiarism and source evaluation.

Duration: 15 minutes

Materials: Enough copies of the quotation worksheet (two pages; after Procedure section) for each student

Preparation: Students should be exposed to the idea that text can be potentially biased or "slanted."

Suggested Reading: Birk, Newman P., and Genevieve B. Birk. "Selection, Slanting, and Charged Language." *Language Awareness: Readings for College Writers*. Eds. Paul Eschholz, Alfred Rosa, and Virginia Clark. 9th ed. Boston: Bedford/St. Martin's, 2005.

A summary of the article can be found at http://thor.clark.edu/smitgm/102/Birk.htm (Key words: "Selection, Slanting, and Charged Language Clark College"). The full text of the article can be found with a Google search of the article title in quotation marks.

The Birks' article, "Selection, Slanting and Charged Language," argues, essentially, that virtually any "fact" is subject to a "slanting" process which must be taken into account whenever writers do research. In the Birks' estimation, this is a natural process. Two factors contribute: (1) apriori experience, knowledge, and dispensation (which affects how people determine which facts are valid or not); and (2) the effect of language, word choice, and document design (which can change the perceived validity of facts). Certain words (adjectives and modifiers, for instance) can also change the perception of fact. It is impossible, according to the Birks, to avoid this slant because it represents the speaker or writer.

Procedure: Give students the worksheets with the quotations on them.

Read instructions at the top of the worksheet: Students are to—

1. Select one of the quotations
2. Rewrite/edit it for three separate audiences (five to eight minutes)
3. Have students read what they wrote aloud and discuss the implications of "slant-ing."

Editor's Note: Instructor might be prepared with closing comments about language, and/or the importance of evaluation, and/or the importance of objective source material.

Author's Note: In later class periods, I come back to this kind of activity, asking students to bring in a researched article they've read, looking closely at the ways in which the writer introduces and paraphrases its sources, and trying to identify the "slanting" that may be taking place in subtle ways so as to reinforce the writer's argument.

Rationale: The exercise should help students to see ways they are shaping a reader's view of a source when they incorporate it, based solely on how they introduce the source.

In addition to teaching the basics of academic integrity and how to avoid plagiarism, this exercise seeks to teach students the subtle complexities of incorporating sources strategically.

This involves the strategic framing of source materials, and a clear distinguishing of the student writers' voices and views from those of the sources they cite.

This exercise is not associated with any specific assignment but is groundwork for future exercises related to how students incorporate research materials into their academic writing.

Because it happens early in the semester, it is a good way of getting students to see the subtle ways in which they might agree/disagree with the authorities they cite. (Often, the very idea that a student writer has the authority to "talk back" to sources is itself a challenging and illuminating one.)

Potential Problems: Students may see the exercise as "fun but purposeless" if not followed up with an application in the context of incorporating researched sources into students' own writing.

WORKSHEET

Your Mission ... (Yes, you have to accept it!)

Select one of the quotes below and reproduce it / some portion of it in an effort to communicate its meaning to three different audiences (as described). You may either paraphrase or quote some/all of it, and you may make a different choice for each audience. The bottom line: reproduce its gist, using the lessons you've learned about slanting, without changing its basic meaning.

"The Holocaust was an obscene period in our nation's history ... this century's history.... We all lived in this century. I didn't live in this century." (Dan Quayle, then Indiana senator and Republican vice-presidential candidate during a news conference in which he was asked his opinion of the Holocaust.)

"Whenever I watch TV and see those poor starving kids all over the world, I can't help but cry. I mean I'd love to be skinny like that but not with all those flies and death and stuff." (Mariah Carey)

"I haven't committed a crime. What I did was fail to comply with the law." (David Dinkins, New York City Mayor, answering accusations that he failed to pay his taxes.)

"Outside of the killings, Washington has one of the lowest crime rates in the country." (Mayor Marion Barry, Washington, D.C.)

"After finding no qualified candidates for the position of principal, the school board is extremely pleased to announce the appointment of David Steele to the post." (Philip Streifer, superintendent of schools, Barrington, Rhode Island)

1. Someone who likes and supports the speaker. (E.g., what Birk and Birk term *slanting for*.)
2. Someone who loathes the speaker. (E.g., *slanting against*.)
3. Someone who feels neutral about the speaker. (E.g., slanting both for and against.)

"Where in the Heck Is Matt?"

Evaluating Global Cultures Project and Writing "Context" Papers

• Lauren Matus •

Abstract: Students learn to use a library database by researching the famous "Where the Hell is Matt" Internet phenomenon, culminating in a series of short "context papers."

Duration: This combination of small exercises can take three or four class periods.

- First class: Repeated viewings of the "Matt dancing" (videos average four to five minutes).
- Second class: Discussion of the videos, possible work on Internet database.
- Third class: (Optional) Student work on Internet databases.

Materials: Overhead projection

This works best in a fully mediated computer classroom where students have individual computers or laptops.

I use the following video as an invention technique for a larger, multi-part project: (key words "where the hell is matt") http://www.wherethehellismatt.com/

The video shows a man (Matthew Harding) "dancing" (if you can call it that!). The video is set to poignant music and shows Matt performing his unique dance in different locations throughout the world, such as Papua New Guinea and the DMZ.

Editor's Note: Videos of Matt dancing are also readily available on YouTube.

Preparation: Familiarize yourself with the phenomenon. Look up "Where the hell is matt" and/or "Matthew Harding."

Procedure:

First Class

I show the video several times in class and we discuss what scenes students liked best and why.

Then I ask them to review the video at home and select three scenes that pique their interest for any reason, but they must explain what is so interesting.

Second Class

In the next class we have a group discussion, and I show students how to conduct scholarly research through our library's website. I ask students to research their scenes—where was the scene filmed? Who was in the scene? What was in the scene? Etc. This takes some time, but I encourage students to spend the necessary time just getting used to researching using databases.

Third Class

Conducted in a computer classroom. Students research their topics on the library databases. Once students have conducted some research, I ask them to narrow their scope to one scene.

Homework: Students are asked to write three short "context papers" covering such things as history, politics, fashion, architecture, language, economics, industry, education, etc. These context papers are the building blocks to the larger research project. For example, after watching the video, a fashion design major was interested in the clothing worn by the Huli Wigmen of Papua New Guinea. Through her research she learned about the history and political system in Papua New Guinea, eventually leading her to write a critique of missionary education in that country.

Rationale: I show the video as an invention technique and use small writing assignments and class discussion to guide students into developing umbrella, target and research questions. I use this assignment as the first part of a longer argument or research paper.

—⁂—

"Post-Secret" Rhetorical Analysis
Knowing Your Audience
• Alexandra Oxner •

Abstract: Students examine "post-secrets" (short, anonymous messages posted in public places or in secret) and then write their own post-secrets as an exercise in cultural and rhetorical analysis (exercise includes specific examples from the Internet).

Duration: 30 minutes

Requirements: Internet, projector screen

Preparation: Find some examples of your favorite "post-secrets."

Editor's Notes: Try a simple Google search using the key words "post secrets"; results include "PostSecret.com," "Post Secret Archive," "PostSecret Community," and "Post Secrets from the Past" (although instructors will want to be careful: many of these post-secret notes are risqué or obscene).

Procedure: Explain that "post-secret" is a community of people who anonymously write their secrets on post-cards. They then mail them, transformed into pieces of art, to an individual who makes them all public. The secrets can be purchased in book form, read on the Internet, and so on.

Most of your students will probably be familiar with "post-secret," and this relate-ability makes the lesson plan more effective. If some students do not know what "post-secret" is, emphasize that it is a form of writing.

Show some examples to your students using the projector screen and lead a discussion to analyze the idea of "post-secret."

Questions could include:

- Who is the intended audience of these secrets? Why? What does that mean?
- Would you share your secret in this way? Why or why not? Is it a good/bad idea?
- What are the moral/ethical implications of this practice?
- Now examine individual examples of "post-secrets."

Example 1: (key words "post secret I spend 90 percent of my time staring at a screen")
Webpage: http://2.bp.blogspot.com/-LyGfcvZ8AMM/UegPKiEqvmI/AAAAAAAAY
78/9iwWDlaQdvM/s1600/screenteam.jpg

The secret reads: "I spend 90 percent of my free time staring at a screen." Begin a discussion.

- Do you relate to this secret? Why or why not?

Talk about this secret in the context of the age of technology we live in. Ask:

- Is it really a secret? Why or why not? If this person were your friend, how would you help them?

Example 2: (key words "post secret I know my ex follows twitter")
http://3.bp.blogspot.com/-UN-cBFYnZa8/UegPt73xd6I/AAAAAAAAY88/Rie9qlO
gI10/s1600/twoobs.jpg

Author's Note: This example contains nudity. You do not have to use this secret. I blurred out the background a bit when I used this example in class.

Discuss this secret. It may be helpful to examine in within the context of a cultural lens or through gender or ideals of femininity.

Questions could include:

- Why might this woman have shared this secret?
- What does it mean that she had to keep it a secret? Etc.

Ask your students to take out a sheet of paper. Ask them to write down one of their secrets, but remind them not to write their name anywhere on the paper. They may include a drawing or other illustration if they wish. Warn them that you are going to share some of the secrets with the class, so they should not write anything inappropriate.

Collect the secrets and shuffle them in front of the room. Analyze two or three of the secrets (quickly read them first and choose milder ones). Lead a discussion in which you collectively examine the students' secrets, but be cautious not to offend the writer.

At the end of the activity, ask your students a few concluding questions. Do they view this form of writing as cathartic? Is it uncomfortable, or can it be used as a means of release? Would they ever send a secret to "post-secret?" Why or why not?

Potential Problems: In general, students really enjoy this activity. Sharing their own secrets may scare them at first, but if it is kept *anonymous*, they seem to understand the purpose of this practice. Try to lead a discussion which focuses on the cultural implications of having or sharing secrets. Examine the secrets in the context of gender/social class/race/etc., and push your students to think critically.

Bibliography and Citation Style

In-Text Citations Exercise

Working Through Incorrect MLA Citations to Learn Style

• Becky Adnot-Haynes •

Abstract: Students review the rules of MLA citation and then work through a series of mock-entries to determine which are correct and which are incorrect (worksheet included after exercise).

Duration: 15 to 20 minutes

Materials: A document camera or overhead projector is helpful; alternately, instructors may pass out a copy of the worksheet to each student.

Instructors may want to acquaint students with the Purdue OWL.

Preparation: A general familiarity with MLA style.

Procedure: First I go over the basic rules of in-text citations.

Second, I review several correct examples (included on the worksheet below) with the class.

Third, I ask them to "fix" the examples on the worksheets below on their own so that they are in correct MLA style.

Fourth, I review the examples one by one, asking students to share their answers.

Rationale: This exercise can be used to emphasize the correct use of MLA style in-text citations, which are often the most problematic part of MLA style for students.

WORKSHEET

Some basic rules:

1. When quoting or paraphrasing, the sentence should include the author's name (required), the page number where the information appeared (required), and, if it seems relevant, the name of the source it came from (optional).

2. Put the citation in parentheses following the quote or paraphrase.

3. When the author's name is included in the sentence, you don't need to include it in the citation (see numbers 3 and 4 below).

4. You are not on a first-name basis with the author. Refer to her by his or her last name or full name.

5. Names of longer works, such as books, magazines, journals, or television shows, should be *italicized* or <u>underlined</u>.

6. Names of shorter pieces, such as stories, articles, or poems, should be put in quotation marks.

From the article "Defending *South Park*: Social Commentary in Animated Television Programs" by Nancy Rutherford:

> Many people are too quick to dismiss *South Park* as a bunch of perverse nonsense. While the show can be—and often is—perverse, it is also entertaining, informed, and potentially thought-provoking. It irreverently tackles the issues of today, from celebrities to politics. *South Park* is intelligent, witty, and timely in its subject matter [13].

Some examples of correct MLA in-text citations:

1. The author argues that *South Park* is a show that is "intelligent, witty, and timely in its subject matter" (Rutherford 13).

2. Cultural anthropologist Nancy Rutherford believes that *South Park* is both smart and funny (13).

3. I agree with Rutherford, who calls *South Park* "intelligent, witty, and timely" (13).

On Your Own

Here are some examples of in-text citations that may or may not be incorrect. Working on your own, fix them so that they conform to MLA style.

1. The author calls *South Park* "entertaining, informed, and potentially thought-provoking" (Rutherford, 13).

2. In this article, Nancy argues that *South Park* is more than "perverse nonsense" (13).

3. In *Defending South Park: Social Commentary in Animated Television Programs*, Nancy Rutherford argues that the show is "intelligent, witty, and timely in its subject matter" (13).

4. Rutherford argues that *South Park* is "entertaining, informed, and potentially thought-provoking" (Rutherford 13).

5. The author argues that viewers who dismiss *South Park* quickly are missing out on the show's merits (p. 13).

6. Rutherford argues that *South Park* is an intelligent show, pointing out that it irreverently tackles the issues of today, from celebrities to politics (13).

7. In her article "Defending *South Park*: Social Commentary in Animated Television Programs," Nancy Rutherford calls the show "intelligent, witty, and timely in its subject matter" (13).

8. Rutherford believes that *South Park* is both smart and funny (13).

—m—

A Works Cited Group Exercise

• Rita D. Costello •

Abstract: During group work, students collaborate to write a Works Cited or References page while using guidebooks.

Duration: 50 or 75 minutes

Materials: MLA or APA handbooks to be assigned as homework.

Teachers need to select and bring in a variety of sources of different types and mediums. The content of the sources does not matter; the trick is finding variety and selecting sources that are light enough to carry them all to a single class.

Procedure: I tend to do a few exercises on constructing Works Cited pages throughout the semester, but this one is always the first one I do in the first class in the composition series.

1. Assign the handbook section on MLA format as homework to be completed for this class. (This should work as well for APA format or any other citation system, but our students begin with MLA.) When I assign the homework, I tell students not to try to memorize any part of the handbook or worry if they do not understand any part, but they need to know how to use this section to look up different types of sources and understand the logic of the system.

2. Bring to class a variety of types of sources to hand out to the groups. I always include: several scholarly articles, at least one html database article, several books with different situations—a translator, multiple authors, an author and an editor, etc.—a DVD, a CD, a poem or story in a literary journal, a newspaper, a magazine article, and so on. For several of these, I place a sticky note on the front specifying that I only want one particular part to be used (as in: use the essay that begins on page 210 or use track number four on this CD).

3. Divide students into groups of about three or four students and pass out a variety of types of sources to each group. I typically give about five sources to each group.

4. Ask students to take out their handbooks, a piece of paper and a textbook from another class (only one other textbook is needed for the entire group).

5. The goal for each group is to write a complete and correct Works Cited page for an essay that has used all of the sources their group now has in hand. (That should be about six sources including the textbook from one of the group members' classes.) Allow students to structure the process any way they need to in order to get the work done—some will work on each entry together, others will give each person a source to get started and then compile them. Note the processes they use, but do not force them to use a pre-determined process.

6. Circulate around the room to answer questions and to give hints when noticing a group going astray.

7. When all of the groups have finished and turned in their Works Cited page, ask students to take out their notebooks and go through citing the textbooks for the current class on the board. Ask students to call out what comes first and require them to look up the necessary information in the handbook and in the actual course textbooks. If the class includes an anthology, go through both citing the entire book and citing a single work in the book. Remind students to write down the sample entries. Also, remind them that if they have taken accurate notes, they now have a template for citing the texts of the class (they need never have a wrong citation for the class texts because they have exact models to follow).

Potential Problems: As with any group work situation there is the risk of some students doing more work than others; the best one can do is note this or try to prod students with questions. Circulating the room and interacting with each group sporadically is essential.

Constructing a Works Cited Page
For Group Work or Homework
• Rita D. Costello •

Abstract: Using the following worksheets, bibliographic information is provided on a variety of sources, which students are then tasked with converting to correct MLA (or APA) citation style and answering questions about the citations.

The attached exercise can be given as homework or in-class group work. The exercise is written for MLA format, but should translate equally well to other citation formats.

Duration: 50 minutes

Materials: Handouts, enough for each student

Handbooks or format guides

Procedure: The worksheets are fairly explanatory.

Below, find worksheets comprising 15 different entries. Each entry contains the essential information that students would use to make a correct Works Cited or References page.

Students first write out by hand the individual entries and then rewrite them as they would appear on the final citations page of a research paper.

Included with each series of entries are study questions on format and citation style.

Author's Notes: This exercise can accompany any essay where sources are used, but it is probably most appropriate for the end of a first composition course—e.g., an English 101 level—or the beginning of a second composition course—e.g., an English 102 level.

Potential Problems: There are no particular pitfalls to the exercise. However, it is advisable to go through student answers to the follow-up questions at the end of each individual exercise. In order to make a more compact handout, the spaces to write each collection of sources could be removed and replaced with instructions to write on a separate piece of paper.

WORKSHEET

While in-text citations vary depending on what information a particular style/format values—for example MLA values the page the material was found on, but APA values how recent the information is—they always refer readers to further bibliographic information. Aside from the fact that bibliographic entries are needed to avoid plagiarism, they also tell readers how to find the source on their own; there are many reasons a reader might want to find a source used in an academic essay. When researching, one might read an article that cites a source and know that the source used in that article is exactly what is needed for one's own research. Looking up the entry for that source on the bibliography page tells the researcher all the information needed to go find that source. On the other hand, readers might be skeptical of the way a source has been used or the claims quoted from that source and want to verify the reliability of the original for themselves. Again, looking at the bibliographical entry tells those readers all the information needed to obtain the source and verify it.

Implementing a style/format system is one of the few times that academic writing has right and wrong answers. These are not answers one typically needs to memorize for tests, but one does need to know how to look up the appropriate bibliographic form. Even experienced writers occasionally need to pull out a handbook or stylebook to verify how to write the bibliographic entry for a particular type of source. Thus, if a student takes the time to look up the proper format, the student never needs to lose points on an academic writing assignment for not using the style/form properly.

For the following exercises, use your handbook to answer the questions and construct a complete Works Cited page. You will *not* always need every piece of information provided, but everything needed is included.

Exercise 1 (sources for an essay)

Information from a Real Source	*Write the Proper MLA Works Cited Entry for the Source*
BOOK IN A LATER EDITION *Author:* David H. Richter *Title: The Critical Tradition: Classic Texts and Contemporary Trends* *Edition:* 3d edition *Publisher:* Bedford/St. Martin's Press *Place of publication:* Boston, MA *Date of publication:* 2007	
A WORK IN AN ANTHOLOGY *Author:* Michael Wolfe *Article title:* "How Does It Feel?" *Editor:* Jonathan S. Cullick *Book: Religion in the 21st Century* *Publisher:* Pearson/Longman *Place of publication:* New York, NY *Date of publication:* 2009 *Pages:* 189–192	
BOOK WITH A TRANSLATOR *Author:* Albert Camus *Title: The Myth of Sisyphus and Other Essays* *Translator:* Justin O'Brien *Publisher:* Vintage Books/Random House, Inc. *Place of publication:* New York, NY *Date of publication:* 1983	
JOURNAL ARTICLE (IN A PRINT JOURNAL) *Authors:* Mohan K. Menon and Alex Sharland *Article:* "Narcissism, Exploitative Attitudes, and Academic Dishonesty: An Exploratory Investigation of Reality Versus Myth" *Journal title: Journal of Education for Business* *Volume:* 86 *Issue:* 1 *Date of publication:* January/February 2011 *Pages:* 50–55	

Information from a Real Source	*Write the Proper MLA Works Cited Entry for the Source*
WEBPAGE ON A WEBSITE *Author:* Margaret Atwood *Page title:* "Siren Song" *Website: Poetry Magazine* *Sponsoring organization:* Poetry Foundation *Originally published:* 1974 *Page last updated:* 2011 *Page visited on:* 13 June 2011	

Now put the above entries together in a proper Works Cited page using all five sources:

_____

_____

_____

_____

_____

_____

_____

_____

_____

_____

_____

_____

_____

_____

_____

_____

_____

_____

_____

_____

_____

_____

_____

_____

_____

_____

Double check a few issues before we move on (check your answers using your handbook):

- What determines the order for entries placed in the Works Cited?: _____

- What type of word is first in every entry for this Works Cited page?: _____

- Was this a Work Cited page or a Works Cited page (and what is the difference)?:

_____

Exercise 2 (a second essay)

Information from a Real Source	*Write the Proper MLA Works Cited Entry for the Source*
BOOK WITH AN ORGANIZATION AS AUTHOR *Compiled by:* American Society of Magazine Editors *Title: The Best American Magazine Writing 2010* *Publisher:* Columbia University Press *Place of Publication:* New York, NY *Date of Publication:* 2011	
PUBLISHED INTERVIEW *Authors/Interviewers:* Stephanie B. Goldberg and Henry J. Reske *Interview subject:* Janet Reno *Title:* "Talking with Attorney General Janet Reno" *Journal title: ABA Journal* *Volume:* 79 *Issue:* 6 *Date of publication:* June 1993 *Pages:* 46–49	
JOURNAL ARTICLE FROM A DATABASE (HTML) *Author:* Herbert B. Dixon, Jr. *Article title:* "The Black Hole Effect: When Internet Use and Judicial Ethics Collide" *Journal title: Judges' Journal* *Volume:* 49 *Issue:* 4 *Date of publication:* Fall 2010 *Database:* Academic Search Complete *Visited:* 14 June 2011 *Pages:* 38–41	
SONG ON A CD *Singer:* Billy Bragg *Song:* "Against Th' Law" *Composer:* Woody Guthrie *Album: 'Til We Outnumber 'Em: The Songs of Woody Guthrie* *Record company:* Righteous Babe Records *Date of publication:* 2000	
TELEVISION SHOW *Director:* Tristram Powell *Writer:* Anthony Horowitz *Episode name:* "Foyle's War: All Clear" *Series name: Masterpiece Mystery!* *Performers:* Michael Kitchen, Honeysuckle Weeks, and Anthony Howell	

Information from a Real Source	*Write the Proper MLA Works Cited Entry for the Source*
Network: PBS *Local channel (call letters):* LPB *Location of local channel:* Baton Rouge, LA *Date aired:* 14 June 2009	

Now put the above entries together in a proper Works Cited page using all five sources:

_____
_____
_____
_____
_____
_____
_____
_____
_____
_____
_____
_____
_____
_____
_____
_____
_____
_____
_____
_____
_____
_____

Double check a few more issues before moving on (check the answers using your handbook):

- What shape is each entry (compared to a paragraph)?: _____

- What indicates to readers where a new entry begins?: _____

- Are the entries numbered?: _____

- How is University Press written in a Works Cited entry?: _____

Exercise 3 (a third essay)

Information from a Real Source	*Write the Proper MLA Works Cited Entry for the Source*
BOOK WITH MORE THAN THREE AUTHORS *Authors:* Julie Ault, David Deitcher, Richard Elovich, Andrea Fraser, Coco Fusco, Douglas Grimp, Holly Hughes, Lewis Hyde, Lucy R. Lippard, Kobena Mercer, Martha Rosler, Kathleen M. Sullivan, Carole S. Vance, Michelle Wallace, David Wojnarowicz, Philip Yenawine, George Yudice *Editors:* Brian Wallis, Marianne Weems, and Philip Yenawine *Title: Art Matters: How the Culture Wars Changed America* *Publisher:* New York University Press *Place of Publication:* New York, NY *Date of Publication:* 1999	
POPULAR MAGAZINE ARTICLE *Author:* Tim Dickinson *Article:* "The Fox News Fear Factory" *Magazine: Rolling Stone* *Issue:* 1132 *Date of publication:* 9 June 2011 *Pages:* 54–66, 82–84	
GOVERNMENT DOCUMENT *Author:* Library of Congress *Title: The Federal Theatre Project Collection: A Register of the Library of Congress Collection of U.S. Work Projects Administration Records on Deposit at George Mason University* *Publisher:* Library of Congress *Place of Publication:* Washington D.C. *Date of Publication:* 1987	
FILM ON DVD *Title: Everything Is Illuminated* *Production Company:* Warner Bros. *Director:* Liev Schreiber *DVD release date:* 2006 *Original release date:* 2005 *Performers:* Elijah Wood and Eugene Hutz	
ARTWORK (VISUAL IMAGE) *Artist:* Karen G. Bourque *Title: Just Like a Tree* *Medium:* stained glass and stone *Location (institution):* The Ernest J. Gaines Center at University of Louisiana at Lafayette *Location (geographic):* Lafayette, LA *Year of creation:* 2010	

Now put the above entries together in a proper Works Cited page using all five sources:

_____
_____
_____
_____
_____
_____
_____
_____
_____
_____
_____
_____
_____
_____
_____
_____
_____
_____
_____
_____
_____
_____
_____
_____
_____
_____

Double check a few last issues (check using your handbook; there are correct answers):

- If the sources from all three exercises above were used for a single essay, which entry would be first on the Works Cited page?: _____

- When a book has both authors and editors, where do the editors go in the entry?:
  _____

- Of all the entries in all the exercises, which is the only one where the state abbreviation should have been included after the name of the city?: _____

- There is more than one way to cite a film; what determines which you use if both are the same film in the same format?: _____

- Do you have to cite notes, blackboard pages or other handouts from a class you are taking (or took) in order to avoid plagiarism?: _____

- What is the difference between the following abbreviations Ed., Eds., ed. (in the first unit of the entry), ed. (if it is in a unit of the entry after the title of the work):
  _____
  _____

Annotated Bibliography and Beyond
In-Class Critique and Development
• Roslyn Reso Foy •

Abstract: In a four or five class period sequence, students generate topics as a group in class; research on library databases, summarize, and create bibliographic entries; write critiques of their articles; and present their research to the class.

This exercise works well to introduce library databases and online research.

Duration: Approximately four or five 50-minute class sessions, depending upon class length and size.

Preparation: Instructors will need to set up a library tour or be familiar enough with their campus library to conduct a tour of their own. Likewise, instructors should be able to demonstrate how to utilize an electronic database; overhead projection is recommended.

Materials: Computer classroom for student research.

Procedure:

First Class Period

We begin by spending the first class period discussing ideas of interest to students as individuals. I ask them to think of topics in which they have a particular interest and already know something about or one that they have always wanted to pursue but failed to for lack of time.

Second Class Period (Library and/or Computer Classroom)

We then go to the library (or use technology in the classroom if available), and we explore how to access scholarly articles through academic databases. This is a perfect opportunity to define and show how peer-editing within the classroom mirrors what takes place with peer-edited journals on a scholarly level, and this helps establish a degree of authority for them as they see that their own critical thinking skills may be applied to writing that has already been examined by experts in a given field. Students should use this period to research and find at least two articles on their subject matter.

Once students have discovered two articles (or perhaps an article and a book chapter) on their individual topics, they create a bibliographic entry that follows a specific style guide (for me it is MLA format); they then write a fairly straightforward *summary* of the main idea presented in each argument. This develops analytical skills and also illustrates the difficulty of saying only the most essential things in a paragraph or two. As 17th century philosopher Blaise Pascal wrote in his 16th Provincial Letter to the Jesuit Fathers, "The present letter is a very long one simply because I had not the leisure to make it shorter"; in other words, it takes more effort to summarize concisely and delineate key information than it does to ramble.

Third Class Period

Next, the assignment demands that they add a solid paragraph or two that *critiques* the main argument presented in this published work. This approach allows them to put to use the skills we have discussed throughout the composition classroom.

The author suggests that students use the following criteria to evaluate their articles:

- Discover flaws in argument/reasoning
- Illustrate why the article did or did not engage or inform them satisfactorily
- Explain that it did or did not use enough information or authoritative sources to convince them
- Examine what was or was not effective overall in the article or chapter
- Explain how the ideas that were presented enlightened (or failed to enlighten) on the subject in question
- State what may or may not be useful in the paper students will eventually prepare for submission.

Overall, students should understand that not all published work necessarily engages or informs sufficiently and generally establish a sense of analytical authority and knowledge that they themselves have critical thinking skills to apply to any published piece of writing. All this they accomplish in writing on a document of one to one-and-a-half pages. They are required to attach a copy of the article in question to their summary/evaluation.

Fourth/Fifth Class Period

Finally, I ask them each to choose one of the articles they researched and prepared and to present the ideas in the article to the class. Generally, this part of the assignment takes two class periods, depending upon the size of the class and depending upon how much the students interact with and respond to the ideas presented. Each student has up to 10 minutes to put forward the main argument of the article, explain why he/she chose that article, clarify how effective or ineffective it was, discuss how it changed or did not change his/her thinking about a particular topic, and project how that student might use it or integrate it into a future essay.

By the end of this class period, students have established individual intellectual authority because they have chosen a topic of interest to them specifically. They interact with each other's comments by exploring things we have discussed in class related to analyzing texts and ideas and to writing in general, and they see that the skills they have acquired in their own peer-editing groups serve them well on a higher level. In effect, they now can act as independent critical thinkers and writers. Students occasionally question each other about topic choices, offer approaches or sources to enrich the idea, and create a true seminar atmosphere in a freshmen-level classroom. In fact, the entire exercise involves students at every step.

Additional Notes: This activity culminates with their last major paper that involves research in a new way, one that means something specific to them and allows them to approach this essay, as stated earlier, from some sense of authority and originality. It not only empowers them as writers, but it discourages plagiarism or hasty, thrown-together papers because they have spent approximately two weeks just gathering information and thinking before beginning to write the paper. They now not only validate their own intellectual and research skills, but they also approach papers from an educated and scholarly investigation of their own making.

Rationale: Most freshmen understand something about doing research, but few have experienced what it means to do scholarly research in peer-edited journals from a variety of academic disciplines. This exercise familiarizes them with university library research using databases and sources that are most legitimate for the sorts of scholarship they will pursue in the future. It clarifies for them what serious research entails, allows them to choose articles that are of interest to them or that are of relevance to their own fields of study, gives them the opportunity to use their analytical skills in assessing major arguments presented in the articles they choose, and most of all offers them a sense of authority as they examine and critique what is valuable in a particular essay and what is not. In effect, it is an exercise that will not only contribute to their own writing skills, but it will also aid them in future academic pursuits— all the while strengthening their own self-worth through the process of gradual accomplishment.

Potential Problems: Occasionally, I may encounter a student who is shy or who has not adequately addressed the article because these articles or chapters are usually of a higher intellectual level than what they may have been previously assigned. Hopefully, since this exercise comes near the end of the semester, students all know each other and have interacted with each other in some way. If the atmosphere of the classroom is one that is nurturing, open, non-threatening, and non-confrontational, even the weaker and less verbal students find a way to rise to expectations because they see how involved and supportive others are.

I include a copy of the assignment below for your information.

A S S I G N M E N T   S H E E T

An annotated bibliography is a bibliographic citation (for this assignment in MLA style) of your source followed by a short summary and analysis of your source. It is simply a *summary* of the main argument in a particular article or book chapter. You will have to find two sources by the date assigned and prepare an annotation of each as described below. Proper research is time-consuming and must be done with enough lead time to have your bibliography prepared on the due date. This assignment is designed to introduce you to proper documentation and preparation for research and to deepen your critical thinking, reading, and evaluation skills. You may find the articles/chapters you read will lead you to a topic for a future paper or may open ideas to new ways to think about a text.

The MLA Bibliography lists titles of all articles and books published in peer-edited journals over the years. This is one of the best resources for books and journal articles on literary topics. Depending upon your topic, you will look at other databases that apply to the topic you choose (JSTOR, Academic Search Complete, Literature Resource Center, LEXIS/NEXIS, or databases focusing on a particular discipline). We will discuss these during our library session. Once you locate a title that sounds interesting, then you need to find out if there is a full-text copy online or if you need to put your feet in the library itself to find your source. If the library does not have a journal in question, you can access Inter-library Loan (ILL) and request that the library find a copy from another university for you. You pay for this service in your university fees. Do not hesitate to use it. The librarians are generally very helpful and the service is efficient. Occasionally, however, such requests take time. You need to plan for at least a week or two of waiting if you see an article that looks significant. You can also ask the librarian for assistance relating to anything outside literary sources. Much of cultural research can be done on the Internet *only* if it appears in legitimate print sources as well.

The Assignment

The sources should have been published within the last 10–15 years. Read the articles (or chapters of books) carefully; be certain that you pick a topic in which you are interested.

Once you have two articles or chapters of books—no need to read entire books for this assignment—you can then write a brief *summary* of the author's argument and comment on how your think the argument works and if it may be useful to your topic. What are the biases of your source? Assumptions? Weaknesses?

The summary should be no longer than two paragraphs and the comment one or two. In your final paragraph or two evaluate the source. Was it worth reading? Why or why not? Did it offer you information that increased your knowledge in a particular area or that made you look at a familiar topic in a different way? Each summary/evaluation should be approximately one to one and a half single-spaced, typed pages, 11 or 12 pt. font—no longer—and should capture the main argument of the essay along with your assessment of its quality.

Once you have completed the written portion of the assignment, you will be asked to choose one of your sources to present to the class. You will give a 10-minute explanation/presentation of the main aspects of the article you have selected, and then clarify for your fellow students what were the strengths and weaknesses of the article and how you think it may or may not assist you in the development of your final essay. Your classmates are encouraged to offer their responses and suggestions for further investigation.

Format: At the top of each summary, document source citation correctly according to MLA guidelines (see example). If you do not own a current English handbook, the MLA Style Sheet is available online. If you do not know how to document sources properly or cannot understand the MLA website, please see me before you hand in any paper to be graded. If you use a book chapter, identify the title of the chapter in the text of your summary. You *must* include a copy of the article or chapter being annotated.

Attach a copy of the article to your summary/evaluation when you turn it in.

Web sources must come from a legitimate print source to be included. For this assignment, you need only document two sources. This assignment helps prepare you for research and documentation.

Example

Place proper documentation for source at the top of the page:

Articles

Hirshfield, Jane. "Justice: Four Windows." *The Virginia Quarterly Review* 84.1 (Winter 2008): 126–37. Web. 2 Feb. 2010.

Morrissey, L. J. "Inner and Outer Perception in Joyce's *The Dead*." *Studies in Short Fiction* 25.2 (1988): 21–29. Web. 3 October 2009.

Books

Rawls, John. *A Theory of Justice.* Cambridge: Harvard University Press, 1999. Print.

Sword, Helen. *Ghostwriting Modernism.* London: Cornell University Press, 2002. Print.

If you do not quote, cite, or paraphrase (with proper credit to source) appropriately and accurately in these two assignments, you will not pass this project. START NOW. Research is very time-consuming and must be done with care. Make this assignment worthwhile. If you would like to use sources that come from a phone interview or a personal interview with someone who has some authority on the topic, you may do so in your paper, but for this assignment, I would prefer that you use print sources.

—◆—

Avoiding Plagiarism
Integrating and Citing Sources
• Debra Rudder Lohe •

Abstract: Students correct improperly cited or misused source materials.

Duration: 20 minutes

Materials: Printed worksheets, enough for each student

Preparation: This exercise requires that students have read at least one text that can be summarized and that instructors have designed a number of incorrectly written citations, or the instructor can use the worksheet prepared by Lohe below which includes a passage from a source and several responses to the source that cite it improperly.

Suggested Readings: Harvey, Gordon. *Writing with Sources*, 2d ed. Indianapolis: Hacket, 2008).

Rome, Dennis. "The Social Construction of the African American Criminal Stereotype." *Images of Color, Images of Crime,* 3d ed. (Eds. Coramae Richey Mann, Marjorie S. Zatz and Nancy Rodriguez. Oxford: Oxford University Press, 2007).

Procedure: This exercise happens early in the semester as a way of testing students' knowledge about the different ways sources can be misused and to test their knowledge of the content covered in Gordon Harvey's *Writing with Sources.*

After assigning Gordon Harvey's first three chapters, I take an excerpt from a class reading we've already done (in the case of the attached sample worksheet, Dennis Rome's essay), and I devise a variety of sentences that "use" content / ideas from the excerpted passage.

All of them "misuse" the source material in at least one way, as described in Harvey's book.

The worksheet asks students to identify which statements misuse content and to revise them so they meet Harvey's standards. What I know and they don't: ALL of the sentences have something wrong with them. One or two students usually get it, but most don't, and this leads to a great discussion about the subtle ways they can go astray in source use without knowing it.

This is not associated with a specific assignment, but is groundwork for future exercises related to how students incorporate research materials into their academic writing.

Rationale: To test students' learning from Gordon Harvey's book and to have them practice correcting the misuse of sources in their own work.

Additional Author's Notes: This exercise was conducted in a Composition Topics course called Engaging Research. The course was a one-credit workshop for students who needed additional instruction and practice in the responsible use of research materials. One of the primary goals of the course is to help students to learn the subtle ways in which sources can be used—and misused—in researched writing. (Often, students think that avoiding plagiarism is as simple as putting in quotes and page numbers, and they don't know other ways—e.g., structural plagiarism—they can be misusing sources.)

WORKSHEET

Source Material: "In short, then, an important merit of the conceptual entrapment by the media imagery schema is that it helps elucidate the connectedness of crime and its control with the society from which it is conceptually and institutionally constructed by human agents. Through it, media and crime scholars are able to recognize, as a fundamental assumption, that crime is both in and of society. My wish is that this schema is a first step in abandoning the futile research for causes of crime because such research simply complicates distinctions that maintain crime as a separate reality while failing to address how it is that crime is constructed as a part of society" (Rome 85).

Rome, Dennis M. "The Social Construction of the African American Criminal Stereotype." *Images of Color, Images of Crime*. 3d ed. Ed. Coramae Richey Mann, Marjorie S. Zatz, and Nancy Rodriguez. Los Angeles, CA: Roxbury, 2006. 78–87.

For each of the following statements, determine whether the source material is handled responsibly. If it isn't, try to identify the type of problem you're seeing and revise it so that it meets Harvey's standards for Academic Integrity.

1. Dennis Rome asserts that one essential value of his concept of entrapment by the media is that it clarifies how connected crime is to the society from which it is theoretically created by people (85).

2. Here, Rome sums up what he calls a "media imagery schema" that "entraps" African Americans and that partially explains the existence of "crime" as both a reality and a social construct. Rome proposes that his "schema" can be used, along with other approaches, as a way to truly understand the complex intersection between race and crime in American culture and to begin to move away from a preoccupation with the factors that lead to real crime.

3. In this passage, Rome proposes that his view of the circular relationship between race and crime is the only way to really convince researchers to "abandon[ ] the futile research for causes of crime" (85).

4. In Images of Color, Images of Crime, Rome shows how "crime is both in and of society," and he suggests that his approach to the "conceptual entrapment by the media imagery schema" is one way to begin to break down common scholarly views about crime (85).

5. Rome offers his own view of the conceptual entrapment of African Americans as a way to break down common views about race and crime; these views, he suggests, contribute to the idea that crime is a separate reality, and they fail to address the ways in which crime is socially constructed (85).

6. Here, Rome summarizes his complex views on the relationship between race and crime, but he worries that his views are "futile [in] the research for causes of crime" (85).

Citing Together
Plagiarism and Source Exercise
• Ben P. Robertson •

Abstract: Beginning with a discussion of plagiarism, students work in groups to complete MLA citations and write short summaries of the sources (second class).

Author's Note: This exercise is intended primarily for first-year students who are already familiar with MLA documentation style but need a reminder about its major features. For those who are not familiar with MLA style, the exercise serves as an introduction to the basic elements of citing sources using MLA style. The assignment may be altered in a number of ways and may be used for APA documentation style, Chicago, Turabian, and so forth.

Duration: Extended exercise: five class periods

Materials: Before the first class period begins, the instructor needs to have prepared enough sources so that each group can have one source at a time. The sources should be similar to the types of sources the students will be required to cite in their papers during the semester.

My usual sources are as follows:

- A simple, one-author book
- A short item in an anthology
- A journal article
- A magazine article
- A page on a web site
- An article from an online database like *EBSCO* or *JSTOR*

Procedure: The class first needs to be divided into small groups. At my university, first-year composition classes have 24 students, so I divide my students into six groups of four students each.

First Class Period (Plagiarism Discussion)

I always preface this assignment with a discussion of plagiarism and the importance of citing one's sources properly while writing college-level papers. This discussion may take a class period or more, especially if the instructor shows examples (which I do) of texts that are plagiarized and texts that are not.

I point out that the students need four items for each source that they use in their papers:

1. Signal phrases to introduce each inclusion of material from each source (I point out that this avoids the problem of "dropped quotations")
2. The material from the source, whether quoted directly or paraphrased
3. The MLA-style in-text citation to acknowledge the source
4. The Works Cited page entry for the source

Second Class Period

I separate the class into groups and then give each group one source. Their job is to create the MLA Works Cited entry for the source they have been given.

Because the students are in small groups, they may help one another with the task, and—

of course—they're allowed (nay, *encouraged*) to use their MLA reference guides as they create the entries. Thus, the exercise facilitates group learning in which the students help one another, but although their answers may all be the same, each student must complete his or her own paper.

As they complete this task, I circulate from group to group to answer questions. Typical questions include books with multiple publication cities and how to create an entry for an anthology item (most need to learn the term *anthology*).

When groups finish creating their first entries, I ask the students to trade sources with another group that has finished. Their task is then to complete the MLA Works Cited entry for the new source. By the end of the process, each group should have entries for the same six sources.

Keep in mind that some groups will work more quickly than others, so groups may have to wait for their next sources. Depending on the length of the class period and the ability of the students, this first step may take more than one class.

Third Class Period

After each group has completed all six works-cited entries, as a class we check each entry for correct MLA style. I sometimes act as scribe and write out student entries as they read them to me.

Note: some databases provide entries at the end of each article; however, these entries often are not correct. It is useful to point out the differences to students so that they will be aware that simply doing a copy/paste function to move entries from the articles to their papers does not always suffice.

Also, some students will want to use entry-generating software as available on sites such as Easybib. These are not always correct either and should be double-checked. Additionally, this might be a good stage at which to discuss source evaluation, especially in terms of electronically-available material.

One good discussion, for example, involves the appropriateness of using *Wikipedia* or Spark Notes for a college-level paper as opposed to using *EBSCO* or *ProQuest* database services.

Finally, this might also be a good time to discuss the importance of including access dates for electronically available sources.

Fourth Class Period

Once the students are sure they have the correct Works Cited entries, I ask them to write six sentences—one for each source. The sentences should use:

- signal phrases,
- direct quotations or paraphrases from the sources,
- and in-text citations.

This stage provides a good opportunity to discuss how to cite sources (such as those online) that do not have page numbers. Additionally, this stage is a good point to discuss what material from the Works Cited page must be included as part of the source citation in the student's text. I always emphasize that the item against the left margin in the Works Cited list absolutely must appear, either in the signal phrase or in the in-text citation. Other material, such as an article title or the title of a book can appear as well, but the item against the left margin (author's name or, in the case of anonymous items, the title of the selection) must appear.

Fifth Class Period

Again, we discuss possible correct answers to this part of the exercise. Like the Works Cited entries, this part of the assignment can be done collectively or individually. At this point, each student should have all four required items (signal phrase, source material, in-text citation, and Works Cited entry) for all six sources.

Rationale: Ideally, when this assignment is complete, each student will have personally handwritten the correct citation material for a variety of source types. Having worked on the project as a group—with the help of the instructor—the students ideally should have the experience to cite any kind of source by following the models in the MLA handbook. The assignment familiarizes them with their MLA reference books, builds group cohesion, and—if used early in the semester—helps the students and instructor to learn one another's teaching and learning styles.

Additional Author's Notes—On Sources: Of course, other types of sources can be substituted. When possible, I bring the actual source itself, not a photocopy, so for items "a" through "d," I bring a regular book, an anthology, a journal, and a magazine, and I mark a selection ahead of time with a sticky note or some other marker. I set aside older items to use for this purpose (like an issue of *PMLA* from 1989) that I probably will not need so if the students should happen to damage one of them, there'll be no harm done. For items "e" and "f," I print the relevant web page and the article so that the students can consult printouts in the way they might do after making a visit to the library.

Idea and Thesis Generation

Silent Discussion
Method for Generating Class Discussion
• Laura L. Beadling •

Abstract: After assigning a reading (or giving a short reading in class), have each student write down a discussion question at the top of a clean sheet of paper. This will then be passed to the student next to him or her; the next student will then write an answer to the question and pass this to the next student who will respond in turn, and so on...

Duration: One 50-minute class period

Preparation: Assign a reading; however, the point of "Silent Discussion" is not text specific, so virtually any text which challenges students to think would be usable.

Procedure: If this is the first time you have done this exercise in class, briefly go over what makes a good discussion question (e.g., open-ended versus closed, examining the major ideas of the reading rather than trivialities, etc.).

After students write a discussion question, have them exchange papers with nearby students and give everyone five minutes to respond to the question in writing.

Then, have them switch papers with a different student and ask them to read the question and the first response, and then give them another five minutes to add their response, asking them to engage with the other response. Do this four or five times, depending on the length of the class.

At the end, ask them to switch one last time (so the person who ends up with the paper isn't necessarily in the discussion) and ask anyone to read what they consider an interesting exchange. Students will then read or summarize the discussion. Ask for further responses. Discuss until there is no further input, and then ask another student to read or summarize another conversation.

Author's Note: The first time I did this, I was surprised at how engaged the students were, not only in writing but also in the discussion after the writing portion. Something about hearing people summarize their ideas emboldened even quiet students to participate. This is also useful because every student must write on a variety of questions; everyone is engaged in the silent portion of the discussion, not just the same handful of students who always talk. This can also help a quiet group become more comfortable with whole class discussions because they have something to read from instead of having to jump in with their own ideas. I have used this very successfully to help create a lively discussion even with a shy or withdrawn group of students.

Variations: I have both asked students to come in with a discussion question already prepared and used the first five minutes for students to write their questions in class. If I am in a computer lab, I have asked students to open a new Word document on their computer and type their question at the top. Then I ask students to physically stand up and move to a new computer. If this is the case, I also have students email me the documents at the end of class, and I post them on our course management software.

Rationale: Often, when having discussions of readings in class, only the same few students participate and the others are frequently disengaged. This exercise can help ease first-year students into discussions because they don't have to speak out loud. It can also get everyone to engage with the ideas of a reading, which can be especially helpful if the material is particularly critical to the course goals or particularly sensitive and controversial, which might make students reluctant to discuss it out loud without some warm up. This exercise also makes discussion more student-centric and less instructor-intensive.

—m—

Creating Personal Profiles
Five Prompts for Developing Persona
• DeMisty Bellinger-Delfeld •

Abstract: In the following five writing prompts, students are asked to generate a personal profile.

Duration: 40 minutes

Preparation: Before beginning this exercise, have a discussion with students about focusing personal essays on one or a very few aspects of themselves and maybe on one or a few events.

Also, whenever I talk about personal essays with students, I remind them that their topic, although about themselves, must be relevant to an outside audience. That is, someone should be able to relate to your thesis without knowing you. While they are free-writing, students may feel encouraged to recreate as much of the event as possible and practice their writing and recalling skills.

Suggested Reading: Lopate, Phillip. "The Personal Essay and the First-Person Character." In *Telling True Stories: A Nonfiction Writers' Guide from the Nieman Foundation at Harvard University* (New York: Plume, 2007).

Procedure: *Part A:* Have students write on these sample situations (at least seven minutes for each), or any other workable situation:

- An important conversation you had with your parents or another adult figure.
- A memorable talk you had with a group of people, such as a band, a dance troupe, or a team. The only stipulation is that it should be at a time of leisure—for instance, in the locker room.
- A conversation you shared with a significant other. It can be a boyfriend or girlfriend or your best friend.

Part B: This is where writers must pick themselves apart. Students will use the writings they created in Part A for this section (10 minutes for each):

- Take some time to look over each conversation. Pick one of the situations you have just written about.
- Who were you during this conversation? How old were you? How was your hair? Where were you living? Think about every relevant detail of yourself at that time, and write a personal profile of yourself then. If it is difficult to write in first person now, it is okay to use third person to talk about yourself.

Students can share their profiles if they wish. Sometimes, students use profiles in their essays to offer a reflection on the story they are relating to their audience. Since there is no required reading before the exercise, there are not any real problems. Still, sometimes students have trouble recalling. If they feel too stilted by the prompts, invite them to use one of their own just to get them writing.

Additional Author's Notes—Advice for Students: Lopate states that we "turn ourselves into characters every day" in different situations. "Turning yourself into a character in your writing," Lopate continues, "requires the understanding that you can never project your whole self. You must be able to pick yourself apart." Early writing students often offer too much of themselves in personal essays. Like newspaper writers, the personal essayist has to present her audience with a profile of her subject: herself. She must be able to "pick herself apart" at the time that the piece takes place and present the most meaningful information. For example, if her religion is important in the story, she has to tell her readers about her faith. But if her religion has no bearing on the story at all, she should not add it to her piece.

This free-writing exercise allows students to put themselves in different situations and create a profile of themselves in at least one of the situations. For example, if they were to free-write on the first situation under "Sample Situations," they would probably tell us how old they were at that time, where they were (city, building, etc), the time period, their likes and dislikes, and, of course, how that conversation affected them at that time in their lives and maybe how it affects them now. Also, students can see that they can apply meaning to certain events in their lives.

—⁓—

From Topic to Position
A Thesis Statement Exercise
• Rita D. Costello •

Abstract: Students generate a broad list of potential research topics and, following a series of prompts, write about why they chose their topics, and in so doing narrow their list to a workable few subjects.

This assignment would be a good preface to research.

Duration: This exercise can be done in a 50-minute class period without any outside time; however, I prefer to give Step One as a journal assignment leading into the class in which we do the exercise in order to allow more time for sharing, class discussion, and modeling of the process on the board.

Although it would reduce the effectiveness because less class interaction, the entire exercise could also be accomplished in 20 minutes.

Editor's Note: This exercise is the third in a sequence from the author and can be done in conjunction with "Division and Classification Exercises," "Exhaust All Questions," "Analyzing Creative Sources" and "Division and Classification Exercises," elsewhere in this book.

Preparation: Assign the "list" (20 topics the student finds most interesting) as homework during the class period previous to the exercise—this is optional as the entire exercise can be done during classtime.

Procedure:

1. Task each individual student with making a list of 20 topics that they find most interesting. [The number (20) is intentionally large to push students to think beyond the surface as well as to provide variety to choose from when pursuing the later steps. Sometimes secondary criteria are included in this section and sometimes it is left as a free-for-all. I have tried some variations in the past: include at least one topic for each class you are taking; include at least 5 topics that relate to your major or future profession; and so on.]

After selecting your topics, write a brief paragraph explanation how you chose your topics and what makes these topics interesting to you.

2. Choose 10 topics from Step One and explain (in a sentence or two) why other people should also care or how you could convince other people to be interested.

3. Choose five topics from Step Two and, for each topic, answer both of these questions:

    (a) What is an issue within this topic on which two reasonable people could disagree?
    (b) Which of the two people would you side with in the argument?

[In research-based courses, I have changed the two questions to reflect investigation rather than argument; however, by then, students are aware that I expect argumentative thesis statements regardless of the topic. An example of that variation is: (a) what do I already know about this topic? and (b) what would I like to learn about this topic?]

4. Choose one of the topics from Step Three and write one to two sentences that state the student's position on the issue for someone who does not know that there is disagreement on this issue. Make sure when you re-read your sentence(s) that someone could disagree with you and not be deemed crazy.

(When going through these steps in class, I tend to ham it up a bit to make the process fun; however, I simultaneously play devil's advocate to much of what students say at each stage. On the board, I often follow two sets of examples simultaneously through each stage ... one that takes an off-the-wall and fun topic and one that is more serious. By the end of class, both topics end up in a viable academic thesis statement. I often include student participation in revising what I write on the board at each stage as well.)

Rationale: This exercise can accompany almost any paper assignment and works at both the developmental and the English I and II levels; I have also used it with Early Admittance and Dual Enrollment high school students. I tend to use it most often leading in to a first paper in English I when discussing how college academic writing differs from earlier experiences with scholastic writing in high school. The goals of this assignment include increasing audience awareness and emphasizing the need to engage readers; establishing the need to take a position in most academic thesis statements; demonstrating through discussion of the exercise the difference between fact (right/wrong) and position; illustrating that it is not necessarily the choice of topic but the approach to the topic that determines if a piece is academic writing; and providing students with a repeatable strategy or thought process to reach a thesis statement which can be applied—though typically on a smaller scale—to almost any academic writing situation.

Potential Problems: If assigning part of this out of class, only Step One should be included in the homework portion. While students can easily deal with steps two through four with teacher/class interaction and explanation, when assigned as a journal/homework, it is often easy for a student to misinterpret the assignment and go astray.

—⁓—

From Image to Thesis
Description and Observation Exercise
• Martin J. Fashbaugh •

Abstract: During group work, students list details found in selected images and then write thesis paragraphs based on their observations.

This exercise has elements of visual rhetoric.

Duration: 30 minutes

Preparation: Photographs, enough for each group of students in the class

Procedure: When I teach the descriptive and observational essay, I usually design a 30-minute activity in which I break the class into groups of three or four and assign each group either a photograph or a collection of photographs depicting a particular place (restaurant, public park, coffee shop, neighborhood, etc.).

I ask the group to look and discuss the picture(s).

Over the course of the discussion, each student is to record what they observe individually and as a group.

Next, students are to review the list of details in order to write a thesis statement recording their overall impression of the place.

Next, one student will volunteer to write a paragraph-length response with a main observational point followed by the key supporting details.

Each student contributes a list of observations so that everyone remains engaged.

Finally, another student is assigned the task of reporting to the class their overall impression while referring to the details that support this impression.

Rationale: Prompt students to utilize their descriptive and observational skills and to understand the interdependent relationship between the two. Students develop a heightened awareness of the purpose of description which leads to an overall argument or impression.

Potential Problems: A common problem is the uneven degrees of participation among group members. In anticipation of these potential problems, it is important for the instructor to monitor closely the progress that each group makes to ensure that everyone stays on task.

—⁓—

Liberating the Conversation at the Start

Narrative Freewriting Exercise

• Martin J. Fashbaugh •

Abstract: Following narrative prompts, students free-write to begin the writing process.

Duration: 25 to 35 minutes

Preparation: Instructors should be prepared to discuss the parameters of a narrative essay. A list of narrative prompts (author recommends four to six).

Editor's Note: There are numerous prompts for narration online. Most of these deal with memoir and personal interactions. Instructors might consider the following:

- Breaking up with a best friend
- First day on the job / school / team
- An experience which was embarrassing / illuminating / frightening
- A blessing in disguise.

Procedure: I hand out four to six narrative prompts, one of which will become the topic for a major paper assignment.

After explaining the objectives for the paper, I have them freewrite for four or five minutes on each prompt.

Rationale: The main objective of this exercise is for students to discover the topic on which they are most comfortable writing. The exercise, therefore, eliminates for most students the out-of-class time spent deciding on a topic.

A second objective is to help students overcome writer's block. By asking that they continuously write in five-minute intervals, they are encouraged to write down as much as possible without worrying about grammar, sentence structure, or organization.

Potential Problems: The drawback with such an assignment is that a student's choice of topic is sometimes determined by the order in which the prompts are listed.

I have noticed that the first prompt they freewrite on has a higher probability than the others in becoming the paper topic for the major assignment because the students are generally the most energized during the first five minutes of the exercise. By the fourth, fifth, or sixth prompts, fatigue may set in and prevent students from writing as unreservedly as they had on the first one or two. In an attempt to avoid this problem, I give a two- to three-minute break after the second and fourth prompts.

—m—

Moving Beyond Summary
Ten Prompts for Critical Reading and Analytical Writing
• Priscilla Glanville •

Abstract: The following handout provides an excellent introduction to the foundational tools one uses in literary analysis.

Particularly well suited to freshman literature surveys and to writing courses for non-majors, it will help students to:

- Explore the differences between summarizing a text and analyzing a text,
- Avoid common pitfalls that lead to plot summary—particularly when exploring conflict, characterization and theme,
- Recognize a work of literature as the product of a cultural sensibility,
- Recognize interpretation of literature as individualized, and legitimately so, yet reasoned and logical.

Suggested Use: I always begin the term with a discussion of this handout, which I post online, ask the students to review in advance, then reference in a full class discussion. I reserve an hour for a thorough discussion of the handout, with ample time for questions, the solicitation of examples and further discussion. In ENC 1102, which features fiction, drama, and poetry, I find it helpful to begin the term with the fiction unit, as the students see it as the most approachable unit. I use this handout to provide the first and most basic description of what literary analysis involves. With the two successive units, we add discussion of devices, conventions and standards common to drama and poetry. When primary texts are assigned for homework, students are asked to keep these prompts in mind while reading, and to either take informal notes in response to them, or to formally respond to more specific prompts that build on the concepts they introduce.

WORKSHEET

I. *Focus*

- Is the overall thesis statement subjective? Does it present a specific opinion in need of proving, rather than a fact or vague idea?
- Does the paper keep the exact promise made by the overall thesis statement?
- Is each subtopic thesis statement clear, specific, subjective and adhered to in the paragraph it opens?
- Does each subtopic thesis statement fit the entirety of the paragraph it opens?
- Does each subtopic thesis statement reflect a specific opinion regarding something in need of developing? Would a reasonable person argue an opposing position?

II. *Development*

- Is each point fully developed with specific convincing evidence? Does the writer interpret that evidence if he or she must do so in order for the reader to see how it is relevant to the point being made?

- Does the development avoid summarizing plot and instead analyze what's happening below the surface of the text? Is it interpretive, or does it just restate things that happen—things that will be obvious to anyone who reads the work in question?
- Does the development clearly support the specific idea presented in each subtopic thesis statement?
- When the writer incorporates evidence from the text, is that evidence well selected, necessary, meaningful and smoothly incorporated? Is it always worked smoothly into the writer's own sentences? Is it always clear whose words or ideas are being represented?
- Are all sources appropriately cited, both parenthetically and in corresponding Works Cited entries?
- Is the evidence interpreted when interpretation is necessary in order for the reader to understand why or how it supports the point it supposedly proves?

III. *Organization*

- Is the system of organization clear, consistent, and free of interruption?
- Are the subtopics well organized around specific thesis statements?
- Does the writing make fluid transitions between ideas?

IV. *Language, Syntax and General Mechanics*

- Is the language used clear and appropriate for the writing situation?
- Does the paper contain proofreading errors, and do they interfere with clarity?
- Does the writer avoid overusing vague verbs and pronouns? Is the sentence structure somewhat varied, through the use of transitions and embedded clauses? Does it combine long fluid sentences with contrasting short sentences? Does the writer use variety and contrast to add tension and emphasis, at significant points in the study?
- Does the paper use punctuation well, for both variety and correctness?
- Does the writer stay in the eternal present tense when analyzing literature?
- Do the nouns and verbs agree—in tense, case and number?
- Does the writer avoid using fragments and run-on sentences?

V. *Overall Assessment*

— ⋅ — ⋅ — ⋅ — ⋅ — ⋅ — ⋅ — ⋅ — ⋅ — ⋅ — ⋅ — ⋅ — ⋅ — ⋅ — ⋅ — ⋅ —

ASSIGNMENT SHEET

Directions: While reading texts assigned for this course, you should keep the following prompts in mind. Although this is not an exhaustive overview, it can be an excellent starting place as you begin to explore a work's central ideas and conventions. Take informal notes, jot down your questions, and come to class prepared to share your thoughts.

I. *The Author's Literary Movement and Zeitgeist*

Always begin here, as the cultures and events surrounding a writer will influence that person's understanding of the world and everything in it. This perception then shapes the individual's art, which both reflects and sustains cultural forces. Literature thus explores a writer's sense of what it feels like to be alive at a certain time and in a certain culture—sometimes by critique, sometimes by emphasis or exaggeration, sometimes by idealizing an alternate environment.

Questions to Consider:

- When was the piece written?
- Is it chronologically linked to a cultural or literary movement?
- Does the speaker voice concerns common to the author's culture and literary movement?
- Are there biographical features that give us clues about the author's objectives, perception, style, and conventions?

II. *Characterization*

Think about the work's main characters, their past and present lives, and the emotional, psychological, and physical characteristics that define them. Also, pay attention to the secondary characters and the roles they play in advancing the plot or revealing important qualities of the more central characters.

Questions to Consider:

- Who are the main characters of the story?
- How do they interact with each other?
- What do their speech and actions reveal about them?
- Are they honest and self- aware?
- The author presents each character a certain way in order to make the readers react to them in a specific way, and perhaps teach a lesson. What does the author want us to think of his or her characters?
- Is there anything telling about the dialogue between characters in what they say or what they don't say? Pay attention to the silences and to unexpected points of conversation that diverge from what is socially appropriate or conventional. What people don't say can be as important as what they say.

III. *The Narrator: The Person Telling the Story*

Remember not to confuse the narrator with the author. The narrator is an artificial construct: a being created by the author for the purpose of sharing the story. When the narrator is also a participant in the story, you should analyze him or her as you would any other character.

Questions to Consider:

- Who is telling the story?
- If this person is also a participant in the story, is he or she objective and trustworthy?
- Is he or she self-aware?

Is he or she aware of all the other characters' actions, thoughts, and motivations, or does he or she have a "blind spot?"

IV. *Rhetorical Conventions*

Pay close attention to the writer's use of language, which reflects an adoption or rejection of standard principles and rules of composition.

Questions to Consider:

- Does the author use grammar, syntax, diction, or punctuation in an unusual way?
- If so, what function does this usage serve?
- Is it just to make the piece sound a certain way?
- Does it further develop characterization or help to prove a specific point?

V. *Setting: The Environment in Which the Story Takes Place*

Setting refers to the time and location of the story, and your discussion of it should illustrate its influence on the characters and events featured in the story. Remember that everyone is the product of his or her environment.

Questions to Consider:

- Where and when does the story take place?
- How does this environment motivate the characters, their actions, the events that take place, and the attendant consequences?
- Does the setting suggest the influence of fate or heredity? If so, and as we are all products of our environment, does the setting direct or excuse the characters' thoughts or behavior?

VI. *Conflict: The Struggle at the Heart of the Story*

Conflict refers to the struggle from which the story develops, and a story can contain many forms of it at once. This is what engages the reader, who wants to find out how the struggle will be resolved. Critics generally recognize five forms of conflict in literature:

- The protagonist vs. himself or herself
- The protagonist vs. another individual
- The protagonist vs. nature
- The protagonist vs. God
- The protagonist vs. society

Questions to Consider:

- What are the work's central conflicts?
- Are they resolved?
- If so, how?
- If not, is there a message behind this lack of resolution?

VII. *Plot: The Sequence of Events in a Story*

Beware of confusing plot summary with critical analysis. Plot refers to the structure of the work's pieces and the order in which they are placed, like the arrangement of pieces in a puzzle. When you tell us what happens in a story, you are repeating the structure of its events without adding your own opinions. In comparison, when you analyze a story, you go below its surface to show us the meanings and symbols hidden in those events. You don't tell us what happens. You share your specific opinion on what it means. Summarizing plot is like drawing a map on how to get from Miami to Orlando, instead of explaining which spots are most worth stopping at—and why. There may be times when you need to discuss the structure of events. Just don't confuse this with analysis, which is much more personal. Ask yourself, "Am I repeating the sequence of events or sharing my personal interpretation of things the events hide or hint at? Am I investigating or passively observing?"

Questions to Consider:

- How does the structure of the piece build tension?
- Is tension built through actions, words, or plot twists?
- Why does the author structure the piece this way?

VIII. *Symbolism: Using Something Concrete to Represent Something Abstract*

Symbolism occurs when something physical and concrete is used to symbolize something non-material and non-specific like an abstraction or emotional condition. For example, a dove is generally seen as symbolizing peace, a heart as symbolizing love, and a lit candle as symbolizing remembrance.

Questions to Consider:

- Are there recurring images (like a candle in the window) or patterns of image types (sources that show light or shadow) in the work?
- When symbols are repeated, they are meant to draw a reader's attention to something important. What do the repeated symbols draw your attention to?
- Do the symbols represent something specific for individual characters?

IX. *Theme: The Writer's Agenda, or Purpose, in Sharing the Story*

There is always an agenda. Each piece of literature emphasizes something or offers a lesson, and its creator wants you to leave it with specific awareness of something. Even in a work designed to show you that art can be beautiful without being instructive, that in itself is a lesson. Your goal is to figure out the writer's agenda.

Questions to Consider:

- What is the work designed to emphasize or teach us?
- In doing so, does it employ direct critique, example, exaggeration, satire, or another means?
- What specific conventions does it use in order to present this theme?

X. *Context: Further Considerations*

Once you have developed a nuanced and individualized analysis of the work's theme, and the devices and conventions that support it, you will be able to better position it within a literary movement. In this way, you are now ready to take your analysis full circle and re-examine the work in its artistic milieu.

Questions to Consider:

- Does the speaker voice concerns common to the author's culture and literary movement?
- Does the writer employ devices and conventions in ways that are typical for that literary movement or that present a clear divergence from the standard?
- If the work clearly diverges from the norms of the movement its author is associated

with, does this divergence represent the emergence of a new set of standards or a period of experimentation on the part of the writer? If the latter is the case, does the author's work demonstrate the influence of this experimentation?

—⌇—

Introducing the Conclusion
Writing the Final Paragraph to Focus the Opening Thesis
• John P. Hazen •

Abstract: Provides students with practice constructing clear and concise conclusions as well as critical reading experience.

This exercise is also a peer review exercise.

Time: 25 to 35 minutes

Preparation: It is helpful to generate a list of topics ahead of time if there is a desired focus: however the class can spontaneously generate the topics as well.

Procedure: Begin by having the students pick topics to write about. This topic can be from a pre-generated list or spontaneously created at the time of the exercise.

Have each student then write a conclusion for a paper on their chosen topic as if they had written a paper on it. Give the students 10–15 minutes to write the conclusion.

Next, have the students pass their work (or change workstations) with a random classmate.

Once each student has a new conclusion (one they did not author) in front of them, have them write the introduction for the paper that would accompany the conclusion. Again, provide 10–15 minutes for this.

Finally, have the students pass the work (or change workstations) again to a new paper. This time, give the students five to 10 minutes to read the introduction and conclusion and write what they believe to be the thesis of the paper. Additionally have the students make any revision suggestions.

Rationale: If the conclusion of the paper is written clearly and concisely, the second student should be able to extrapolate an introduction for the paper. Additionally, the exercise provides students with critical reading experience in order to disseminate the information from the conclusion to write an effective introduction. Finally, it provides peer review experience.

Additional Author's Note—Variable Methods: The writing order can easily be reversed to provide focus on the introduction. I have used both methods to shift focus from one aspect to the other.

—⌇—

Journaling the Headlines
Finding Paper Topics in the News
• Kathleen Maloney •

Abstract: Students keep a journal of news items, practicing MLA bibliographic style, which culminates in an essay about one topic that students have researched.
This exercise includes citation practice, issues of source evaluation, and peer review.

Duration: Extended assignment: two to three weeks of the semester

Preparation: Editors recommend orienting students to library databases and print resources.

Materials: Students need access to news sources. They can select articles from local, national, or international newspapers (on some campuses, students have access to daily newspapers). They can read magazines (the library has a number of popular and academic periodicals). They may also read online news sources or websites, watch news programs (local or national news, news channels, cable news shows), or listen to radio programs (likely on NPR or other talk radio).

Students will also need a notebook or computer in order to record their reading journal, as well as access to citation guide in order to write the bibliographic information.

Author's Note: I work to assist students to learn how to learn. In the past, I found that centering course discussion on popular culture texts and issues enabled students to find their voice. However, I have recently decided that students should have control over deciding what topics we discuss in the course. To this end, I created the assignment I am sharing with you below.

For the first few weeks of the semester, students read the news and keep a research journal to record summaries of news stories and impressions about these stories. At the end of this period, students write a two to three page essay in which they discuss an issue/idea that they have read about in the news and think their fellow students should also read about.

In class, the day the essay is due, we read all of the submissions. Then students vote on what topics they are most interested in. I write the assignments for subsequent essays based on this vote.

Procedure: What follows is the text of the essay assignment that I give students: As you have already read on your syllabus, you will be keeping a research journal about the reading you are doing of the news. You should type your journal entries and consider keeping them as a single computer file.

Each week, you should read three to five articles about any topic which interests you. You should explore a variety of topics rather than research a single topic. You can select articles from local, national, or international newspapers; can read magazines; can read online news sources or websites; can watch news programs; can listen to radio programs. Be sure to note the bibliographic information, so you can cite these sources.

After finding and reading these articles, you should write a journal entry including the bibliographic information (see website about MLA citation), a summary of the article/source, and your perception/impression/questions/concerns.

You should bring these journals with you to class—either on the computer or printed versions. I will let you know which days I would like you to bring print sources with you to class. We will use the information you are working with to study reading and writing.

As you read and keep your journal, you will need to begin to think about writing a two to three page essay in which you explore one issue/topic/idea you have learned something about. You will suggest why you think this topic is important, why you think your fellow students should learn about it, and what more you would like to learn about this topic. We will read these essays in class and decide what the topics for Essays 2 and 3 should be.

While students work through this essay, in class we discuss what writing is; the writing process; rhetorical considerations of audience, purpose, and form; organizing information; and integrating sources. One day of class time is devoted to peer response on this first essay.

Students are asked to bring an extra print copy of their final draft with them to class on the day the essay is due. In class, we sit in a circle and read and make notes about each essay. Students are given two to three minutes to read each essay and then pass it on to the next person. At the end of the class period, students vote in writing for their top three essay topics. I compile the results and use these in order to construct the subsequent essay topics.

Rationale: I have found this assignment to be very successful. Not only do students get thrust into the research process immediately, but they also bear a significant responsibility for the course materials. And they have an immediate rhetorical situation to consider—convincing their classmates that the topic they have selected is worthy of further study. Unfortunately, the students in the class are not savvy readers and fall victim to particularly seductive arguments—which they later regret—so that we have essay assignments on stem cell research, oil addiction, competition and steroids, immigration, and the war on terror. While many of these topics might have appeared on my "please never write about list," the beauty of this assignment is that the students must carry the responsibility for these topics. Their increase in responsibility allows me to be the classroom teacher that I want to be—the one who assists students to make the best of the situation, to assist students to find some interest in the topic, and to remind them of just how important reading and writing are.

—⁓—

Jump-Start Your Introduction
A Getting-Started Checklist
• Christine Photinos •

Abstract: Students write increasingly specific thesis sentences in class; the exercise includes an in-class worksheet on narrowing topics from a very general statement to a very specific statement.

The exercise is meant to accompany any thesis-driven or question-driven writing project.

Duration: 15 minutes

Author's Note: Some students will finish swiftly and others will take more time. So that no one feels hurried, there should be some other task lined up for early finishers.

Preparation: This exercise is best used after students have had some time to think about their paper ideas and do some preliminary research and prewriting. When the time comes to begin drafting a formal piece of writing, many students have trouble pushing past the dreaded blank page. This exercise provides a structure for getting students started on their drafts.

Instructors might consider generating good and/or bad introductions, good and/or bad first sentences, etc. as examples for their students.

Materials: The only requirement is some means of drafting. Pen and paper alone are sufficient. Indeed, a central purpose of the exercise is to demonstrate that writing can be accomplished under less than perfect circumstances.

Procedure: In class, I go over the exercise (worksheet included below), emphasizing especially the importance of breaking down larger tasks into smaller and more manageable tasks, and of liberating oneself from the belief that writing can occur only under ideal circumstances.

Read through the worksheet with students, emphasizing each of the three steps (one sentence introducing topic; one narrowed sentence on the topic; a one sentence thesis statement).

The exercise models for students how to break down potentially intimidating writing tasks as well as the importance of getting started in avoiding procrastination.

Potential Problems: Occasionally there will be a student who has fallen behind the rest of the group and thus is not yet ready to produce even a rough draft of the introduction. This student might use the allotted time for make-up work.

WORKSHEET

"Nothing is particularly hard if you divide it into small jobs."—Henry Ford

"There is no perfect time to write. There's only now."—Barbara Kingsolver

When the time comes to write an introductory paragraph, some people freeze. The trick to pushing past this kind of block is to break the task down into smaller tasks. Right now, here in class, write a rough preliminary draft of your paper's introduction. Use the list below to focus on one task at a time, but begin with whichever item you please.

Write at least one sentence introducing the general topic.

Two tips:

1. Be general, but not *too* general. Here is an example of a too-general introductory sentence: "The Internet has brought many changes to American society."
2. Avoid clichéd openings such as "In today's society..." and "Throughout history..."

Write at least one sentence introducing your narrowed topic.
Write a single sentence expressing your thesis statement or research question.

With the task broken down like this, you should be able to produce a beginning draft of your introduction in very little time, and regardless of the setting. (For example, even those who prefer to compose their papers at a computer can write a few sentences in longhand.)

An example:

[general topic] The first video games appeared in the 1970s with simple graphics and minimal, abstractly-depicted violence. [narrowed topic] Since then, highly realistic representations of violence have become a major feature of video games and a matter of social concern and debate. [research question] Do violent video games cause some players to commit violent acts in real life?—OR—[thesis] Very little support exists, however, for the widely-held belief that video games lead to real-life violence

Try it!
Write a rough introduction for your paper that contains all three elements listed above.

"Complainstorming"
Brainstorming with Complaints
• Nichole E. Stanford •

Abstract: Students brainstorm subjects that trouble them, using any technique that helps them generate ideas, and create lists based on these subjects; students then share their lists with the class.

This exercise works well with argumentative assignments.
Duration: Generally 15 minutes
Materials: A chalkboard or whiteboard is helpful for post-exercise discussion. Students will need pen and paper.
Preparation: Students should pick a topic of local importance which they will develop into an argument paper.

Instructors may chose to link the "complainstorming" exercise to a reading or learning unit in the class.

Procedure: Explain complainstorming: Students will make a list of everything that "gets under their skin" regarding some topic for 10 minutes. They're welcome to break off into freewriting, doodling, or any other helpful brainstorming method as they try to think of more complaints, but they should keep coming back to the list. I let the students know I won't be picking this up, so they can write whatever they want.

Create broad parameters. If it's for a paper, choose a theme or topic. If it's for class discussion, ask an opinion question about the assigned reading or an opinion question about the day's topic. My theme (and readings) for this unit is education, so I have my students write their papers about something they'd like to change in their own education experience. To launch the complainstorming, I write on the board, "What annoys you about school?"

Provide a few examples to get students going. My students are usually reluctant to complain in the presence of authority (even though I won't see their papers), so I start them out with "It can be anything—tuition, parking, course prerequisites, the registrar's office, so-and-so's critique of standardized testing, the article we read about the sorting function of schools..."

Ask questions to jog the students' memories. Here are some of my memory joggers:

- What do you always complain about to your friends regarding school?
- What would your mom or dad say you hate the most about school?
- Complete this sentence: "School would be great if only..."
- Did you ever have a bad day here? What made it bad?

When time is up, have students share their complaints (and add to their lists if they think of anything else). I ask for student responses and write everything on the board. I remain sympathetic and nonjudgmental. With every response, students usually volunteer more and more from their lists, and sometimes that prompts more ideas.

Rationale: "Complainstorming" is a form of brainstorming that helps students connect their outside interests with writing assignments in the classroom, resulting in more interesting assignments for both students and teachers.

Additionally, this exercise is useful for:

- helping students brainstorm for paper topics (especially argument, persuasion, and research papers),
- starting or encouraging a class discussion, or
- generating topics in a problem-posing curriculum.

Additional Author's Notes: Since I use this exercise to help my students choose topics for their persuasive letters, my next step is organizing students into groups according to their interests to discuss possible solutions. I've gotten great results with complainstorming every semester I've used it, and I've passed it on to fellow teachers who have also used it with success. The only potential problem I can anticipate is students feeling too uncomfortable to share their complaints after the exercise. To avoid that, I recommend waiting to use complainstorming until mid-semester.

I created this exercise when I was planning a writing assignment in which students would be required to demonstrate problem solving (or "critical thinking") as they write a persuasive letter to a local administrator or politician. I wanted them to choose topics that were interesting enough to encourage good writing and local enough to discourage plagiarism, and I also hoped it would model for them how to take action with other complaints in their lives, from relationships to social problems.

—⚬⚬⚬—

Grab Bag
Free-Writing Order Out of Chaos
• Beth Walker •

Abstract: In groups, students will create situations or scenarios that feature objects, words, and phrases pulled from a grab bag then will freewrite individual stories or poems based upon them.

This exercise also teaches the elements of plot construction.

Preparation: You will need about six bags full of magazine cut-ups of words, phrases, photographs, and illustrations. Aim for three or four visuals and at least a dozen words/phrases for each bag. Add a few (two to four) small objects from junk drawers to each bag. Anything as simple as paperclips, cereal box toys, old lipstick, or matchbooks can be evocative. I also like to throw in a crayon: color is always evocative. Try cutting phrases apart to make them more ambiguous or mysterious. Also take the time to tape or glue the words and pictures to construction paper; they will last longer with repeated handling.

Assembling the bags will take two to three hours, or you can build the bags slowly throughout the semester. Once the bags are ready, however, this activity requires minimal prep and in-class set-up, and of course the bags can be reused. In fact, this exercise is handy for any time during the semester that you want to shake things up a bit and get the creative juices flowing. And it works for a variety of ages and skill-levels—just choose your items for the bags accordingly.

Author's Note: Instructors may wish to consult Natalie Goldberg's *Writing Down the Bones* (Boston: Shambhala, 2005.)

Procedure:

1. Ask your students to gather in (or assign them to) groups of three to five people.
2. Give each group a bag with the cut-up magazines and other objects.
3. Ask the groups to discuss the contents of their bags.
4. If they get stuck, ask them to answer the 5WH questions: Who is involved? What is the problem or situation? Where and when is the setting? Why and how is the situation developing? Mingle among the groups if necessary.
5. Then ask each student to freewrite his/her own vignette based on the contents of the bag.
6. The vignette can be a brief story or poem and does not have to follow the group's discussion. A student can return to the group's discussion for ideas if he or she gets stuck. Remind students not to stop writing until time is called.
7. Finally, ask for read-aloud and discussion.

The activity should take the entire class period, so adjust your minutes for discussing and writing accordingly. For a 50-minute period, try 10 minutes of discussion and 20 minutes of freewriting, followed by another 10 minutes of read/aloud and reflection. That should leave about 10 spare minutes for announcements, set-up into groups, and final comments.

You may choose to collect the assignment at the end of the period or ask for a revision. Used in the creative writing unit of my freshman composition class, this exercise easily generates both flash fiction and poetry. Most students tend to write a two-page vignette, which can then be revised into something longer and more structured if needed.

Author's Note—A Script to Use in Class:

Background Script: The Grab Bag Analogy

Ever won a grab bag at the carnival? You know that it is going to be full of junk, but you are still curious about what might be in it. Something might spark the imagination, and suddenly it is no longer junk; it is treasure. This is why many of us write—not because we know what is going to happen, but because we want to discover. We are curious by human nature; hence, we are writers. There are worlds of possibilities, worlds of adventures, if we just open up our imaginations and see what comes.

Sometimes, however, we are not adventurous. We panic at the thought of writing. But resistance, as the Borg say, is futile. Put something down on paper even if you have to grab onto the unlikely, the improbable—even if it looks like junk, even if it seems completely and utterly wrong. There are no right or wrong answers, only interpretations.

Let's face it: writing is not always easy or fun, not even for the best of writers. Writing is sometimes panic, sometimes chaos. That's okay. We simply take what we are given and work with it. Here is chaos on paper in front of us: now we must find a pattern. Look for basic information that is part of any good story: *Who is involved? What is happening? Where is it happening? When is it happening? Why is it happening? How is it happening?* These questions are the building blocks for vivid writing: character, plot, setting, time, motive, method and, of course, appropriate detail.

The Activity Script: Grab a Bag, Discuss, Write, Share

Now I want you to divide into groups of four. Each group will select a bag. Open your bag and arrange the contents for everyone in your group to examine. Your instructions for the next 5–10 minutes are to discuss the contents of your bag. Take notes if you wish. I will be mingling in and out of the groups in case you have questions. [*Discussion.*]

Now that your group has discussed your grab bag, there will be no more talking, only writing. Do not worry about spelling or mechanics; just keep your hand moving for the next 20 minutes. If you are stuck for something to say, write about these questions: *Who, What, Where, When, Why, How?* [*Writing.*]

Does anyone need more time? If not, let's be wrapping it up.

I would like someone from each group to tell the rest of us what you talked about. [*Discussion by one of the groups.*] Would someone in your group please read what you have written? Can the rest of the class see the connections? [*Reading and comments about this group's bag.*] Thank you. Next group?

Now that we have heard some of the things that were written, can someone tell me how this exercise could help with your writing? Where can you go from here?

Pedagogy Script: Rationale for What You Just Did

Thank you for your comments. If you can write something coherent from a bag full of unrelated words, you can write about anything. If you are stuck for a topic to write about, pick a word or an object (or more) and fit them together in a piece of writing as if you were trying to put together a puzzle. Ideas can come from anywhere and everywhere; often, a word, a phrase, or an object can be the catalyst for good writing. Naturally, if you find a detail (a word or object) that just does not seem to fit with everything else, put it aside; it does not have to go into your writing. You do not have to know the whole story; you can discover that as you go along.

If you like what you wrote today, you may expand and revise this for a formal essay, story, or poem. But for now, someone once said that you need two things to create a work of art: a title and a signature. So put an appropriate title on your piece of writing, sign it, and pass it up to me. Thank you for your participation.

Rationale: The activity calls for the practice of oral participation, timed in-class freewriting, and listening/read-aloud skills. The activity especially will appeal to kinesthetic learners since students will be handling the objects from the grab bag, just as if they were examining clues.

Application to Reading and to Special Teaching Units: I use this activity to supplement Natalie Goldberg's classic text on the freewriting process, *Writing Down the Bones*, but no special reading or preparation is required of the students. This activity also works well when discussing the elements of fiction—e.g., what is the conflict? exposition? climax?

To develop practical writing skills, the activity teaches the importance of placing relevant details within an appropriate structure: give students the details (the items from the grab bag), and they will provide the structure (the vignette) that holds the details together.

Potential Problems: Students who were absent will become bewildered if you hand over this activity for individual make-up work (and you might not get your bag back). It is the group dynamic that makes coming up with likely scenarios fun and the in-class timed writing that cuts through resistance.

—⟋⟍—

Following "The Black Cat"
A Descriptive Essay Assignment
• Dennis A. Yommer, Jr. •

Abstract: Students follow the example of E.A. Poe's "The Black Cat" to construct an essay with a striking central image; included on the assignment sheet are prompts for writing style, organization, process, and experimentation.
This exercise also teaches creative writing and symbolic analysis.

Preparation: Instructors should be prepared to cover elements of creative writing prior to this assignment including character development, using dialogue, plot progression, and symbolism prior to assigning this essay. Descriptive writing deserves a solid class lesson.

Also review basic citation style so students can incorporate a properly cited image into their paper.

Assignment: Homework: Poe's "The Black Cat."

Discuss with the class the central image that animates the story—obviously the unfortunate cat itself. The idea that students should come away with is that an image can serve as a central theme or idea in a piece of writing.

Following the worksheet (below), students should "Select a general idea, theme, or genre that you feel a good story may exist within."

Make sure students follow prompts for formatting, elements of creative writing, and style.

Important Lesson Topics: This assignment is designed to be one of the first essays in a composition course. Concepts learned from an image-centered text—such as tone, organization, descriptive writing, citations, and style—easily transfer to other genres such as "Compare and Contrast" or "Analysis" papers. Also, the accessibility of a creative focus allows students to gain confidence in their writing and gives them an assignment they truly enjoy.

Potential Problems: Instructors want to warn students away from hackneyed narratives, such as "My Favorite Football Game," which generally result in a bland recollection of the event. This does not mean that these types of stories will always fail, but they do tend to stall the creative process. Additionally, three to five weeks of class are required to introduce creative writing concepts such as character development, plot construction, etc.

ASSIGNMENT SHEET

Overview

This essay does not need to have a clear argumentative thesis or any outside sources. You may use both logical and emotional examples in your writing and the use of narrative language (the use of I) will be acceptable. I would still suggest that you do not address your audience directly (you), but this suggestion may not apply to all students. An image to accompany your writing will be required, and a proper MLA citation must also be included for this item.

Topic

Remember that a topic is a generally broad category that provides a starting point for your paper. You will narrow your topic as you formulate the first draft for your paper. Your topic is as follows:

After discussing "The Black Cat" by Edgar Allan Poe, we learned that a story can be defined by a strategically selected image. For this tale, the most obvious choice is a "black cat," but there may be other options as well (axe, brick wall, single cat eye, etc.).

Select a general idea, theme, or genre that you think will make a good story.

For example, you may choose to write something that takes place in prehistory. A story from this era might include a dinosaur, meteor, caveman, etc.

Or you may chose a photo taken sometime in your family's history and write a story based on it.

After selecting an image, write a story that represents what the image symbolizes. You may use a variety of techniques including personal narrative, fiction, creative non-fiction, or biography.

Your story should be between four and five pages in length.

You may also begin by writing your story and then selecting an image after your work is completed, or change/alter your image to better suit the needs of your tale. This story must have a beginning, middle, and an end and contain proper grammar, spelling, and punctuation. Keep in mind that the image does not need to directly appear in the story, but instead must be (in some way or another) a symbolic representation of the piece of writing that you produce.

In short, your assignment is as follows: "Compose a descriptive story of moderate length that is accompanied by a symbolic image that represents this story." Your topic, however, is of your own choosing.

Language, Style and Organization

The language you use in this paper may be one of a variety of styles. As long as the language works well with your chosen writing style, it will be accepted for this assignment. As discussed above, you may use humor, sarcasm, narrative or any other form you wish. Your word choice (vocabulary) must be appropriate for your subject matter. Regardless of which style you choose, you will want to be as descriptive as possible.

Each essay should contain the following:

- Writing that is descriptive and precise. This will ultimately bring your story to life.
- An introduction that draws the reader into your story.
- A middle that contains the support, progression, conflict, or details of your story.
- A conclusion that brings closure to your paper/story and answers any previously unanswered questions. A "cliff hanger" may be appropriate.
- Transitions (in one form or another) that appear throughout and help your story flow.
- An image that is printed as a cover for your paper that is relevant and unique. Regardless of your genre or topic, a proper MLA citation will be required for this item.

The Writing Process

This course is designed to emphasize writing as a process instead of simply a product. For this essay, a proposal and two prior drafts will be submitted during the designated days marked on the daily schedule. The first draft must include some form of prewriting and a start to your actual paper. If you do not generally prewrite, you may simply have a page or two of what you plan to use for your paper. For those of you who brainstorm or freewrite, you may bring this work and a paragraph or two of your paper.

The second workshop day will be used to review an actual rough draft of your paper. A rough draft is not simply some writing that may be used in your paper: it is a virtually complete version of your assignment. At this point, most of the work should be done and only fine tuning should remain. Each of these drafts will be used in a workshop during class time. The workshop procedures will be discussed and reviewed prior to these sessions. As a reminder, never write something that you do not feel comfortable sharing with your classmates or instructor.

Important Points to Note

- This is the first essay of the semester, so show me what you can do.
- Do not be afraid to experiment with a genre that is currently unfamiliar to you.
- As an author, always take into consideration who your audience will be. For this paper, the audience may only be myself or your classmates.
- Your objective for this essay is not to persuade or convince your readers—it is simply to entertain and captivate them.
- Symbolism and description are of the utmost importance for this assignment.
- Most "good" stories have implied meanings as well as direct plot events. Try not to compose a tale that is impossible to analyze as a reader.
- Many stories change over time. During the writing process, do not be afraid to experiment with new actions, endings, characters, and images.
- Though this is a formal graded assignment, creative writing is often done simply for pleasure. Be sure to write about something you believe you will truly enjoy.

Language Usage
and Grammar

Teaching Spelling, Grammar, Punctuation and Citation Through Unintentionally Humorous (Anonymous) Student Errors

• Svetlana Bochman •

Abstract: An in-class grammar, spelling and punctuation exercise which can also be adapted to teaching quotation marks and quoted material for research papers; errors are taken from student papers and corrected by the class.

Duration: 20 minutes

Preparation: Look through drafts of student essays and make a list of student errors, quoted from the original essays (without listing student names).

Author's Note: It helps to focus on a particular type of error—misspellings of easily confused words (like "your" and "you're"), lack of parallelism, or misuse of quotation marks, etc. It also helps if the errors are unintentionally humorous.

Make a handout of 10 of these errors, leaving room for students to make corrections.

Procedure: Give the students 10 minutes to correct the handout.

Have volunteers come up and correct the errors on the board, asking whether the class agrees with each correction as it is made.

Author's Note: I do this exercise twice: at the beginning of the semester to work on spelling, grammar and/or punctuation, and towards the end of the semester to work on proper use of quotation marks and appropriate introduction of quoted materials in research papers.

Potential Problems: Sometimes students will reveal which errors they committed, only to be poked fun of by their classmates. Other times, students may go from laughing at the errors to making fun of the anonymous writers. A brief warning at the beginning of the class usually prevents such situations.

—◦◦◦—

Mapping Language
A Metadiscourse Exercise

• Christine Cucciarre •

Abstract: Students discuss where and when they encounter "metadiscourse" in the real world, analyze the language, and then search for examples of metadiscourse in an excerpt.

115

Duration: 50 to 75 minutes

Preparation: Teachers must find a section of text that has moments where the writer is directing the reader instead of actually communicating the topic of the passage.

Suggested Reading: Strossen, Nadine. "Everyone Is Watching You," in *Contemporary & Classic Arguments,* pp. 155–161, edited by S. Barnet and H. Bedau (Boston: Bedford/St. Martins, 2005).

Materials: Copies of an excerpt which demonstrates metadiscourse to be read in class

Procedure: I start by having students discuss how they get to destinations.

Students talk about Google maps, Map Quest, GPS devices such as Garmin or TomTom, and their smart phone navigation applications.

Write on the board the actual language generated by these devices: "After 200 yards turn left," "Bear right to get on the highway," "In 40 yards turn right and then make a sharp left," etc.

Discuss how you provide directions to other people (ex., using landmarks and counting traffic lights).

Segue into a discussion about the manner in which we provide directions to our audience in writing. I explain that what those moments are called is "metadiscourse"; students then brainstorm the ways writers do this.

I sometimes have to prompt them by explaining that metadiscourse not only provides directions, it also instructs the reader about the writer's judgments on how they are handling the material, much like a navigation system chooses the path one will take.

For example, if a writer writes "on the other hand" they are saying to the reader (with only four words), "Reader, I am about to tell you the opposite of what I just wrote, or at least I consider it the opposite of what I just wrote."

We then follow by discovering what other moments of metadiscourse tell the reader to do and what those words, phrases and sentences really argue in that moment. Words and phrases such as "however," "clearly," "but," "in sum," "although," "therefore," "in other words," etc. constitute metadiscourse.

We also discuss the importance of choosing metadiscourse wisely. The example of "moreover" indicates not only an additional statement, but that the writer thinks the next example or idea is even *more* important than the previous.

After we discuss all these possibilities for metadiscourse, I have students read the chosen excerpt and circle all the moments that have nothing to do with the content of the paper but are strictly for the reader. I warn students to be careful not to circle adjectives or adverbs if they are describing part of the topic.

I have a very generous definition of metadiscourse, and, as we go over the passages, I often say that I would argue that some examples are metadiscourse, where others may say they are not. But the point of the lesson is for students to heighten their awareness of leading the audience through the writer's thought process.

This exercise can be done for any type of paper because it is for the writer's audience. I introduce it midway through the students' drafting of their first paper.

—〰—

Digital Diagramming
Adapting a Tried and True Pedagogy to a Digital Environment
• Mary Lynne Gasaway Hill •

Abstract: Sentence diagramming has been updated for use on modern technology. This is an extended discussion which requires a good working knowledge of Prezi. **This exercise teaches elements of visual rhetoric.**
Duration: Once prepared, approximately two one-hour class periods are necessary:

- one for the Prezi workshop to teach the class the software and
- one for the student presentations of their sentence analyses.

The process runs smoothly when students work in groups or dyads, with one student managing the computer while the other student(s) present the analyses.

Preparation: For the instructor outside of class, the time commitment is approximately one hour to learn the basics of Prezi.

Materials: For this exercise, a computer classroom with Internet access and an overhead projector, and Prezi, is necessary.

Instructors and students will also need to set up a Prezi account (which are offered free by the company). If students are to work in groups, then an account can be set up for each group with all members (including the instructor) having access to the account. This permits students to log in at different times and for all to contribute to building the presentation-diagram. This also allows for the instructor to see who is contributing and who isn't.

If the instructor is not familiar with Prezi, then s/he can learn it from the video tutorials available through the Prezi website (www.prezi.com) or Atomic Learning (www.atomiclearn ing.com). These are user-friendly videos that allow one to pause and re-play as necessary.

Author's Note—Why Prezi?: Because parsing sentences with traditional diagramming strategies, particularly tree diagrams, can become unwieldy as the sentence grows more complex, we decided to explore digital options such as Prezi. As an interactive canvas, Prezi operates in a fluid, dynamic fashion, allowing students to zero in on a particular component of a structure while not losing sight of the entire structure.

Procedure: The main objective of this exercise is for students to learn to identify, analyze and manipulate basic syntactic forms and functions within their own writing. Finally, the hope is that Prezi provides a fun, interactive environment that encourages imaginative play with words.

After completion of this exercise, assessment measures may include a pre and post quiz over various structures or a pre and post comparison of a short writing assignment that includes the structures analyzed in the exercise.

Before the Prezi Workshop for Students

Before the Prezi workshop for students, the instructor should review the structures to be highlighted in the exercise with the class. Also, if this is to be graded, provide the students a rubric that details instructor expectations for the assignment. This might simply be a rubric based on the eight parts of speech or basic sentence, phrase or clause structures. Also, if the instructor is not conducting the workshop, be sure to meet with the individual who is to ensure coverage of all pertinent material.

Be prepared to spend a bit of extra time with prepositions as well as subordinating conjunctions. Prepositional phrases are often tricky because the same structure can function to describe a noun or a verb depending on its position in the sentence. For example, "The dog is sleeping on the porch." In this sentence, the prepositional phrase "on the porch" acts as an adverb by telling the reader "where" the dog is sleeping. However, we can move the same prepositional phrase so that the sentence reads, "The dog on the porch is sleeping." In this sentence, the phrase acts as an adjective because it tells the reader "which" dog is sleeping. Subordinate clauses often seem to be tricky because in "text talk" or "tweets" subordinate clauses are treated as complete sentences instead of a dependent structure. So a review of subordinate conjunctions is generally helpful.

Procedure:

Choosing Sentences: Instructors may either assign certain sample structures to be used for practice in the workshop or have students write a series of sentences related to their current writing assignment: one simple sentence, one compound sentence, and one complex sentence. Ideally, one of these sentences is a working thesis statement for an assignment or is meaningful to the students in another way. Another take is to have students identify sentences from previous assignments that were problematic and parse those.

Instructors may also want to start with structures smaller than the sentence such as a prepositional phrase or a noun phrase. However, if the class is more advanced, then introduce more intricate sentences. For example, have students choose from a list of sentences that open famous novels such as:

- "Call me Ishmael."—Herman Melville, *Moby-Dick* (1851).
- "Ships at a distance have every man's wish on board."—Zora Neale Hurston, *Their Eyes Were Watching God* (1937).
- "It is a truth universally acknowledged, that a single man in possession of a good fortune, must be in want of a wife."—Jane Austen, *Pride and Prejudice* (1813).
- "riverrun, past Eve and Adam's, from swerve of shore to bend of bay, brings us by a commodius vicus of recirculation back to Howth Castle and Environs."—James Joyce, *Finnegans Wake* (1939).
- "It was a bright cold day in April, and the clocks were striking thirteen."—George Orwell, *1984* (1949).

The Prezi Workshop

1. Choose Template

In the workshop, have the students choose a Prezi template. Because the templates, themselves, can be distracting, instructors may wish to choose one template to be learned by all during the workshop. The one presented below is called "The Journey."

Begin by clicking in the Title Area boxes to add appropriate text for your assignment. For example, "Simple Sentence Digital Diagram" in the top text box with the simple sentence to be parsed in the text box below it.

Simple Sentence Digital Diagram

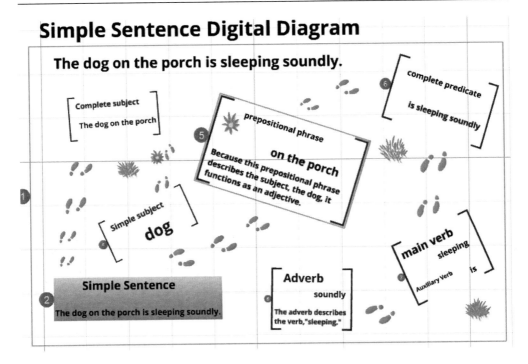

Sample sentences:

- "The dog on the porch is sleeping soundly."
- "The environmental efforts of the United States should be focused on the increase of carbon dioxide in the atmosphere."

2. Fill the first frame of the template.

Once a template is chosen, students write the largest structure, such as a simple sentence, to be parsed in the first frame.

Simple Sentence

The dog on the porch is sleeping soundly.

Simple Sentence

The environmental efforts of the United States should be focused on the increase of carbon dioxide in the atmosphere.

3. In subsequent frames, students parse the appropriate constituent parts of the larger structure. Below are sample ways to parse the complete and simple subjects of the two sentences from above.

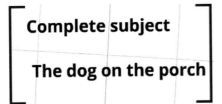

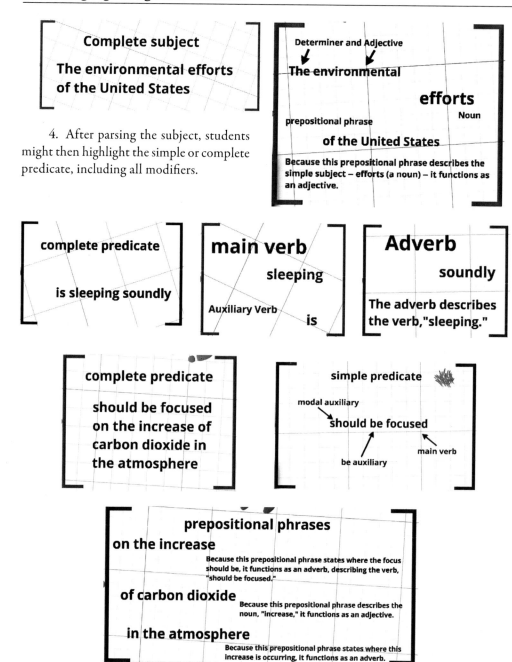

4. After parsing the subject, students might then highlight the simple or complete predicate, including all modifiers.

Student Presentations

It is much more time efficient to have a single computer, which all students will use to present, instead of having students connect their own laptops to the projector.

Encourage student interaction with their peers during the presentations. Odds are that more than a few errors will occur in the student analyses. Pause and invite students to comment and assist in clarifying or correcting the errors. Walk softly at this stage as students can become terribly uncomfortable or embarrassed if the instructor does not facilitate a positive environment for the exchange. These errors, however, often provide the richest learning interactions for all in the classroom. Also, remember that ambiguity often occurs in syntactic and semantic relationships. There just may be more than one way to analyze a particular structure. Encourage students to consider alternative views if actual ambiguity is involved, but carefully distinguish such ambiguity from a misunderstanding of a part of speech or a particular structure. Be sure to leave time at the end of each presentation for questions as well as follow up conversation when all have been completed.

At the conclusion of the student presentations, consider offering a more challenging structure or two that the class can work on together. Students are usually relaxed after their presentations and are willing to risk engaging in a more detailed analysis now they that have made it through their own work. For example, below is a detailed analysis of the opening line of Zora Neale Hurston's *Their Eyes Were Watching God*, based upon the system of sentence analysis offered in the Kolln and Funk text, *Understanding English Grammar*. This analysis includes identification of the noun phrases functioning as the subject and direct object, NP1 and NP2, respectively, as well as the type of verb used, transitive (Trans—V), along with applications of the Noun Phrase and Verb Phrase Expansion Rules. The sentence is what Kolln and Funk have labeled a Sentence Pattern VII, which contains a subject, transitive verb, and direct object.

Grading

The grading or assessment of the digital diagramming exercise should be based upon a clearly articulated rubric available to the students prior to the start of the exercise. In the rubric, be sure to clarify which structures the students are to identify in the presentation. For example, if the exercise is worth ten points total, then assign points for each structure to be explored: prepositional phrase for two points; subordinate clause for three points; independent clause for three points; complete subject in subordinate clause for one point; and complete predicate in independent clause for one point.

Also, if the students are working in groups, develop a peer evaluation in which students state their contributions to the process as well as providing feedback on the contributions made by their fellow group members.

Summing Up

Overall, the Prezi environment offers students an interactive format to learn the analytical thinking skills developed through traditional sentence diagramming on paper. Along with phrase, clause, or sentence level structures, this activity may be adapted to work with larger discourse structures as well. For example, it can be particularly helpful when students struggle with transitions between paragraphs. Students can type in the final sentence of a paragraph in one text box in a frame and the first sentence in the following paragraph in another text box within the same frame. Students can then insert a transition text box between the two sentences that clearly links them and write a transition based upon the key words of the preceding and proceeding sentences. Another example is using Prezi to track the development of a metaphor or a motif through a poem, designating the various elements with lines or arrows within or between frames. Whatever the discourse level, don't hesitate to break open the beauty of a string of words for your students using this innovative technology. Enjoy exploring!

Author's Note: Thanks to my students Charlie Lopez, Roxana Miranda, and Justine Hernandez, who generously offered feedback.

—ɯ—

Practical Punctuation
Applying Grammar Rules in Context
Laura Beadling *and* Russell Brickey

Abstract: On the day that graded drafts of students' papers are handed back, provide students with a text that has had all the punctuation marks removed and ask them to add punctuation back in. Then hand back students' minimally-marked papers to correct grammar and punctuation.

Duration: Anywhere from 20 minutes to 50 minutes, depending on instructor approach.

Preparation: Cut and paste a text (1,000 words approx.) into a Word document and remove all capitalization and punctuation marks. Print up enough copies so that each student has one.

Be prepared to discuss the rules of punctuation and grammar.

Procedure: Pass out the text without the punctuation and capitalization to students. You can either ask students to read the text on their own or you can read the text aloud as a class. If you choose to read it aloud, read through the text quickly, trying to keep your voice as flat as possible; the point of the exercise is to force students to apply the rules of grammar without the aid of instructor inflection.

Students work on their own or in small groups to correct the text.

After about 10 minutes, regroup and read the text aloud a final time, asking students to voice corrections as you go. It is a good idea to stop and either ask students what rule they are following or why they "instinctively" inserted punctuation.

Hand back student papers that have been corrected using minimal marking, in which the instructor merely places a check mark at the beginning of a line or sentence that contains a grammar, punctuation, or other mechanical error. Allow 10 or 20 minutes for students to go through the same correction process with their own papers as they did with the sample text.

Rationale: Generally, students enjoy the hands-on, practical aspect of this exercise, and it tasks students with actually using grammar in context.

Potential Problems: Students may not want to speak up for fear of stating an incorrect answer in front of the class. One way to lighten the mood is to explain that grammar and punctuation are rarely taught in the classroom, and so no one should feel embarrassed for an incorrect answer.

—ɯ—

Meaningful Text Assignment

Short Paragraphs Explaining the Importance of Writing

• Lauren Matus •

Abstract: Students choose three texts that were self-produced and three texts created by others, write a short paragraph on each of their texts explaining why each text is important, and share at least one selection with the class.

Duration: Two or three classes

Author's Note: Taxonomies are not just for the science classroom! A taxonomy is a system of classification into categories; this assignment helps students to understand new ideas by classifying concepts and keywords into categories. The Class Taxonomy can be used in any course to introduce new concepts or to reframe existing understandings. Not only does the Class Taxonomy assignment push students to question their current understandings of a concept, it also helps students understand the mutable nature of knowledge. Further, students can add to, manipulate and change their taxonomies as their ideas develop throughout the semester.

I have used the Class Taxonomy in many different types of courses, but the idea is the same: begin with what students already know.

Procedure:

First Class

I will begin the class with a very brief overview of what a taxonomy is, why it is valuable to produce such a document, and why we should closely examine our preconceived notions.

Then, I will begin the activity by writing a word on the board. (While in mediated classrooms it might be easier to type up the list and project it on a screen, I enjoy using the board.)

- For example, *writing*. I ask students to "throw out" any words or phrases related to writing, and I begin to list them on the board.

We don't stop until the board is completely full or we have at least 40 to 50 keywords.

Second Class

I will type up the list and distribute it to pairs of students in the next class.

Pairs are asked to categorize the keywords and provide a rationale for how they define each category and why each keyword "fits" into the selected category.

This task is very challenging and requires students to ask themselves what values underpin their current understandings.

Following Classes

Each pair presents their taxonomy to the class and we discuss why the taxonomies are different, even though all of the keywords are the same. As a class, we create a Class Taxonomy that reveals our collective understanding of the idea. As we move through the semester, we will revisit the Class Taxonomy, add to it, and change it as our collective understandings change.

Author's Note: This assignment can precede any type of reading or writing assignment, but is particularly useful for argument or critical analysis papers.

The Class Taxonomy helps students to think critically about broad ideas and concepts, and therefore gives them practice defining key terms, and developing arguments.

Potential Problem: The most common issue that I have seen is that some students are hesitant, initially, to take ownership of their own taxonomy. This hesitation does not last long once they realize that there are no right or wrong answers.

—⁓—

Making Connections Between "Like" and "Dislike"
Effective Transitions
• Alexandra Oxner •

Abstract: Students learn about transitions by linking lists of their own "likes" and "dislikes" in a short in-class essay.

Duration: 20 minutes

Editor's Note: This is the third of three exercises in a series designed to teach revision (see also "Oxner and Bouier: Genre Bending" [1] and "Oxner: Underlining the Plot" [2]); each exercise can be used as a standalone or as part of the sequence.

Preparation: Instructors may want to compile a list of popular "transition words." Examples of these lists can be found on the Internet.

Procedure: Students can inadvertently resist incorporating effective transitions into their writing; they are sometimes attached to common "transition words" ("firstly," "secondly," "lastly," "meanwhile," "furthermore," etc.).

Show students a list of like examples. Explain to them that adding one of these words to the beginning of a paragraph will not always effectively demonstrate a shift in their paper.

To illustrate this problem, ask students to complete the following writing activity without using any of the trigger words you provided.

Have your students fold a sheet of paper in half, or draw a line down the middle. (It should feature two columns.)

Students should label the first column "Likes" and the second column "Dislikes."

Choose a subject for the students to write about. Example: "List what you like and dislike about being a student at (your university)."

Direct them to include at least seven items in each column. Then ask them to randomly circle two items from each column.

Now, they must alternately number these ideas in this order: 1. Like, 2. Dislike, 3. Like, 4. Dislike.

(Example: 1. Close to beach, 2. Writing is hard, 3. The girls/boys are hotties, 4. My roommate is loud.)

Ask them to write you a four-paragraph personal narrative about their first experiences at their college or university. The trick is they must use these four ideas as the topics of their four paragraphs.

Because they are such disparate ideas (they are meant to be opposites), the students will have to find ways to make each paragraph lead into the next. Encourage them to create sub-thesis statements that will incorporate both ideas, rather than planting a "transition" word at the beginning of the paragraph.

Ask student volunteers to share their essays with the class. Begin a discussion about "rough" transitions. If a student uses a "rough" transition (if they jump between ideas without any attempt to connect them), ask your class to help come up with ideas to help their class-mate.

Rationale: This exercise aims to teach students how to construct transitions and make meaningful connections between paragraphs with seemingly disparate ideas.

—⅏—

Your? You're? There? Their?
Spelling Exercise
• Christine Photinos •

Abstract: The exercise can be used on an as-needed basis—ideally at a point in the class when students are being asked to produce carefully-edited prose. For example, the exercise might be useful during a class session that takes place after students have submitted rough drafts of an essay but before they submit final versions of their work.

Duration: On average the exercise will take about 15 minutes, but some students will finish swiftly and others will take more time. So that no one feels hurried, there should be some other task lined up for early finishers.

Materials: The exercise assumes Internet access.

Procedure: Students should work through the following worksheet with the instructor.

Rationale: This brief spelling exercise begins with an acknowledgment of the challenges of English spelling. It then illustrates some quick ways to double-check word meaning using widely available online tools. Finally, it asks students to practice using commonly misspelled words in the context of their own sentences.

Potential Problems: On rare occasions, a student will work through the exercise in a hurried way, skipping past the lookup part of the exercise. One way to mitigate this problem is to ask students to trade work with peers at the end of the exercise and to discuss any differ- · ences in their respective understandings of how the words are correctly used.

WORKSHEET

Introduction

English spelling is complicated. To illustrate this, supporters of English spelling reform point out that the made-up word *ghoti* could be pronounced the same as the word *fish*.

What?

Well...

In the word "rough," gh is pronounced with an "f" sound.

In the word "women," o is pronounced with an "i" sound.

In the word "nation," ti is pronounced with a "sh" sound.

Spelling reform supporters such as the playwright George Bernard Shaw have long argued that English spelling is unnecessarily complicated and ought to be changed so that spellings more closely match pronunciations of individual letters, as they do in languages such as Greek and Spanish, where each letter of the alphabet produces (for the most part) just one sound. With these more "phonetic" languages, you can read words out loud without memorizing a bunch of exceptions, and your guesses about how words ought to be spelled are usually correct or close to correct.

Some of the challenges of English spelling have been alleviated by computer spell checkers, but it is very important to remember that a spell checker can never replace human judgment.

Whenever a spell checker recommends a change, you must make sure the change actually makes sense. This can be quickly accomplished online. For example, in Google you can simply type the word followed by "define." For example: conscious define

You might also wish to bookmark an online dictionary—for example, the online Merriam Webster dictionary at www.merriam-webster.com—or, even better, download a dictionary app that works offline.

Hardest to avoid are look-alike/sound-alike spelling errors. These are errors that occur when two words sound or look the same (or similar) when they actually have very different meanings. For example, you might write "air" (meaning atmosphere) when you meant to write "heir" (meaning one who inherits property). Note that a computer spell checker will not flag this mistake since "air" is correctly spelled.

In the exercise below, you will review some of the most common spelling errors. To reinforce the lesson, you will write your own sentences using the words.

Practice

Go online to quickly review the word distinctions below. For example, for ACCEPT vs. EXCEPT, simply type accept vs. except into Google (or whatever search engine you use).

Then write your own sentences, using the words correctly. Rather than copying sentences that you find online, write your own original sentences. This is what's going to reinforce the distinction for you and prevent you from misusing the words in your own writing.

ACCEPT and EXCEPT
1. Write a sentence using the word "accept"
2. Write a sentence using the word "except"

AFFECT and EFFECT
3. Write a sentence using the word "affect"
4. Write a sentence using the word "effect"

ITS and IT'S
5. Write a sentence using the word "its"
6. Write a sentence using the word "it's"

PASSED and PAST
  7. Write a sentence using the word "passed"
  8. Write a sentence using the word "past"

THAN and THEN
  9. Write a sentence using the word "than"
  10. Write a sentence using the word "then"

THEIR, THERE, and THEY'RE
  11. Write a sentence using the word "their"
  12. Write a sentence using the word "there"
  13. Write a sentence using the word "they're"

YOUR and YOU'RE
  14. Write a sentence using the word "your"
  15. Write a sentence using the word "you're"

—◊—

When *Ethos, Pathos* and *Logos* Are a Crime
Rhetoric Scene Investigation
• Gary Vaughn •

Abstract: In small groups, students answer a series of prompts concerning ethos, pathos, and logos. Each group then elects a "spokesperson" who then presents the group's analysis.

Duration: Varies: 50 minutes or two classes

Materials: Optional: An on-line course system like Blackboard, student laptops, and overhead projection.

Preparation: I introduce this in-class activity by locating it within our previous discussions of rhetorical context and rhetorical devices.

Procedure: I bring up the popular series *Crime Scene Investigation* and suggest that any text can be examined as "a scene of rhetoric."

Break the class into three groups and ask each group to examine the rhetorical issues involved in an assigned reading.

One group focuses on *logos*, one on *pathos*, and one on *ethos*.

I ask the same questions of each group:

- What is *logos / pathos / ethos*?
- How does the author employ this rhetorical device? (Use at least five specific examples of evidence from the text with page numbers)
- How is the author effective in this area and how could this area be improved?
- Who is the intended audience for this text, and what is the author's purpose?
- What do you think is the driving need for the author to write on this topic?

Have students elect a "note taker" who will record the responses and post them to the Discussion Board on Blackboard.

Each group also needs a "spokesperson" who will later read the group's responses to the class.

Circulate among the groups, offering encouragement and hints.

Finally, each spokesperson reports their group's findings.

The entire class discusses the quality of each group's investigation, focusing on the persuasiveness of the evidence.

Sometimes different perspectives on the responses might be offered, especially to issues involving audience and purpose. I ask students to argue for their viewpoint, supporting it with the clues they have found in the text.

Author's Note—Follow Up Exercise: Later in the term I supplement the rhetoric-scene questions with questions on the author's style and use of specific rhetorical tools, such as rhetorical questions, figurative language, and tone—to put the text under even closer examination.

Rationale: Students work collaboratively to develop analytical thinking skills and gain appreciation for writing as a craft that involves rhetorical tools and deliberate authorial decisions. It also emphasizes the importance of discovering and citing supporting evidence and arguing for a perspective while remaining open to rebuttal. Furthermore, recording the groups' findings on Blackboard gives students a review aid that they can refer to later when they use the text for an essay assignment—including, of course, rhetorical analysis and synthesis.

Potential Problems: At first, students might stumble with *logos*, *pathos*, and *ethos*, but the re-iteration of those terms quickly leads to understanding. That understanding is expanded as the students grapple with more subtle rhetorical techniques.

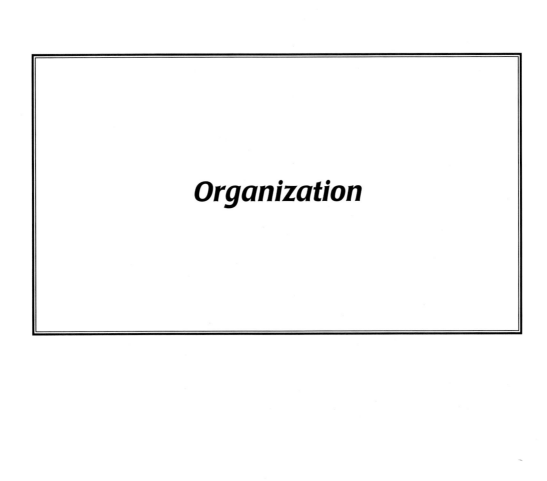

Organization

Division and Classification Exercises
Learning the Process of Classification
• Rita D. Costello •

Abstract: Using both familiar and unfamiliar objects brought in by the instructor, students categorize these objects by articulating criteria.

Editor's Note: This exercise is the first in a sequence and can be done in conjunction with "Exhaust All Questions," and "Analyzing Creative Sources," elsewhere in this book.

Duration: I always feel the need to do at least two class days on this particular exercise below because often, even if students seem to have it at the end of the first day, the information gets lost or confused once students leave the classroom.

Depending on the particular group of students only one or two may be needed. However, there are five separate exercises included in this sequence, this first of which sets the stage for the others. If all of these exercises are used in the classroom, the sequence would take a full week of classes; if some are used as handouts or homework, the rest could be put into a single class. I tend to incorporate all of them into lecture days and use the board; exercises are written here so that they could be given to students as handouts as well. I also tend to vary some of the topics from semester to semester.

Materials: For the first exercise, it is necessary to collect familiar (e.g., a pen, a butter knife, etc.) and unfamiliar objects (e.g., Chinese ear cleaner—explained further in the exercise).

Preparation: Spread your collection of articles on a table in the classroom where students will have access to them. Divide the class into groups (three to four students per group) which will then work together to classify the articles according to a criteria of their own choosing.

Procedure: *Classifying Unknown Objects*:

In real life, one of the ways we make sense of the new and unfamiliar is by trying to categorize it with other familiar objects. I do this exercise during the first day of the sequence on presenting division and classification ideas. When it comes time for the exercise, I lay the objects out on the desk or table and have students gather around to look at them. I allow students to physically handle the objects (although I imagine, depending on what objects are used, not everyone might feel the same about allowing students to physically handle and move objects; be careful of bringing anything too delicate or valuable to class).

- **Example objects:** *(familiar)* fork, knife, spoon, chopsticks, q-tip/cotton swab, a bowl, candy (I usually bring both an American candy and an Asian candy); *(unfamiliar)* a

Chinese ear cleaner (it is a thin metal stick with a minuscule spoon/scoop end), a piece of pottery in the style of an ancient Japanese hand-fitted rice bowl (it looks more like decorative pottery, rather than being identifiable as a functioning bowl), an art object (such as a blown glass paperweight) and a few other random food/cleaning/utensil/personal hygiene type objects.

- **First round:** I ask students to sort objects into at least three groups of three (they can leave out any objects they do not see as necessary). Usually, the organizing principle students first utilize relates to food consumption: utensils, dishes, edible objects. If I ask them to do this a second time, the process usually involves either shape (sharp, blunt, round) or students attempt two categories of two and lose steam by the time they attempt a third (decorative, functional..., or food, hygiene,...).
- **Next round:** When the categorizing runs out of steam, I ask students to focus on one of the unknown objects and try to categorize it based on the identifiable qualities. Most are not successfully categorized by the end, but students have fun trying, and in the end I tell them what the unidentifiable item is and how the qualities they noted work toward its function. (With my objects, the Chinese ear-cleaner is particularly satisfying—and amusing to students—because they tend to categorize it with utensils using the same qualities that make it functional as an ear cleaner.)

The sequence of exercises teaches ways that division/classification are useful and are designed to go with division and classification, but they can also work with any type of writing that requires scientific thinking skills. In our semester, this tends to fall about six-weeks or a third of the way into the first composition course.

Rationale: In our first year composition sequence, Division and Classification mode is the first instance where there is a significant shift in the level and type of critical thinking required of students, so it often takes several different types of examples and exercises before students start to really understand the purpose and uses.

Potential Problems: Instructors will need to bring in objects which will inspire conversation and categorization.

—w—

The Paragraph Game
A Collaborative Game to Teach Paragraph Structure
• Francesco Crocco •

Abstract: Students are divided into teams, and each team member is given a specific task while the team compiles a paragraph collaboratively; this is a competitive classroom game.

This exercise also teaches a number of writing issues: idea generation, topic and supporting sentences, argumentation, and summary.

Duration: Each round of play takes about 15 minutes. At least four rounds are recommended so students can play all of the roles. This will take about an hour.

Materials: Chalkboard and timer

Candy and stars may be awarded at the instructor's discretion.

Preparation: Students list topics as starting points for paragraph construction (or students may choose their own topics for homework before class).

Suggested Reading: Graff, Gerald, and Cathy Birkenstein. *They Say/I Say.* New York: Norton, 2007.

Procedure: Students will assume the following roles on the team:

- writing a topic sentence,
- writing supporting sentences,
- writing an argument rebuttal,
- and writing a summarizing sentence.

By rotating through these roles, each student learns to write a complete paragraph. Teammates may help each other, and each team competes with other teams to write successful paragraphs. In every round, each student plays a different role.

Groups

Randomly group students into teams of four. Tell them they will be writing paragraphs together.

Topics: Write a list of topics on the board.

Group Roles: Assign each player a different role, perhaps by counting off:

STARTER: This person begins the collaborative paragraph by writing a topic sentence stating an argument about the topic. He/she then passes the sheet of paper to the next person.

SUPPORTER: This person adds a few sentences that offer supporting details. These may come from facts, statistics, examples, analogies, logic, explanation, quotations, anecdotes, comparisons/contrasts, or some other means of support. Pass the sheet.

REBUTTER: This person anticipates possible counter-arguments by stating and rebutting them in a few sentences. Pass the sheet.

SUMMARIZER: This person sums up the main idea and draws all conclusions, thereby finishing the paragraph. The paragraph is now ready to be read aloud to the class.

Writing Phase

Starting with the first topic on the list, have each team begin the collaborative writing process at the same time with the same topic. After one team successfully completes a paragraph (by signaling with raised hands), use the wall clock or a watch as a timer to give the remaining teams 60 seconds to finish their paragraph.

Challenge Phase

Once the writing period is over, the game enters a "challenge phase" in which each group reads its paragraph aloud and can be challenged by another group based on paragraph form or content. The challenging group must state its rationale for issuing the challenge. The other groups each get to cast one vote to resolve the dispute. If the paragraph wins the vote, the group that wrote the paragraph receives a point. If the paragraph loses the vote, the group that issued the challenge receives a point. Each paragraph that makes it to the end of the challenge phase (whether challenged or not) receives an additional point. Finally, the team that finished their paragraph first receives an additional point as long as their paragraph is not voted down.

Tally Phase

At the end of the challenge phase, the professor tallies each group's points on the board.

Rounds

The game proceeds to another round using the next topic on the list; the players in each group must rotate roles. Repeat steps 4, 5, and 6.

Ending the Game

The game ends when one of three conditions is met:

(a) the list of topics is exhausted;
(b) a preset point threshold is crossed by one or more teams; or
(c) time is up.

I suggest giving the winning group(s) an appropriate prize (candy, stars, a minor privilege, or even extra credit points will do). Written paragraphs may be collected for further evaluation.

Potential Problem: The only potential problem with this exercise is that students may need help assessing each other's paragraphs during the challenge phase. The professor may choose to step in and provide or vet rationales for or against each paragraph.

Rationale: Use this exercise to teach paragraph structure. This exercise can also be used to teach reading and citation skills by using quotations instead of topics as starting points. These quotations may come from course readings to which the students must respond with a close-reading and analysis.

—⟆⟆⟆—

Structure as Shape
Using Poetry to Teach Reader Response
• Chad Engbers •

Abstract: Students learn revision by reading an original poem (included below), graphically mapping the contours of its argument, and then applying the concepts learned to their own papers.

This exercise has elements of organization and visual rhetoric.

Duration: 50 minutes

Preparation: The author suggests a PowerPoint presentation of the poem below.

Materials: Overhead projection.

Students should bring their essays to class.

Procedure: The exercise follows a very basic pedagogical archetype: introduce a concept, show an example, have students apply it to their own work.

Reading the Poem

I begin by telling the students that we're going to read a poem, but that we're going to read it very slowly, line by line, in order to get a more thorough sense of how the meaning of a text unfolds in time. I observe that no one reads a book or even a single sentence all at once: we experience texts in time, one sentence after another, and changing the arrangement of those sentences changes the experience. And that is one of the writer's most basic tasks: arranging a reader's experience. So I ask students to keep track of their reactions to each line of the poem.

I use PowerPoint to present the poem silently, without reading it aloud, because I want students to listen to their own inner voices "saying" the poem, and I pause for four or five seconds on each line before revealing the next one.

We then discuss the poem line by line, always asking questions such as these: How did you react to *this* line? How did this line affect your opinion of the speaker? And how does this line confirm or change the expectations you have from the lines that came before it?

"Drawing" the Poem's "Shape"

The next slide in the PowerPoint spins the poem on its side, with the lines running vertically, and a basic graph appears above it. I announce to students that we're going to undertake the somewhat silly business of graphing the intensity of each line of the poem. "Intensity" is, of course, a vague and subjective word, and I confess that my graph has no scientific precision. But it's true that our relationship to the poem tends to change as we read it, and it can be useful to think visually about how and where those changes happen. So I suggest a basic graphing of the poem, trying to draw from reactions that students described during discussion.

If time permits, I also show them an alternate version of the same poem—using almost exactly the same words, but in a different order—to demonstrate how a reader's experience changes when the structure changes. The order of the words is every bit as important as the words themselves. "When you think of structure," I say, "don't just think of an outline of your paper. Think of structure as the rising and falling and swerving of readers' interest. Structure is the shape of your reader's experience. And you get to manipulate it. In fact, it's your *job* to manipulate it."

Application to Students' Own Drafts

Ask students to number the paragraphs in their own drafts. Extremely long paragraphs might need two numbers, and dialogues of several lines might need only one. Then I ask students to graph the "intensity" of their own narratives on the back of the last page—how can they draw the "structure" of their reader's reaction to their essay? In other words, what is the "emotional structure" of a text?

I have found these shaky little graphs to be extremely helpful in getting students to think and talk about structure. When I meet with students individually in the days following this class session, I can get quiet or shy students to talk about their writing by walking me through their graphs and explaining why the intensity rises and falls in different places. When students ask me whether a particular change would be a good idea, I ask them how they think it would affect their "graph." And often students themselves will begin a conference by flipping over their paper and saying, "I think I've got a problem right here," literally putting their finger on the problem.

End the class session by displaying some common structural problems, complete with little graph lines to show what each problem looks like. "Too much intro" is a low, flat line with a little mountain at the right end of it representing the actual story on which the author should focus. "Too much aftermath" is the reverse: a little mountain at the beginning, followed by a long, flat line. "Multiple climaxes" has several mountains—exhausting and bewildering for a reader.

Later

In the class session after this one, I often run a separate workshop specifically on pace—the speed at which a reader experiences the rollercoaster that we graphed in the previous session.

I sometimes also use images of hedge mazes to help students visualize structure. An outline of a paper, or a graph of it, is like a hedge maze viewed from above: you can see the paths and how all the twists and turns are laid out. That's a useful perspective for the revising writer, but a reader experiences a hedge maze on the ground level, seeing only the turn immediately in front of him or her.

I return to the technique of graphing for the big persuasive essay at the end of the semester, too, but there I graph not the intensity of the story but rather the reader's resistance to the author's argument. I provide a few sample graphs for the same argument if it were structured as a classical oration, a more Rogerian conversation, and a few others. A reader can experience the same argument in many different ways, depending on how that argument is structured.

The Poem

Although this exercise might work with nearly any short poem, I've had good luck with the anonymous one printed below:

> Woman,
> Of all the mysteries
> In my life,
> You
> Are number three.
> But don't feel bad
> For coming in third:
> God beat you out,
> And me.

Student reactions to the poems vary widely, but wherever the conversation takes us, I make sure that our focus ends up on the middle line of the poem. I observe that there are four lines before it and four lines after it, and it has a different relationship to each of those four-line chunks. In relationship to the first four lines, line five comes as a surprise. Most students get the sense from the opening lines that this is another sappy love poem, a hazy Hallmark card full of dreamy hyperbole. The word "three" snaps the poem out of that mode. "One" would make better sense. It would be tempting to present that line with a blank at the end and ask students to fill in the blank. They probably wouldn't fill it with "three." (I've never done that, because it would disrupt the flow of reading the poem.)

At the same time, that central line works in relationship to what follows, because a reader simply must wonder what numbers one and two are. This is where I introduce my students to the notion of suspense, which is not just a matter of literal cliffhangers and scary plot developments. Suspense can simply be a pressing question that remains unanswered. (I often take this opportunity to say that there's no need to write about a car crash or the death of a loved one in order to make a narrative essay suspenseful and dramatic.) The suspense of "number three," I point out, isn't resolved until the very last word of the poem. You have to finish the entire thing to answer the mystery created in line five.

The alternate version, which includes most of the same words but in a different order, is this:

> You
> Are the third greatest
> Mystery in my life,
> Woman.
> But it was God and I
> Who beat you out,
> So don't feel bad.

Rationale: I use this exercise to help students think rhetorically about the structure of a text, that is, to think of the structure of their papers not in terms of an abstract outline, but rather as an emotional experience for a concrete reader. The exercise works so well, I think, because it also gets students thinking visually about the processes of reading and writing.

Additional Author's Notes: The exercise works well with other papers, too—I return to it for the persuasive essay at the end of the semester—but the narrative essay is the most natural place to talk about the emotional structure of a text.

Descriptive Outlining, or Fun with Post-Its
Students Learn Essay Reorganization
• Kathleen Maloney •

Abstract: Students use Post-It notes to summarize, outline, and reorganize the structures of their essays.

Duration: 15 minutes, although the exercise can be expanded at the discretion of the instructor.

Materials: Post-It notes, enough so that each student can use them to make multiple notations about the ideas in their essays, and physical space on which to arrange their notations.

Students should bring drafts of their essays to class.

Preparation:

Instructors may want to cover the basics of outlining and revision before this exercise.

Procedure: Ask students to outline their essays and to copy individual ideas on to Post-It notes (one idea per Post-It).

Students should then play with the arrangement of their essay and to consider that now that they are playing if additional ideas/Post-Its are necessary.

Author Notes: The following exercise can be used near the beginning of an essay sequence, as a part of peer response workshop, or as a revision exercise. I have successfully used this exercise in both composition and general education literature courses. The idea here is to ask students to think about their essay or outline and to reconsider organization.

Students seem to both enjoy this activity and find it helpful in seeing their essay in a different way—at the end of the exercise—students should have a new version of their outline and should be ready to start writing.

Alternately, if this exercise is used as a part of the revision process, I ask students to read their essay one paragraph at a time and to write the main idea of each paragraph on a Post-It. This helps in two ways: first, many students realize they have more than one idea in a paragraph and second, students realize that the organization that made sense when they were planning the essay may no longer make sense. Once the students have completed their descriptive outline on Post-Its, they begin to play with the organization or to see what they have omitted, where they went on a tangent, what they need to add as a part of the revision process.

This assignment works well with most essay types. I generally use it for argument essays.

This assignment can be used for a 15-minute exercise or might be expanded for a full class period depending on the level of writers and the part of the writing process they are working on.

—⁂—

Deciding Their Own Fates
Facilitating Student-Created Rubrics
• Chelsea R. Swick •

Abstract: Student groups are responsible for creating 10 open-ended questions which the instructor will use to grade student writing.

Duration: One hour to an hour and 15 minutes; conceivably two 50-minute class periods

15 minutes for students to work in individual groups
15 minutes for recording of all the questions
30 to 45 minutes to debate and revise the rubric

Preparation: Students should have drafts of their papers underway.

Materials: Overhead projection

Procedure: Student groups create 10 open-ended questions designed to evaluate important aspects of the paper assignment that they are working on. Typically, the questions begin with "How well" in order for the answer to be open to a range of answers. Some classes might need example rubrics to help them get started.

For instance, "How well does the paper engage with complex issues?" or "Is there enough evidence to provide a thorough overview of the main thesis?"

In addition, the class should already be in the midst of creating their assignment in order to have them understand what the assignment is and what the key parts of the assignment are.

Once the students are finished creating the questions, have the students read them aloud and write them on the board. As each question is written, the teacher should ask if any other groups have similar questions. This allows for the questions to be grouped prior to the revision process.

It is important to encourage all students to participate. No question is rejected in this time. Everything is written on the board.

Once all of the class's questions have been exhausted, the class should discuss each grouping of questions. The class should discuss how they might most effectively ask the question in the grouping. Debate typically ensues at this point.

Once each grouping has been discussed and revised, each question needs to be assigned point values; students assign the values. Classes can decide that all questions are equal, or they might decide that higher order concerns are weighted heavier than lower order concerns.

The end product becomes the rubric the instructor will use to assess the assignment.

Rationale: By having a stake in the assessment process, students feel more attached to the assignment and are able to apply the concepts when drafting and revising their assignments. In addition, by creating questions designed to evaluate the important aspects of the assignment and debating both the aspects and their relative importance, students gain a better understanding of the nature of the assignment and how it will be evaluated, thus demystifying the grading process.

Potential Problems: Arguments can ensue. The teacher needs to facilitate the conversation so hostility is not present. As well, during the recording of all the questions, the teacher should make sure every voice is heard. Some students will raise low order concern questions (e.g., Does it fulfill the page requirements?), and these must still be recorded. These questions often are deleted during the debate process.

—〰—

"Trimming" the Information
Reassembling Student Papers with Scissors and Tape
• Virginia Tucker •

Abstract: Using scissors and tape, students literally cut their papers apart and then reassemble them to learn the concept of reorganization.

This exercise also teaches revision.

Duration: 50 minutes

Materials: Scissors, tape, stapler, or any other adhesive to reassemble student papers

Preparation: Students will have to bring early drafts of their papers to class.

Procedure: To help students "re-see" their papers, I cut their drafts into paragraphs and shuffle the pieces.

Upon returning their drafts, I ask students to re-organize their papers using cues in their thesis, topic sentences, and closing sentences. I note that these are the same cues readers use to pre-determine their expectations in reading a work.

While students re-piece their papers, they see that the chronological order of the paragraphs do not necessarily coincide with the hierarchy of information presented in their thesis.

Additionally, they take notice of paragraphs that simply don't belong or merely reiterate previously discussed information.

Author's Notes: The class is often taken aback when the stack of paragraphs that was once a word processed paper lands on their desk, but the activity is often a welcomed change of pace and a favorite among students who value practice in effective revision strategies

The most time-consuming part of the activity takes place when I am cutting the papers. This frequently takes me well over an hour depending on how many students are enrolled, but I typically have had the papers for a week as I am responding to them in draft form. Care must be taken not to give clues to their original layout so students don't simply return the paper to its original state. The title and header information as well as any end comments I provided for the draft are separated from the paper's paragraphs while page numbers are discarded. The paragraphs must then be shuffled. I often place the conclusion paragraph on the top to have students begin by questioning whether it is an introduction paragraph.

Rationale: For some students who really struggle to integrate research, the workshop aids them in visually connecting choppy paragraphs full of ideas into more cohesive, logical units of information. While students are quick to cut and paste during the computerized writing process, they rarely ever make such dramatic rearrangements once the paper is in hard-copy form. By cutting their papers into paragraphs, I ask them to "re-envision" their papers as part of a more effective revision process.

Potential Problems: The only problems I encounter are with those students who do not submit drafts or who submit weak drafts. In these cases I ask them to help another student out, or I will cut their weak drafts into sentences for sentence-level revision. Students will make jokes and scowl about their papers being cut up, sometimes remarking that these papers must've been really terrible if I hacked them up. However, by the semester's conclusion most indicate in their portfolio cover letters that the organization workshop was the most helpful and interesting of all the workshops, with some admitting that it was even a bit fun.

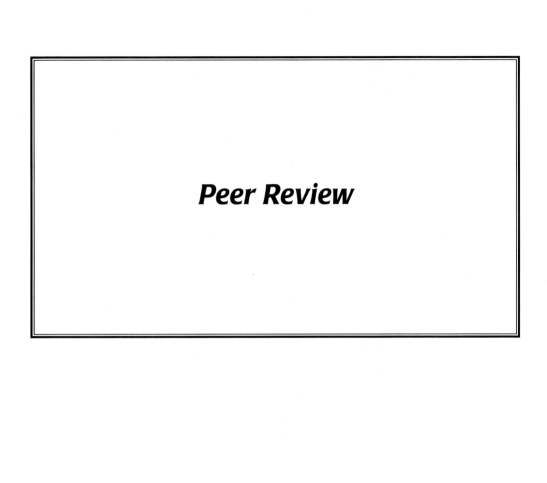

Peer Review

Double Take Peer Review
Checking Revisions Between Drafts One and Two
• Mary Jo McCloskey •

Abstract: Students review their partners' papers twice, first in an initial peer review, and then in a second follow-up peer review to gauge how well the author made revisions.

This exercise also teaches citation style.

Duration: Two 50-minute classes

Materials: Students should bring both the first draft and the second draft of their papers to class.

Enough worksheets (see below) for each student in class; alternately, prompts could be projected.

Instructor might also provide MLA/APA guidebooks or example papers.

Procedure: This exercise may be used with all essays that incorporate research, including but not limited to comparison/contrast, description, narration, and cause/effect, and using any formatting style. For my purposes, I use this with a research argumentative paper that requires MLA format. Having taught writing for 10 years, I have found this exercise to be the most productive *and* enjoyable for students as they work on the ever-dreaded research paper. This exercise reinforces their grasp on how to incorporate research, follow formatting guidelines, and achieve an essay's rhetorical purposes.

Day 1

I return the first drafts of their research papers. I assign the following homework:

1. Revise the essay.
2. Highlight the feedback on the first draft after you have addressed it in the second draft. You may use any color highlighter or any colored ink.
3. Bring in both drafts next class. Do not staple them, as they will be viewed side-by-side.

I remind the students of the current, detailed goals of our class, which usually fall into the broader categories of incorporating research, following formatting guidelines, and achieving the essay's rhetorical purposes.

Day 2

The students should pair up and work as partners. If there is an uneven number of students in attendance, there will be one group of three students.

I put the following parameters onscreen with the overhead projector *or* on the blackboard/wipeboard *or* I distribute them in a handout:

Composition Peer Review Workshop Exercise Parameters

1. Sign your name above your partner's name on the revised draft.
2. Read the revised draft, referring to the first draft as necessary and handwriting any notes (on either copy) that come to mind.
3. Fill out the Composition Peer Review Workshop Exercise worksheet.
4. Discuss your findings with your partner.
5. Paper clip the worksheet atop the revised draft, atop the first draft.
6. Do note that your role in this process contributes to your grade on the essay.

After we *carefully* discuss the parameters, I distribute the Composition Peer Review Workshop Exercise worksheet. I also place several MLA handbooks, composition guidebooks, and copies of a sample MLA paper on the desk for them to use as desired throughout the exercise.

The students work on this assignment for the remainder of class time; the duration varies according to paper length, and ranges from one-hour class sessions to two-hour sessions. Throughout the class duration, I walk around to each set of partners and guide them as necessary. At the end of class, I distribute paper clips, they paper clip the worksheet atop the new draft, atop the old draft, and I collect them.

WORKSHEET

1. What is your name?

2. What is your partner's name?

3. How many of the revisions did your partner make?
   a. All
   b. Most
   c. Some
   d. A few
   e. None

4. Did your partner highlight the moments on the first draft that he/she revised in the new draft?
   a. All
   b. Most
   c. Some
   d. A few
   e. None

5. Describe one element of MLA format that your partner needs to address:

6. What are three suggestions, guidelines, recommendations, etc. that you want to give your partner?

    a.

    b.

    c.

—ɯɯ—

Three Versions of Peer Review
Worksheets for the Classroom
• Mike Farmer •

Abstract: In the following three worksheets, students review based upon three different writing modes:

Description and Definition
Comparison and Contrast
Cause and Effect

Duration: 50- or 75-minute class

Materials: Copies of the following worksheets, enough for each student

Procedure: Below find *three different forms* that have slight variations in the questions asked to reflect three different modes of writing—descriptive/definition, comparison/contrast, and cause and effect.

Author's Notes: Students are encouraged to make connections between the writing they review and their own writing. In fact, one of the review questions says "What mistake do you see made repeatedly? Do you have a tendency to make the same mistake? Maybe recognizing that mistake in someone else's paper will help you to realize the error you've made in your paper."

The following worksheets also ask reviewers to check for sentence order and clarity; I ask students to remember an image we discuss in class to describe the process of linking sentences and ideas together: "Venetian blinds" or "dominos"—one sentence naturally "pushes" or yields to the next sentence.

Encourage as much creative thinking as possible. Tell the students that they may not have many comments to make on first review, but once they get their papers back with comments written on them, they'll be better prepared to peer evaluate the next paper. This plants the seed that this is a recurring exercise and the idea that revising is a very important step in the process.

Peer Evaluations—Revising—Paper 1

This first hand-out is instruction-heavy, designed to ease the student into the idea of reviewing another student's work. Most students will either not know what to say or will not want to be too harsh for fear that the reviewed student will then be harsh with their paper. It begins with a brief explanation of revising and proofreading. There is an intentional mistake at the outset of the second paragraph for the student to try and catch. Even the final quote has a word omitted intentionally for the students to notice.

A favorite question of mine on this form is at the bottom of page 1—"What is your favorite sentence in the essay you've read?" We are not often asked what our favorite is unless the author is someone like Kipling or Wilde and you really can't go wrong with practically any sentence you choose. However, the responses to this question have been some of the most insightful on the form. I also encourage them to find strengths in the sentence that they like and apply those strengths to a sentence in their own writing that they consider weak. This question has paid off to such an extent that it is on *all* three of the variations. This is more obvious and methodical on the second hand-out

Peer Evaluations—Revising—Paper 2

There is much less instruction here and much more questioning; the number of questions has increased from 13 to 22. The questions are now numbered and points deducted for incorrect or missing answers. The "favorite question-why-sentences like it in your paper" sequence is now more plainly spelled out in questions 6 to 8.

Certain questions are geared now toward the compare and contrast mode of writing, concerning Block or Factor Methods of organization (questions 14 to 18).

Peer Evaluations—Revising—Paper 3

This final form breaks the questions into categories: "global" / assignment, paragraphs, sentences, and writing style. The student is asked many of the same questions, but he or she is being asked to evaluate the paper globally (Does it fit the assignment? Is it truly cause and effect?), on a paragraph level, and on a sentence level. The "favorite sentence" sequence now falls under the "sentence" category (questions 12 to 14).

Concluding Remarks: If the instructor is so inclined, he or she might do as I did one semester and print the three worksheets on three different colors of paper from the printing department. That way, when I was flipping through the "sandwich" of papers submitted, the presence of the peer evaluation was obvious at a glance.

Remarks for Students: "It can be difficult to convince the cut-and-paste generation of the importance of revising, but hopefully, with the addition of this exercise and a marked increase in their paper scores due to a reduction in errors from serious organizational mistakes to the more minor typographical error, the composition can begin to make inroads with our students and their writing processes. There are more steps than just Writing; don't start at step #3 and neglect Pre-writing and Organizing, steps #1 and #2. And don't throw all that hard work away by submitting a paper that hasn't been Revised (step #4) or Proofread (step #5). This exercise emphasizes the importance of having the time to get a second set of eyes on your paper at the Revision stage in order to better craft the paper. Don't submit a rough draft and call it a final draft; Revising is not for the faint of heart. This exercise helps to ensure that all of your good ideas have been effectively communicated."

Potential Problems: The only common problem is non-attendance. I deal with this in several different ways. As mentioned before, if a student shows up without a rough draft, I dismiss him or her and count the student absent. On the first exercise, I will give a 100 for a fully completed paper. This is only a "homework" grade; the paper itself is a "major" grade and worth significantly more in the cumulative score for the course. On the second peer evaluation, I distribute two sheets to each student; they are to complete both in class. One is submitted for a grade; the other is included in the "sandwich" of papers that is turned in with the final draft (final draft, pre-writing, outline, peer evaluation, rough draft, etc.). The copy that is turned in that day is graded and returned with a more precise grade than just 100 or 90 or 80. This is repeated for the third paper. This usually solves any problems of non-participation.

WORKSHEET

Peer Review #1: Description/Definition

Your Name: _____

Name of Student You Are Evaluating: _____

Peer Evaluations—Revising—Paper 1

Editing and *revising* are terms that I use interchangeably. Your *Wadsworth Handbook* makes a distinction between them. What the ... *Handbook* calls *editing* is what I refer to as *proofreading*. I suppose a newspaper editor might make some of the changes suggested by the book; however, there is also a difference between an editor-in-chief, who will edit articles in larger terms, and a copy editor, who is perhaps one step above a proofreader and will be reading for the misspelled word and the misplaced comma. This is why I refer to *editing* and *revising* as changes that are on larger scales—moving of paragraphs, re-ordering of sentences, re-working patterns of development. Proofreaders are looking for the smaller, last-minute correction to be made.

"I'm not a very good writer, but I'm an excellent rewriter."—James Michener. Or as Michener has said it, it's now time to do some re-writing.

You've already engaged *pre-writing* (the exercise on values, the card exercise, reading essays online, the creeds and mottoes, the poem), discussed organizing, and drafted your first draft (*writing*). Today's step of the writing process is *revising* using peer evaluation. Still to come, you will have to find the time for *proofreading* your final draft. All of the steps of the *writing process* are equally important, and none of the five should be neglected out of a desire to "cut corners" or having waited 'til the last minute. If you read closely, there is a very easy-to-make mistake in the first sentence of this paragraph, but when you've already written "engage," it is understandable for your mind's eye to incorrectly "see" the missing "in," especially since that same syllable is in the word "engage." The correct sentence should read "We've already engaged *in...*." That's *proofreading*. *Peer evaluation (revising)* is an opportunity to raise bigger questions than "Does a comma go there?"

- Are the sentences clear? Do they say what the author intended? If not, what is standing in the way of the real meaning? Feel free to question whether the sentences are in the correct order. Remember the picture of the Venetian blinds: the bottom slat pushes the one next to it, and those two together push the third as the blind is being drawn. _____

- Question the order of the paragraphs. Are they all well-developed? _____

- Does the introductory paragraph give you hints about the body paragraphs to come? If it doesn't, work together to discover what the topic for each paragraph actually is. Then make sure that they are mentioned in both the first paragraph *and* the topic sentences of each paragraph. _____

- What is your favorite sentence in the essay you've read? Write it below. Why is it your favorite? Do you have any sentences like it in your essay? If not, where can you make a change or two to include a sentence like it? _____

- What mistake do you see made repeatedly? Do you have a tendency to make the same mistake? Maybe recognizing that mistake in someone else's paper will help you to realize the error you've made in your paper. _____

- What strong points do you see? What weaknesses do you notice? _____
_____
_____

Write your first draft with your heart. Re-write with your head.—from the movie *Finding Forrester.*

In addition to these questions, look at the box on p. 56 of your *Wadsworth Handbook* and consider the suggestions made there. Some are included in the questions above; others are included below.

- What is the essay about? _____

- Does it fulfill the requirements of the assignment? _____

- Is the thesis clearly worded (despite the fact that a good thesis should not make an announcement like "I believe...")? If not, how can the wording be improved?
_____
_____

- Is information missing that needs to be there? Is there information there that doesn't need to be? Suggest additions and/or deletions. _____
_____
_____

- Can you think of any ideas or examples from your own experience or observations that might strengthen the paper? Have you read a particular "This I Believe" essay that you think might be helpful?_____
_____
_____

- Is the introductory paragraph interesting to you? Does it "hook" you? How? _____

_____

- Does the concluding paragraph leave you with a sense of closure? Are there any questions still left unanswered? Would another concluding strategy be more effective?

_____

_____

_____

Between now and Tuesday, you need to find the time to re-write and / or re-type your paper into its final form. Remember that you need to hand in *all elements* of this paper—rough draft, pre-writing, copy of "This I Believe" essay, this sheet, and the final draft. If you have questions, consult the hand-out I gave you on Project 1 that has the illustration of the sandwich on the back.

Proofread carefully to see if you any words out.—Author Unknown

— - — - — - — - — - — - — - — - — - — - — - — - — - — - —

W O R K S H E E T

Peer Review #2: Compare and Contrast

Your Name: _____

Name of Student You Are Evaluating: _____

Peer Evaluations—Revising—Paper 2

Editing and *revising* are terms that I use daily ... and practice in my own life. That's why this peer evaluation sheet is a little different from the first one. This is a graded assignment. No "Yes/No" answers anywhere on this paper.

1. What is the thesis sentence? _____

_____.

2. Are the sentences clear? (No one-word answers) _____

_____.

3. Do they say what the author intended? _____.

If not, what is standing in the way of the real meaning? _____

_____.

Feel free to question whether the sentences are in the correct order. Remember the picture of the Venetian blinds.

4. Look at the paragraphs. Are they all well-developed? (This is not a "Yes/No" question)

_____.

5. Does the introductory paragraph give you hints about the body paragraphs to come?

_____

What are the three sub-topics or "factors?" (a) _____, (b)

_____ (c) _____.

6. What is your favorite sentence in the essay you've read? Write it below.

_____.

7. Why is it your favorite? _____.

8. Do you have any sentences like it in your essay? _____.

In the space below, re-write one of your weaker sentences to reflect the strengths of this sentence you admire in your classmate's paper.

(old, weaker version of the sentence) _____

_____.

(new and improved sentence) _____

_____.

9. What mistake do you see made repeatedly? _____

_____.

10. Do you have a tendency to make the same mistake? _____

(Maybe recognizing that mistake in someone else's paper will help you to realize the error you've made in your own paper.)

11. What strong points do you see? _____.

12. What weaknesses do you notice? _____.

13. What is the essay about? _____.

14. Are the subjects sufficiently alike for the comparison to be logical and meaningful?

_____.

15. Is Factor or Block Method used to organize the essay?

_____.

16. Are the same features discussed for each subject? Are they equally developed?

_____.

17. Which signal devices are used? _____.

18. Is one overused? Can you suggest an alternative to a much-used/over-used word or phrase? _____.

19. Can you think of any ideas or examples from your own experience or observations that might strengthen the paper? _____

_____.

20. Is the introductory paragraph interesting to you? Does it "hook" you? (Again, there are no, "Yes /No" answers here) _____

_____.

21. How does it successfully "hook" you or fail to "hook" you?

_____.

22. Does the concluding paragraph leave you with a sense of closure? Are there any questions still left unanswered?

_____.

You should have two copies of this paper. One will be turned in at the end of class; the other will be returned to the student whose paper you're evaluating. Answer ALL the above questions in complete sentences; one word answers will not be counted.

Proofread carefully to see if you any words out.—Author Unknown

WORKSHEET

Peer Review #3: Cause and Effect

Your Name: _____

Name of Student You Are Evaluating: _____

Peer Evaluations—Revising—Paper 3

Editing and *revising* are terms that I use daily ... and practice in my own life. That's why this peer evaluation sheet is a little different from the first one. As with the last peer evaluation, this is a graded assignment. No "Yes/No" or one-word answers anywhere on this paper.

"Global"/Assignment

1. What is the essay about? _____
_____.

2. Is the paper truly cause-and-effect ? _____.
3. Is the essay about causes, effects, or both? _____
_____.

4. Is the essay organized chronologically or from least important to most important point?
Are there any logical gaps (post hoc, ergo propter hoc)? _____
_____.

Paragraphs

5. Look at the paragraphs. Are they all well-developed? (This is not a "Yes/No" question) _____.

6. Does the introductory paragraph give you hints about the body paragraphs to come?
_____
What are the three sub-topics or "factors?" (a) _____, (b)
_____ (c) _____.

7. Is the introductory paragraph interesting to you? Does it "hook" you? (Again, there are no "Yes /No" answers here) _____
_____.

8. How does it successfully "hook" you or fail to "hook" you? _____
_____.

Sentences

9. What is the thesis sentence? _____
_____.

10. Are the sentences clear? (No one-word answers) _____
_____.

11. Do they say what the author intended? _____.
If not, what is standing in the way of the real meaning? _____
_____
_____.

Question whether the sentences are in the best order. Remember the Venetian blinds.

12. What is your favorite sentence in the essay you've read? Write it below.

_____.

13. Why is it your favorite? _____

_____.

14. Do you have any sentences like it in your essay? _____.
In the space below, re-write one of your weaker sentences to reflect the strengths of this sentence you admire in your classmate's paper. *This is not optional.*
(old, weaker version of the sentence) _____

_____.

(new and improved sentence) _____

_____.

Writing Style/Strengths and Weaknesses
15. What mistake do you see made repeatedly? _____

_____.

16. Do you have a tendency to make the same mistake? _____
(Maybe recognizing that mistake in someone else's paper will help you see the error in your own paper.)

17. What strong points do you see? _____.

18. What weaknesses do you notice? _____.

19. Which cause-and-effect signal devices are used? _____

_____.

20. Is one overused? Can you suggest an alternative to a much-used/over-used word or phrase? _____.

21. Does the concluding paragraph leave you with a sense of closure? Are there any questions still left unanswered? Can you think of any ideas or observations that might strengthen the paper? _____

_____.

You should have two copies of this paper. One will be turned in at the end of class; the other will be returned to the student whose paper you're evaluating. Answer ALL the above questions in complete sentences; *one word answers will not be counted.*

Proofread carefully to see if you any words out.—Author Unknown

Peer Review Postings
Understanding Organization from the Reader's Perspective
• Brianne Howard •

Abstract: Reviewers read their partners' papers and write the topics/subjects of each individual paragraph on Post-Its; reviewers then reorganize the Post-Its for better information flow.

Duration: 50- or 75-minute class

Preparation: Students should come to class with a copy of their most recent draft in progress. Ideally, the students should be in the revision stage of multiple drafts and have completed at least a first rough draft.

Materials: The instructor should bring enough Post-It notes to allow each student the opportunity to use one per paragraph or main idea.

Each student should have a separate sheet of paper or a surface upon which to affix the Post-Its.

Procedure: Students can work in pairs or be given a random draft by the instructor.

Students should read the assigned peer's draft, one paragraph at a time.

After reading each paragraph, students will determine a word or small phrase that they think summarizes the subject discussed in the paragraph and write the subject, along with any necessary notations, on a Post-It. If there is more than one topic found, the student should list each idea on its own Post-It.

To help the author understand what section of the original paper is being addressed, the peer reviewer should number or letter the section on the draft and mark the corresponding Post-It with the same number or letter.

Upon completing a reading and categorizing of each paragraph, the students should have all ideas covered on respective Post-Its and have a visual, moveable outline of all content.

The peer reviewers can then examine the order of information based on the original order of Post-Its displayed and evaluate where paragraphs need to be divided to separate ideas.

Physically move and play with different organization strategies by grouping related ideas together. Reorder the Post-Its to produce a better flow of information within the draft.

After putting the Post-Its in the desired order, students meet to discuss the new organization strategy with the author of the paper. Peer reviewers can provide explanations concerning why one organization strategy is easier to read or creates a better experience for subject comprehension.

The authors of the original drafts can then revisit their drafts, move paragraphs around accordingly, and adjust the necessary transitions as appropriate.

Additional Author's Notes: Another version of the exercise can work with small groups. Students can be divided into groups of three or four and work the exercise for each person's paper as a team. Using the small group version helps give the author additional experience in receiving feedback and making decisions for the final product based on several readers' opinions.

Rationale: Students learn in a variety of ways. The method described here reaches out to visual and kinesthetic learners. The focus is moved from the macro level of the paper as a whole onto the micro level of paragraphs to decide the most effective method of relaying information to the reader.

As writers, it can be difficult for students to see how a reader will understand and interpret information. The peer review approach helps student writers become acquainted with how another person experiences a paper and how different organization strategies can be employed to reach a certain audience and make information accessible through writing.

Reviewing another's paper also exposes student writers to new ideas for organization and style to use within their own writing.

Potential Problems: Students who do not come prepared with a draft of the essay cannot be paired with another student to benefit from having someone else read his or her draft. These students can still benefit from reading another student's draft.

One remedy is to have students come prepared with two copies of their draft. The extra copies can be used as backups for students who would otherwise not get to practice reading another's paper.

I have also made bringing the complete draft a small graded component to motivate students to attend and come prepared.

If possible, another solution is to have students upload their electronic drafts to a communal class website so that more than one student can access a draft at the same time for review.

Reflection Roundtable
Students Evaluate Their Writing Experience
• Afaf (Effat) Jamil Khogeer •

Abstract: A group exercise in which students discuss predetermined questions which ask them to reflect upon their writing experience (prompts included below) with a partner, then switch partners and repeat the process; students are then assigned a summary of their answers, which instructors can use to calibrate their class lessons.

Duration: 45 minutes to 1 hour

Materials: Handouts of discussion questions (suggested questions offered in the "Procedure" section below), enough so that each pair of students has at least one

Preparation:

Editor's Note: The author has provided the following graph and explanations of terms which might be useful either as an in-class or explanatory lesson or for instructor edification:

This exercise addresses all components of the writing process: prewriting, researching, drafting, revising, editing, and publishing, and adheres to the categories in the cognitive domain of Bloom's Taxonomy, which encourage a student's higher-order thought.

Creating
Evaluating
Analyzing
Applying
Understanding
Remembering

Remembering: The questions provided prompt the students to retrieve, recognize, and recall information from their short- or long-term memory about the experience they had completing writing assignments.

Understanding: Students have to construct meaning from what they discuss. Through reflection they address why what they did when writing assignment was important and whether they met their goals.

Applying: Students use the reflection to implement what they have learned. They will be able to improve their writing skills by identifying and correcting problem areas that they had, and applying any new writing strategies they have learned from listening to other students' reflections.

Analyzing: Students break their writing experience into constituent parts and determine how each part relates to another and the overall structure or purpose of their assignments. They can see the patterns or relationships in what they did.

Evaluating: Students make judgments based on the criteria, standards, and rubrics for the assignments. They can determine how well they did on writing assignments, what worked, and what they need to improve.

Creating: Students take what they have learned and decide what they need to do next to improve their writing skills and then create a plan for doing so.

Providing a reflection discussion question allows students to engage in a degree of socialization. It is the act of explaining themselves to their peers, instead of just the teacher, that enhances their learning about writing. They benefit from having another person help them learn. Students increase their ability to monitor their writing during the writing process and become their own editors, instead of relying solely on their teachers.

Procedure: Have students arrange their desks in two concentric circles with pairs of students facing each other. This will result in there being an inner circle and an outer circle.

The teacher can begin the exercise with the following explanation:

We will be having a reflection exercise. Reflection exercises give you the opportunity to think about the class and what you are doing so that you can learn from your experiences. You have the opportunity to discover how the lessons you are being taught can help you with your real-world and academic writing tasks. Discussing your thoughts makes it easier for you to think about them and make connections between what you are being taught and what you are doing when you are writing. Your reflection will also serve as a source of reference and evidence when you are writing compositions in the future. You will be given an opportunity to learn from your classmates as you discuss the answers to the questions that will be asked. Be sure to take notes as you discuss your experiences with your classmates so that you can have them as a future reference.

Give the students a handout containing the following questions and instruct them to respond to them with each other. The list of questions can be added to or changed according to the teacher's needs and requirements.

- What have you learned in the class so far?
- Which course materials have helped you the most?
- What types of writing strategies worked best for you when completing the assignments?
- What have been your successes and/or failures with the assignments? What can you do to prevent future failures and ensure future successes?
- What changes, if any, have you seen in your writing?

- What areas of your writing do you want to improve?
- Which skills or experiences from this course can be applied in your future classes and present/future job?

Have the students discuss the questions with their partners for 15 to 20 minutes. Then have students from either the inner or outer circle move to the desk on their right. They should discuss the questions with their new partners. (If time permits, the students can rotate one or more times during the class period.)

During the exercise, the teacher should act as an observer, and not interject comments unless students ask him/her questions.

Follow-Up: As a writing exercise, instructors can assign students to write a summary of the negative and positive experiences they discussed during the exercise and what writing strategies they will use in future assignments that will help them improve their skills. The information the teacher obtains from their written summaries can help him/her make better decisions about what resources to provide to help students with problem areas and address any concerns the students may have about their learning experience.

Rationale: Providing a reflection exercise promotes a learner-centered environment in the composition class. It is particularly valuable in a composition class, because it is recognized as "a critical component of learning and of writing specifically" (Kathleen Yancey, 1998, p. 6). Providing a reflection question promotes metacognitive learning in that it helps my students be independent, critical thinkers, and conscious of their learning and thought process. According to Luanne Kowalke (1998): "Facilitating thoughtful, metacognitive learning in the classroom is not especially difficult, but it does take time, understanding, and a vision that goes beyond the traditional classroom values."

The end result, however, is an increased awareness for students, not only of what they learn, but how they learn it and what they can do with that knowledge (p. 220).

Students learn by creating new knowledge and understanding through the transformation of experience, and reflection plays a significant role because it provides the bridge between practical experience and theoretical conceptualization.

Potential Problems: Some students may not respond to the questions as much as others. There also may be students who dominate the discussion, which often happens. So, lopsided conversations are not anything out of the ordinary. Discussing their learning experiences may be new for some students and, thus, they may be hesitant to expose themselves to their peers. Most people do not want to publicly announce their weaknesses, and this type of assignment can put students on the spot. However, the teacher should let the students know that this is not a graded assignments and that they should not be critical of each others' responses. Letting students know that this is a collaborative, learning exercise, and not one to evoke criticism will help ensure a non-threatening environment.

—ɯ—

Linguistic Exfoliation
Student Writing Self-Evaluation
• Debra Rudder Lohe •

Abstract: Using a worksheet, students evaluate their own writing for common language and grammar issues (word choice, wordiness, nominalizations, active/passive voice).

Duration: Approximately 40 minutes

- about 20 to talk through the various "dead language" items
- about 20 minutes to work with their own essays during class time.

Preparation: Instructors should be familiar the following concepts explained on the worksheets:

- Pompous language
- Nominalization
- Active vs. Passive Voice
- General vs. Specific Words
- Abstract vs. Concrete Words
- Unnecessary Wordiness

Materials: Copies of the worksheet (four pages), enough for each individual student. Students should bring copies of their essays to class.

Procedure:

1. Distribute and read-through the examples on the worksheet.
2. Students should then use the specific guidelines for language revision in their essays.

- Students can use the spaces on the worksheet for making notes if they so choose

The exercise should help students to see ways they can inject new life and intentionality into their prose and to see "style" as more related to an action (e.g., choosing the way a text looks and feels) than to an adjective (e.g., stylish).

Additional Author's Notes: "Linguistic Exfoliation" was designed for a junior/senior level composition course titled "Exposition"; in it, students were to become more intentional about the choices they made as writers, and to think in new ways about how to sharpen their writerly "eye" and to bring new consciousness to all the writing they did, including their disciplinary work. One important element of the course was an insistence that all writing has "voice," even if that voice is cultivated to seem "voice-less."

This exercise was conducted in class about half-way through the semester. Students were asked to bring a draft of the essay they were currently working on and to be prepared to do some revision work in class. In class, I distributed a handout called "Linguistic Exfoliation"—the idea being to clear away the "dead language" in their prose and to make room for new growth and renewal—which we discussed for about 20 minutes or so.

Then, students were asked to go apply their learning to the drafts they'd brought in, going through and looking for examples of "dead language" and considering new ways they might write the same content. At the very end, we spent a few minutes discussing what they'd discovered and whether or not the changes they came up with were, in fact, improvements. (I wanted them to feel total authority over their work, and we spent some time in a later class discussing how discipline has a lot to do with whether or not they would actually want to edit out some of the things we were looking at together.)

W O R K S H E E T

Dead language can build up in your writing, preventing your prose from new growth and making your voice sound lifeless and dull. When you want to "exfoliate" your writing, try examining it for words and constructions that make writing sound voice-less. Below are some of the most common signs of un-conscious, un-crafted prose.

1. *Pompous Language.* This is unnecessarily formal language; writers often use it because they think it makes them sound smarter. In reality, it is language that calls attention to itself in a different way: it usually seems overly-complicated, like the writer is trying too hard. Sometimes it can come across as insincere, or it can have an unintentionally comedic effect. When you can, opt for the more direct, more common word. It won't make you sound less intelligent; it will make your writing sound more clear. Some examples of pompous language:

Instead of ...	Use ...
Optimal	Best
Ascertain	Find out
Finalize	Finish
Methodology	Method
Utilize	Use
Functionality	Function

2. *Nominalizations.* Many words that fall into the category of "pompous language" are also nominalizations. A nominalization is simply a noun that has been made of either a verb or an adjective. (The name, nominalization, is itself one: to turn a verb into a noun is to "nominalize" it.) Typically, you nominalize verbs and adjectives by adding endings like -tion, -ment, -ence, -ing, and so on. Nominalizations can make your writing sound overly complex, impersonal, abstract. Some examples of nominalizations:

Verb	Nominalization	Adjective	Nominalization
React	Reaction	Proficient	Proficiency
Discover	Discovery	Careless	Carelessness
Assist	Assistance	Different	Difference

Nominalizations are just verbs or adjectives hiding out as nouns. As with nominalizations, adjectives can also be verbs in disguise, and these usually follow the weakest verb in the English language (weak because entirely overused and capable of doing very little on its own): to be. Some examples would be: "fearful of" instead of "fear"; "deserving of" instead of "deserve"; "indicative of" instead of "indicate"; "suggestive" instead of "suggest." To avoid these sorts of dead language in your writing, make sure your verbs are really the actions in your sentences.

3. *The (Unintentional) Passive Voice.* In passive voice constructions, the agent of the verb's action is concealed. If you aren't purposefully concealing the agent, then the passive has the

potential to make your prose wordier than it needs to be, to make your prose awkward, and/or to make it harder for your reader to understand your point. So, for example:

Active: He lost his wallet.
Passive: His wallet was lost [by him].

In this example, you see all of the tell-tale signs of the passive voice: The subject of the active sentence actually becomes the receiver of the action (typically a spot reserved for the object), while the object (here: the wallet, the thing that "was lost") occupies the subject position. Also, a form of the verb *to be* precedes a verb in the past participle form.

Now, many teachers tell student writers never to use the passive voice, but this sort of rule isn't very useful because the passive voice does have its uses. The trick is to try and use the passive strategically—that is, only when you want to conceal the agent of the action because you don't know who it is, because your readers won't care who it is, or because you don't want them to know who it is. For instance, the following example of the passive is a common one for politicians: "Mistakes were made." The beauty of a sentence like this one, for a politician, is that she doesn't have to say, "I made mistakes." She effectively conceals the agent of the action, the person doing the mistake-making.

4. *General / Specific Words.* To keep your reader from having to work too hard, it's important to try and balance general words with specific ones. Look at the degrees of specificity in the following example:

General. Specific
Book . dictionary . unabridged dictionary . 2006 edition, American Heritage Dictionary
Abstractions (which we've discussed already) are a particular form of general word; they express ideas, beliefs, or feelings—things that cannot be perceived by the five senses (sight, sound, smell, tough, taste).

Concrete words, on the other hand, are very specific, and can be perceived by the senses. (Tropes, like metaphors and similes, can also help you describe something in concrete terms.)

When you have a lot of general words/abstractions piled into the same sentence, the effect can be one of vagueness or confusion, and your reader will have to work much harder to understand your meaning. Aim for balance between these when you write.

5. *Unnecessarily Wordy (or Instructional) Phrases.* Many of us use empty phrases like "the reason is because," "due to the fact that," "this is the one that," "what I want to say is," and so on. I call these "instructional" phrases because it's as if the writer wants to instruct us about what he's going to do/tell us, not just do it/tell us outright. Usually, these phrases involve several words where one could suffice. A couple of examples:

Original: What I want to say is that I hate it when I write wordy sentences.
Revision: I want to say that I hate it when I write wordy sentences.
Revision: I hate it when I write wordy sentences.

Original: He was late due to the fact that his sister's car died.
Revision: He was late because his sister's car died.

Generally, these sorts of constructions—like the others described above—make their appearance (read: appear) when a writer is feeling insecure about her ideas/claims. That insecurity is transmitted (e.g., the writer transmits her insecurity) through language that feels suddenly outside of the writer's voice.

—ɯ—

Six Peer Review Strategies
Prompts for In-Class Review
• Tessa Mellas •

Abstract: Following the six prompts below, students (1) learn to pose marginal questions, (2) highlight major ideas, (3) color code (with highlighters) sections that pique reader's interest, (4) color code research to determine ratio of cited material to author analysis, (5) cross-out unnecessary material, and (6) highlight but not fix grammar issues.

Duration: 50 minutes

Materials:

Students will need yellow, blue, and pink highlighters and multiple drafts of their papers.

Procedure: Below are some ideas for guiding student peer-reviews. Some of these steps can be used in the same workshop. However, since several of them use highlighters, some steps will only work if students bring two or three copies of their draft to class and enact different strategies with different drafts. If so, have the students label what each highlighted color means on each draft. Otherwise, the colored markings of the highlighters will get confusing.

1. **Responding with Questions:** While students read their partners' papers, they should only write questions in the margins. Examples: What do you mean here? Can you give an example? Are you saying that women didn't think before the Women's Rights Movement? Is this the right word? Should this point come earlier in the paper? What does this term mean? Would this sentence be more effective as a question? How does this paragraph relate/connect to the previous one? The instructor will need to demonstrate this method for students before they peer review. This can be done on a volunteered student paper on an overhead projector in the first half of class or the class period before peer review. Students should be encouraged to fill the paper with questions. If instructors find that students are finishing peer review too quickly without giving much feedback, they can mandate a certain number of questions per page, say 10.

2. **Organization:** To review organizational cohesion, students can break their partners' papers down into four or five major points, topics, or ideas and assign each a different colored highlighter. They should then go through the paper and highlight all the material that relates to the same topic in the same color. This will help writers to locate any material that is misplaced. This is also a very useful strategy for conferencing individually with students. I always keep several highlighters in my bag to show them material that is off topic.

3. **Hot and Cold Spots:** Students should read through the paper and highlight hot spots (ideas, information, prose that piques their interest) in *pink* and cold spots (places where the writing slows down, gets boring, isn't saying anything new and just feels like filler) in *blue*. The

writer will then have a good idea about what parts of the paper they should develop further and what parts they should cut.

4. **Too Much Research?**: For a research paper, it is helpful to highlight all quotes in one color, all paraphrases in another color, any information that should be cited but isn't in another color, and missing citations as colored stars. This method can show writers the ratio of source material to their own ideas (sometimes source material takes over a paper), and can also point out problems with uncited material and inaccurate or missing citations.

5. **Cutting the Fluff**: Ask students to read through the draft and cross out any phrases, words, or sentences that seem unnecessary. Students might also rewrite sentences so they're stronger, punchier, and more concise. Instructors can challenge students to cut a certain number of words from the paper, say 100, without hurting the quality of the writing. In conjunction with tightening up the prose, students should highlight verbs that are passive or weak in a certain color. They should highlight nouns that are vague (thing, stuff, people, it) in another color. This is a good exercise for students to perform on their own work.

6. **Grammar and Syntax**: To prevent students from getting hung up on sentence-level issues or from simply fixing their partners' grammar mistakes for them, tell students that they should not mark or fix any grammar or syntax issues with a pen or pencil. Rather, they should highlight any grammatical or syntactical problems in a specific color, such as yellow. This strategy might work well with strategy 1.

Rationale: Students often learn best from their peers. In part, the particular learning environment of the peer-review is bolstered by the social structure of the classroom—students often view their peers as less intimidating and are often therefore more open to criticism. Students learn to read closely and practice articulating their observations about writing verbally, which in turn aids both the student-editor and the student-write whose paper is under review. If nothing else, the peer-review is valuable because it forces students to learn actively rather than passively as when simply listening to an instructor.

—⟋ɯ⟍—

Visualizing Causality
A Peer Review and Poster Exercise
• Lori Mumpower •

Abstract: Students build and present causal arguments in poster format, much like a poster presentation for an academic conference.

This exercise also teaches argumentation, visual rhetoric, research, and focusing a research question.

Duration: Extended exercise: Two to three weeks depending upon the amount of time spent on teaching "causal arguments"

Materials:

1. Students can purchase their own poster and poster-making materials, but the instructor will need to bring materials to affix the posters either on the wall (tape) or to prop them (poster stands).

2. If you have access to computers in the classroom, students can present their arguments digitally. However, this presumes that students have some facility with technologies.

3. The instructor should prepare Poster Review Sheets (3 for every student in the class).

Context of Exercise: Students bring a poster to class that illustrates a causal argument, which they will be making later in a traditional (print) format. Students explain their poster orally and answer questions from their peer reviewers about their causal links.

In this unit on causality, I ask students to write an argument that explains the causal relationship between an early technological development and developments in their major discipline. Traditional peer-review sessions are often sequenced after the student has completed a rough draft of the paper but before it is due to be graded. By having students construct posters of their causal arguments before they finish drafting, they can receive crucial peer-review support at a stage in which their claims about causal links need to be critiqued. Students can uncover potential problems in their chains of reasons and have time to research their topic further, narrow their focus, or seek out other causes that could improve their arguments.

Goals for the Exercise:

Students will:

- argue causality both orally and visually
- determine weaknesses and strengths in their own and their peers' causal arguments
- distinguish between causality and correlation

Activity Timeline:

- Explain the day's activities to the class and answer questions (five minutes).
- Divide the class in half, assigning them to Group A or Group B. Ask Group A to tape their posters to the wall or prop their posters against the wall. Group B will serve as reviewers for the first review session. Members of Group B should find a Group A member to review and stand in front of them. Every poster presenter should have one reviewer. Distribute three Poster Review Sheets (Appendix A) to each reviewer. (five minutes)
- Peer Review begins. In five minutes, students should be able to give a brief description of their causal argument and answer questions from their reviewer. At the end of the five-minute review, the reviewer hands their Poster Review Sheet to the presenter. The instructor should tell students when five minutes are up so that the reviewers can rotate clockwise to their next poster. Repeat twice, for a total of three individual reviews. (15 minutes)
- Have Group B tape or prop their posters on the wall. (five minutes)
- Repeat peer review process, but Group B presents their posters to Group A. (15 minutes)
- Class discussion about what was learned and how this process informs their drafting. (five minutes)

Potential Problems:

1. As with many group activities, the noise level of the classroom can distract from the activity itself.

2. Students could place too much emphasis on the visual aspect of the assignment and

not enough on the arguments that they are making. Instructors can mitigate this by handing out, in advance, the Poster Review Sheets (Appendix A) to students, which shows the emphasis on the argument. The Poster Presentation Assignment Sheet (Appendix B) can also emphasize the goals for the assignment.

   3. In the past, some students have complained that they weren't creative enough to complete the assignment. Instructors should be sure to reiterate the goals of the activity, to visually represent their argument. Artistic ability is not required.

WORKSHEET

Appendix A: Poster Review Sheet

Poster Presenter: _____

Reviewer: _____

   Instructions: The presenter should verbally explain his or her poster. Listen closely. Ask questions. Then fully answer the following questions.

   1. What is the presenter's initial cause or causes? Summarize briefly below.
   2. What are the presenter's effects? Summarize them briefly below.
   3. Are there gaps in the chains of causality? Which links are difficult for you to understand or need more explanation?
   4. Are there other potential causes for the effects listed? In other words, could the author be confusing causation for correlation?
   5. Which part of the student's argument is most interesting to you? In other words, what would you like to know more about?
   6. Which parts of the student's causal links are more obvious and don't need much explanation?
   7. In what ways can the poster presenter tailor his argument to print? Are there ways he or she can help readers "visualize" their causal argument?

WORKSHEET

Appendix B: Poster Presentation Guidelines

   What I expect...

   1. Your causes and effects clearly indicated on your poster.
   2. Your grounds (personal experience, chains of reasons, sources, evidence) posted clearly with each link in your causal chain.
   3. Your name, section, and date clearly marked on your poster.
   4. You show up prepared to present your poster the day it is scheduled.
   5. You show up prepared to critique others' posters the day it is scheduled.

   What would *improve* your poster presentation...

1. For you to use graphics/pictures/photos or other media to further present your argument.
2. For you to be creative in your presentation of your argument.

What would *detract* from your poster presentation

1. To not show up the day you are scheduled to present your poster.
2. To show up late for class on presentation days.
3. To forget to do this assignment entirely, or to put in minimal effort.

—ɯɯ—

Composition Exercise Text
Peer Review Exercises
• Abigail G. Scheg •

Abstract: The author discusses the importance of peer review, offers a script for prompting students on peer review, and provides potential prompts for a peer review.

Discussion: In my composition classes, I have my students peer review each of the major writing assignments of the course (so approximately three or four traditional papers—narrative, compare/contrast, cause/effect, and an argumentative research paper). Prior to the first day of peer review, I explain to the students what the process will entail in generally this manner:

Next class period, please bring a printed copy of your narrative into class for peer review. Peer review is the process in which you share your rough draft with a classmate (or two) in order to get one-on-one edits and feedback on all aspects of your writing. So, you will come in to class and split into pairs. Then, you will exchange papers with your partners and take time to thoroughly read through their draft. Feel free to write on their paper with any questions, comments, or concerns that you may have. It will probably be necessary to read through their paper multiple times. Perhaps the first time you read through there are a number of errors with commas, which makes it difficult to read through the sentence. In that case, I would recommend that you read through the paper once and edit the commas to the best of your ability. Once you have the sentences written in a more manageable manner, read through the narrative again in order to understand and evaluate the *story*.

It does not matter if you are not an expert on the subject or on aspects of writing such as commas. Do your best. If you have questions about sentence-level concerns, you can always double check with me or with your textbook. If you do not understand something that the writer has written, check with the author. After you have finished going through the paper a few times, give the paper back to the author and discuss any of your questions or concerns.

It is not helpful to read through others' paper and tell them that everything is great. It may be the nicest thing that you think you can do, but it is also the least helpful. If someone uses commas incorrectly or has a poor story line and you let them know this, it is not a personal attack; it is a way to encourage the writer to succeed with his/her writing and in the class.

If you receive your paper back from your peer reviewer with tons of comments, that is good news! You have an opportunity to make great changes to your paper in order to learn more about a pattern of writing errors that you may have (such as run-on sentences) and to ultimately earn a higher grade on the final draft!

For the first peer review in a class, I do not provide the students with any handouts or additional questions to consider. The first peer review serves as a sort of litmus test to assess the editing and collaboration skills of the students. If the students do well working one-on-one with one another and provide substantive feedback, then I do not provide them with a handout or additional questions for the subsequent peer reviews either.

However, if a class struggles with what to say, what to address, or how to speak to their classmates, then I do provide a list of questions:

I know that it is always easiest to tell people that their papers are "good," but constructive criticism means so much more in the long run.

Some key points to watch and comment on:

- Do they have a clear idea overall?
- Do they provide specific examples in their paper?
- Are they *showing*, not *telling*?
- Do they have correct MLA format for the paper?
- Is the paper logical?
- Is there a good introduction and conclusion paragraph on each end of the paper?
- Does the paper meet the length requirements? At least three full pages? If not, where could they add more information or description?
- What emotions do you have after reading the story?
- Is it a "good" story? Did you like it? Why or why not?
- After reading their essay, please discuss these questions with them at length.
- Ask them: What was the purpose of your essay?
- See if their response to that question aligns with what you read. If not, decide why together.
- If you have any questions, please let me know.

Any unique constraints of various assignments can be substituted in these questions. For an argumentative research paper peer review, I ask students more focused questions about the thesis statement and demonstrating organization through a thesis statement. There are also additional questions about in-text citations and appropriate sources. The above questions are typical questions designed for a first narrative-writing assignment in a composition class. They are basic questions that lead students into more in-depth discussion when they may be at a loss for words or focus with their peers.

Another way that I sometimes provide structure to a peer review is by providing students with a copy of the rubric and ask them not only to go through the paper to provide comments and feedback, but also then to grade the paper using the official rubric. Peer reviewing with the rubric affords the students an opportunity to take a closer look at the rubric and really understand the nuances of how it can be applied to their writing.

Peer review assignments should provide the students the opportunity to become better writers, readers, and editors. Throughout my composition classes, I stress to my students to try to identify any negative patterns in their writing such as an overuse of simple sentences, run-on sentences, passive voice, or other problems. Once a pattern is identified in students' writing, they can learn how to address these elements in order to strengthen their skills for the long run. Peer review can help in this process of identification; it provides a chance to have a close one-on-one relationship with a reader that the student may or may not get from an instructor with dozens or hundreds of students.

Peer review can be done in any amount of time, depending on how it is framed in a class (e.g., whether or not guiding questions are provided or another structure is applied to the discussion). Typically, I provide my students two days of 50-minute class time to participate in peer review. Strong peer review sessions typically last for an entire 50-minute class period. If students finish early, I have them review their work or exchange papers with another early group. Typically I require that students work with a new reader on the second day of a peer review on the same assignment. There are ways to mix this up; perhaps on the first day there are no guiding questions for peer reviewing, but on the second day we use the rubric to guide and assess work. This is certainly up to the discretion of the instructor and the needs of the students.

No special materials are necessary in peer review assignments—only the requirement that students exchange papers in some way, whether printed copies or electronically. I have found that generally students provide more comments when they are able to write on a paper copy as compared to providing them electronically, but that would be different for every group of students or the population of the institution. I typically do not provide printed copies of guiding questions or a rubric to be used for peer review. Rather, I project the documents at the front of the classroom for students to see throughout.

Potential Problems: Peer reviews are one assignment that I find to be deeply personal, with the opportunity to change tremendously from one group of students to another. Some students have peer reviewed in previous classes; others are new to the concept and completely wary. Therefore, I would caution all instructors new to peer reviewing in class to be incredibly responsive to the needs of their students. Perhaps an instructor could have guiding questions ready in case the students are unsuccessful at providing feedback on their own. Once students understand that peer review can have a tremendous positive impact on their writing (and their grade), they are typically more invested in the process.

—w—

Alone in a Crowd
An (Anonymous) Peer Review Process
• Chelsea R. Swick •

Abstract: Students work in anonymous peer-review groups. The author provides suggested prompts.

Duration: 15 to 20 minutes per peer review

Preparation: An instructor-generated list of students who will work together on peer review; students will not reveal themselves to their partners.

Instructors may need to learn how to utilize online dropbox technology.

Materials: Cloud or Dropbox folders online (optional)

Procedure: This process begins with the teacher creating a list of students who will peer-review each others' papers; each student will be linked to four to five other students. The student is told not to share this list with any classmates. This keeps the process anonymous. When creating the lists, teachers should assign each student to multiple other students. This allows each student to receive multiple peer review letters.

Once a draft of an assignment has been finished, the class shares their drafts with one another. This can be done in hard copy, but it is easier to create a shared folder with cloud technology such as dropbox.com. This allows students access to every classmate's draft.

Students are instructed to create letters of peer review to two or three of the assigned peers. The teacher should give the students an outline of what needs to be included.

This will vary from assignment to assignment, but typically the assignment

- Should have the students find and detail what the thesis or purpose is in the assignment,
- Give three concepts that excel in the composition, and
- Three concepts that could use improvement.
- Details should be used to describe the concepts.
- The teacher should encourage the students to point to specific moments in the draft or even quote passages in order to describe where concepts are either executed well or need improvement.

Once the students finish their peer review letters, they send them to the instructor who will then distribute them to the students. This keeps the process anonymous. This can either be done through hard copies or through a shared folder in a cloud, such as the previously mentioned dropbox.com.

Rationale: By having the process be anonymous, students typically feel more comfortable detailing both the effective and ineffective concepts presented; thus they produce more honest feedback for their peers.

Potential Problems: The teacher should read and review the peer review letters in case there is unnecessary negative feedback.

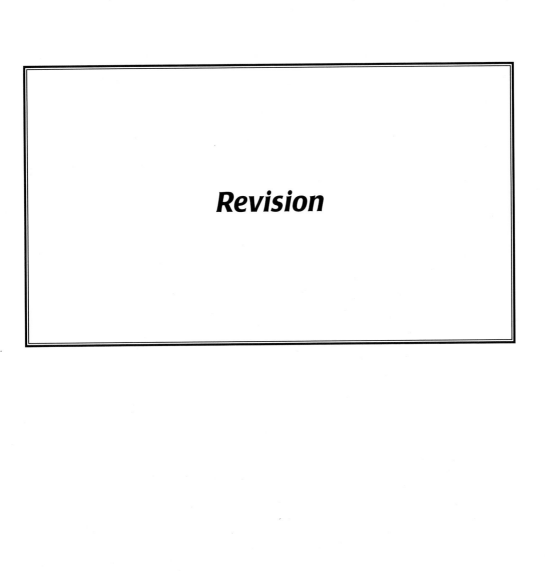

Revision

Revision in Practice
Review and Rewriting Intros in Class
• DeMisty Bellinger-Delfeld •

Abstract: Students perform peer reviews of each others' introductions, discuss their papers, and then rewrite based on student critiques during class time.

Duration: 30 to 45 minutes:

- Five- to 10-minute peer-review
- Five- to 10-minute discussion of review
- 10-minute break
- 10- to 15-minute in-class rewrite of introduction

Preparation: Students need, specifically, the "Introduction" to their papers.

This particular exercise should take place after a paper prompt is given and students have started drafting their papers on their own, but before the first peer workshop (if peer workshops are given, but this would work without workshops).

Procedure:

Five to 10 minutes: This should be a directed reading, where you tell the readers to mark up errors, question text, and write a brief note regarding what they think the thesis of the paper is and how the paper will address the thesis.

Five to 10 minutes: Each partner should do a "say back" (à la Peter Elbow)—that is, have each student orally tell in his/her own words, what he/she read in the introduction. Also, each student should look at his/her own draft and the partner's remarks.

Then, have the students put their drafts away and out of sight. Book bags work well.

10-minute break: Have your students take a break! They can get up and move around or sit silently. You can play a distracting video from Youtube or they can go out and get water. Do jumping jacks together or do other homework separately, like math. The goal here is to get their minds working, but without looking at that first draft and those markings their peers made. They can think about it, but just do something else.

10 to 15 minutes: Now, have the students sit back down and rewrite that introduction with their partners' remarks in mind. They are not allowed to look at their first drafts.

Before leaving class, the students must complete yet another draft of their introduction.

Additional Author's Notes—Variations: I've done this in two ways: a "mean way" and a "nice way."

This is the "mean way": I had a class that knew whatever they wrote was golden and that second drafts were a waste of time. This was the class I first tried this exercise in. I went to a student and read the draft completed in class. It was okay, but I said, "This is terrible!" and ripped it in half. I went to another student and did the same thing. Then I said, "All of you. Rip up your papers! I'm sure they all fall flat." And they did. Then I said, "Write a third draft. When you think that paper is perfect, raise your hand and I'll come and read it. Then you can go." My class got very quiet and busy, writing as if their weekends depended on it. One student eventually raised her hand. "Yes?" I said. "Would you read my draft?" "Are you happy with it?" I asked. "Yes," she said. "Okay, I suppose you're done." After that, I explained about the revision process, the review process, and asked them if their drafts are adequately introducing their paper. I was in grad school, and I felt invincible. It seemed perfectly fine ripping up students' writing, and I had students thanking me for that exercise for at least a year later, but I can't imagine doing that now.

This is the "nice way": Go through parts A and B again with a different peer, and then have the conversation about the revision process and introductions.

I'm sure we all tell our students that revision is more than correcting grammar and mechanical errors, and I am sure our students hear this in good faith. But when they get corrected drafts back, many first year writers only line edit or rework specific sections that were pointed out to them in their subsequent drafts. I noticed this in my first year as a TA and to address it, I created this exercise to help my students see that revision is, as often noted by accomplished writers, re-seeing. In revising, we have the chance to understand better what we have written, what is working, and what is not working. And here, we have the chance to rewrite.

After this exercise is completed, I tell my students of times when I and writers I know have restarted from scratch or rewritten entire sections (a paragraph to pages long). The goal of the exercise is to (1) show what we write is not set in stone, but on mere paper or malleable bits in a word processing document. We are not beholden to those first words and we may change them a little or a lot to create a coherent piece of writing that we can share with an audience; (2) help students understand what they have written through their peers and; (3) see what the introduction should accomplish.

Potential Problems: Each time I do this exercise, there are at least two or three students who did not bring in a working draft. This is okay. In the first five or 10 minutes of class, have them write an introductory paragraph. If anything, this will get them working towards their final paper and out of procrastination mode.

—⁐⁐—

Lessons in Revision with the Beatles and the Declaration of Independence

• Rita D. Costello •

Abstract: After an instructor-lead discussion of correcting, editing, and revising, students compare drafts of the Declaration of Independence and John Lennon's first draft of a song with the final lyrics as well as listen to the song itself. Then, the students discuss the changes made between the versions as well as the impact of the changes.

Revision is the primary focus of the lesson, but it can also be linked to Peer Reviewing.

Duration: 50 minutes

Materials: Overhead projection:

- Drafts of the Declaration of Independence (urls provided below)
- a projection or handout of the versions of The Beatles' song "I'm Only Sleeping" by John Lennon.

Instructors may consider playing aloud the song to the class.

In addition, instructors may want to create a spreadsheet or bookmark the web pages found at the end of the Procedure section.

This works best in a room that allows projection, such as with a SMARTboard; however, it can be translated into handouts or a sequence of BlackBoard/Moodle screens.

Procedure: This is not so much an exercise as a lesson.

1. I begin by differentiating between correcting (fixing definite errors), editing (making surface changes, either of errors or for clarity and style), and revising (making significant changes in order to develop ideas, argument, content, fluidity, and so on). The first two deal more in Lower Order Concerns (LOCs). While revising may incorporate LOCs, the focus is on Higher Order Concerns (HOCs). Emphasize throughout the lesson that revision is not just for students, but for all writing.

2. After about 15 minutes of lecture/discussion, present the initial version of the Declaration of Independence (Thomas Jefferson's draft). Allow for a read-through (either individually with handouts or out loud with a projection) and discuss with students if there is anything that seems unfamiliar or problematic. Parsing the language is okay, but be sure to deal with the major concepts as well.

3. Switch from looking at the full Jefferson draft to the edited copy with additions and deletions made by the Congress. This switch often takes students aback for a moment, so give a moment or two for discussion to get going again. Discuss the rationale for the changes and what it says about our country as well as what it says about the revision process. (I also like to link this stage as a parallel to peer reviewing essays within a composition class. What might have happened if Jefferson had sent his version to the King of England without the Congressional peer review? In a research based course, this could also be linked to the peer review process in academic journals.)

4. As the discussion is winding down, I switch to the view of the finished/final draft. (If time permits, I include another read-through using the text and end on a projection of the image of the document. But this is not absolutely necessary.)

5. The Declaration of Independence takes the bulk of class time and using it alone is enough to get the lesson across; however, if time permits, only five or 10 minutes is enough to add a pop culture reinforcement of the lesson. I use The Beatles song "I'm Only Sleeping." This is not necessarily the most up-to-date reference, but it is the most graphically observable revision I have been able to find and students still recognize it as popular music.

6. Project the image of John Lennon's first draft of the song (several photographs of the

page are available online) followed by the side by side comparison of the draft and the final version of the lyrics. There is no need to say anything at this point (depending on your level of comfort with hokeyness, and your Internet/computer situation, you could also just allow the song to play). Again, my primary purpose is discussing revision, but it is also possible to make the link to peer review in terms of a band member writing a song and then taking it to the rest of the band, which changes the song before recording.

This works best in a room that allows projection, such as with a SMARTboard; however, it can be translated into handouts or a sequence of BlackBoard/Moodle screens. One reason that projection/online presentation is beneficial is because color-coding makes the shifts in the congressional draft of the Declaration of Independence much more apparent to students.

I have saved all the pieces of this lesson into computer files since at least one of them has changed on me since beginning to use this lesson; however, here is a list of sites that can be used to project various parts of the lesson:

Editor's Note: The urls below are all housed on the "ushistory.org" website. They show the various versions of the Declaration complete with successive drafts, including drafts which show strike-outs from the original.

(Key words "us history org declaration of independence")

- http://www.ushistory.org/declaration/document/rough.htm
- http://www.ushistory.org/declaration/document/congress.htm
- http://www.ushistory.org/declaration/document/images/declaration_big_enhanced.jpg
- http://www.ushistory.org/declaration/document/index.htm
- http://msnbcmedia.msn.com/j/MSNBC/Components/Photo/_new/pb-101124-lennon-whalen.photoblog900.jpg

The transliteration of The Beatles lyrics I constructed based on two different images I found online; that resulting document I created is included at the end of the lesson.

7. Students often seem disinterested at the start of the lesson; it is not until the second draft (congressional edit) of the Declaration of Independence that they start to get into the process. I have not developed a means of making the beginning more engaging or moving directly into the point at which students become engaged. However, once I reach the congressional edit, students have always engaged at that point. Also, while projecting the images may not seem necessary to us in terms of the material, they do help many students engage.

Rationale: Students learn that revision is not just academic; more specifically they learn the difference between correcting/editing and revision, as well as that what they learn in terms of revision and peer review in composition classes does have real world applications.

Kick Ass Paragraphs
Using Stronger Language to Bring Writing to Life
• Tessa Mellas •

Abstract: The class reads first a "boring" paragraph and then a "kick ass" paragraph revised by the same hypothetical writer; students then discuss what makes one paragraph better than the other and practice revising additional "boring" paragraphs (examples on worksheet below).

This exercise also teaches language usage.

Duration: This exercise can take anywhere from 20 minutes to a full class period, depending on instructor approach.

Preparation: Giving students context for this exercise can be helpful. Language is often the last thing students think about, which means they sometimes forget about it altogether. Showing students how to liven up their prose to make their writing more vivacious is important toward giving their writing power and punch.

Materials: Instructors will need a computer with a word processor that can be projected onto a screen in order to make revisions to paragraphs as the class discusses them.

Also, instructors will need to check these two children's books out of the library, so the students can see the images in order to describe them more clearly:

- *Flower Garden* by Eve Bunting and Kathryn Hewitt (HMH Books for Young Readers, 2003).
- *The Berenstain Bears Out West* by Jan Berenstain and Stan Berenstain (Harper Collins, "I Can Read Book 1," 2006).

Editor's Note: Unlike a great many books, the two titles listed above do not appear to have many representative images available online, so instructors will probably need the actual books if they plan on using either title.

Procedure: The first two paragraphs on the worksheet (following) demonstrate how an experienced writer would revise a paragraph with stale language, making changes in word choice to make the prose more lively.

Read these two paragraphs together as a class.

Discuss why the writer made the choices he or she did in revision. Talk about the effect of word choices in both the weaker draft and the stronger one.

Then, as a class, revise one of the sample paragraphs with weak language to make the language punchier.

Instructors might consider doing one together as a class, and then break students into groups to revise a paragraph together. You can treat the revision as a competition to see who can make the best improvements.

After working on livening up a paragraph, students can project their rewritten paragraphs on an overhead projector and vote on whose group did the best job. They could also merge every group's draft into one final draft that takes the best sentences from each group.

WORKSHEET

A Boring Paragraph with Boring Language

One important criterion that parents should look for in a good children's book is good pictures. The illustrations in a children's book should be colorful. They should also relate clearly to the story that is being told. Pictures should also be interesting and full of interesting details. If children aren't interested in the pictures, they might not even care about the story. The book *The Berenstain Bears Out West* fulfills this criterion. The pictures are very well done. The illustrators, Stan and Jan Berenstain, use primary colors such as blue, red, yellow, and green. Also, kids will be very interested in the pictures because the bears portrayed are very expressive. The bears are always smiling and their clothes are very detailed. The setting is also detailed. We can even see the pricks on the cactus. The pictures also take up most of the page, which is good. Overall, I think that the illustrators did a great job with the pictures. The pictures make the book even better.

Two Kick Ass Paragraphs with Vivacious Language

In addition to having an exhilarating plot, a children's book must also keep kids glued to their seats with vibrant expressive illustrations. Illustrators must use bold, beautiful colors that leap off the page and grab kids by their eyeballs to hold them entranced. If a book has dull colors or no colors at all, a parent might as well flush it down the toilet because children will be more interested in the pretty colors on the Kleenex box than in the lackluster drab book stuffed in their face. Parents need not worry about color here. Stan and Jan Berenstain certainly know how to make the page pop. Papa Bear's pants are royal blue. Brother Bear's shirt is fire truck red. Sister Bear's clothes are fashioned in a pretty pastel pink, and Mama Bear's dress is a demure aquamarine blue. Any child would approve of this color scheme. It would keep kids staring for hours.

As well as utilizing a rich palette of colors, the illustrator of any children's book should also make sure that the pictures bring alive the story in rich details to help the child follow along with the words in the book. If poor illiterate Skippy Junior wakes up before his parents on Saturday morning and wants to read *The Berenstain Bears Out West* all on his own, he has to be able to figure out what's happening based solely on what's pictured on the page. Stan and Jan Berenstain earn high marks in this category as well. From the very first picture on the cover, kids will understand what's going on. Papa Bear is perched on a bucking horse, his hat held high, a whoop of joy on his face. The rest of the bear family is at the rails cheering him on, their mouths opened wide in mid-holler. The horse has a sly look on its face and its head is bent low as though it is about to buck Papa Bear off his high horse. Nearby is a prickly green cactus. Even a dimwitted child would be able to put two and two together to assemble the plot from there. Poor Papa Bear is going to end up on the cactus. The plot is engrained in the picture and this will help any child appreciate the book even more. The illustrations in this book are colorful and enhance the story brilliantly.

Sample Paragraphs to Practice On:

1. The book *Flower Garden* is also a good pick for the Wood County library because it is multicultural. It is a good idea for a book to show multiculturalism because that opens kids'

minds up to and helps them be more tolerant and less prejudiced in the future. This book is definitely multicultural. The main character and her family are African American, but there are people of other ethnicities on every page. The cashier seems to be Irish, as she has red hair and a fair complexion. On the bus, there is an older white couple, an African American boy, and an Asian mother and daughter. Every time we see a scene of the neighborhood, we also see different ethnicities together. This is good because it will expose kids to multiculturalism especially if they live in a neighborhood all of one race. This will help young kids start to understand that different races can live together happily and enjoy each other's company and culture.

2. Another problem with this book is that the story isn't very interesting. The girl and her father just buy flowers, carry them home, and make a window box for the mother. I guess this is a "nice" story, but it's not really that exciting. It's really pretty boring in fact, and kids will pick up on that and won't want to read it. If kids don't want to read it, then what's the point of having it in the library. Flowers just aren't a very interesting topic. They're kind of lame really. Boys don't care about flowers either, so they won't be interested at all. Overall, the library needs to find a book with a better plot.

3. *Flower Garden* is also a good book to choose because of its physical attributes. The book is really big. It's almost one and a half feet long both in width and length. This makes the pictures inside really big also. Any child will enjoy huge pictures. A kid might have trouble holding such a big book but could easily lay it on the floor and just examine the huge pictures. They would enjoy that. Also, such a big book would be useful for a visually impaired child. It also could be helpful for a teacher to read to a class because everyone would be able to see the pictures. Another great physical attribute is the pages, which are thick and glossy. This will make it easier for a child to turn the pages. The front is also glossy and covered in some sort of plastic coat. I carried the book in the rain yesterday, and it didn't even get damaged. This would be good because the library wouldn't have to worry about it getting damaged by other people. I think the physical attributes really help make this a good book.

4. In conclusion, I just don't think that *Flower Garden* is the best book for the Wood County Library. It does have good pictures, but the story is kind of boring. Also, boys wouldn't want to read it. Also, it doesn't have complete sentences, so kids would learn grammar wrong. It's got big words that would frustrate kids too, and it's really too hard for a kid to hold. There are so many bad things about this book that out power the good. Overall, I think the library could find a better book that everyone would like.

—✳—

A Spatial Approach to Style
Using Tag Clouds for Revision in Narrative Writing
• Kristin Mock •

Abstract: Students upload their essays to Wordle or TagCrowd, choose a typography and design, and then compare the results to learn about graphic design and revision; homework assignment is an option.

This exercise also teaches visual rhetoric.

Duration: 50 minutes

Materials: Instructor will need access and familiarity to "Wordle" online at http://www.wordle.net/.

Suggested Reading: The author suggests excerpts from the following:

Boynton, Robert S. *The New New Journalism: Conversations with America's Best Nonfiction Writers on Their Craft.* New York: Vintage, 2005.

Lazar, David. *Truth in Nonfiction.* Ames: University of Iowa Press, 2008.

See *The New New Journalism* website at http://www.newnewjournalism.com

Preparation: A pre-writing activity can be helpful. Students might benefit from having the chance to see and analyze some tag clouds in class before the assignment. Famous speeches and literary passages they are already familiar with work well, as students can compare what they know about the original piece of writing with the way the tag cloud has interpreted it.

See the website "Word Cloud Analysis of Obama's Inaugural Speech Compared to Bush, Clinton, Reagan, Lincoln's" (use title as key words) which compares several presidential inaugural addresses.

For this portion of the exercise, then, a reliable Internet connection and a projector would be ideal, but it is not necessary. The rest of the activity only requires that students bring in printouts of their essays and tag clouds (or post them to a course website or blog).

Have students read some narrative excerpts from *The New New Journalism* to get a sense of the vast range of forms their essays might take. Talk about the techniques each writer uses and what kinds of craft elements they find intriguing. Frame the discussion in terms of style, convention, and aesthetics (this will help students grasp the concepts before working on their own essays).

Time permitting, instructors might also have students take a look at a selection or two from David Lazar's *Truth in Nonfiction*, which is a comprehensive and stimulating collection of essays that utilize both text and graphics.

Procedure: First, give students the opportunity to write a piece of nonfiction narrative, such as an investigation into their relationship with reading and writing. Ask them to focus on specific details, personal insights, and specific events that shaped their thoughts about literacy.

Next, ask students to upload their essays into a program like Wordle (TagCrowd, while not as interesting as Wordle, is a nice alternative because it allows students to upload files from their hard drives rather than copying/pasting).

If possible, have them choose the typography and design that is most appealing to them and ask them to bring in a printed copy for the next class.

Then, during the next class, have students who wrote on similar topics pair up and compare their tag clouds. Encourage them to carefully study the diction and the way in which the words appear on the page.

Ask them:

- *What is the essence of each Wordle?*
- *How do the passages differ?*
- *Does each one retain the same idea?*

- *What individual stories does each one tell?*
- *How can the students tell whose Wordle is whose and, if so, what does that imply about writing?*

Then, if you'd like to get them thinking about genre and hybridity, you might like to ask them: *Is a Wordle an essay in itself? Why or why not? What are the conventions/tropes inherent to narrative, and how can we break away from or adhere to those boundaries?*

Post-Writing Activity: As a closing discussion, ask them, as a group, to reflect on their findings. Ask them:

- *What did the exercise illuminate about each writer, specifically?*
- *How can using new technologies inform and enhance (or restrict) the writing process?*
- *How can their findings from this exercise help them tackle the revision process, from both a global and local perspective?*

From here, have students take home their work and revise their narratives as informed by the in-class exercise.

Additional Author's Notes: Ideally, as a first essay in the FYC sequence, this exercise would accompany a personal writing assignment. However, the topic can be broad—instructors could have students write an essay about their relationship to reading/writing, a narrative about a specific moment or person from their past, a journalistic essay on a particular event on campus, an expository essay analyzing a short text or film, or a persuasive piece for a newspaper. The options are limitless; however, do ensure that students pair up together who have written on similar topics, as the students will be evaluating each other in terms of the similarities/differences in their prose and approach to the topic, not necessarily the content of the essay.

Depending on the amount of conversation devoted to the post-writing activity, instructors have a lot of flexibility with this assignment. Additionally, it can also be adapted to other assignments and types of essays.

Rationale: In this exercise, which focuses on teaching an awareness of style, Tag cloud programs, while not necessarily designed to provide reliable analytic insight, are extremely useful in the composition classroom because they take the students' work, isolate the most frequently used words and expressions, scramble them by size, color, and shape, and generate a piece of "art" derived from the original content for students to examine and analyze.

In terms of thinking about revision, this visual representation of the students' work can be an excellent way to help basic or developing writers investigate areas for both global and local revision by showing them repetitive words, unclear ideas, or over-used phrases; this, in turn, emphasizes the importance of word choice and encourages a more refined attention to language based on an understanding of voice, diction, and frequency of words and ideas. By doing a genre analysis of the "essay" to bookend this activity, students will re-envision their own work, gain new insights into the personality of their writing voice, and be able to explain conventions of the traditional and non-traditional narrative essay.

Potential Problems: Students often have difficulty understanding stylistic nuances, especially when framed in terms of their own writing. Make sure, as they are working, that they are focusing on *style*—not content. Also, continue stressing that mastering a personal style takes many years of practice and refinement, and that this exercise is aimed at helping them explore their particular approaches to writing.

—∿—

Thinking Like an Editor
Revising Across Media
• Martha A. Webber •

Abstract: In group work, students take on the role of a magazine editorial board tasked with revising an essay for multiple media platforms.

Duration: 50 minutes

Author's Note: I have conducted this activity over a 50-minute class session, and I could see it also filling the span of a 75-minute session as well. I provide a 45-minute breakdown below but I encourage you to add or remove steps as well as experiment with time distribution for the individual steps.

Preparation: Prior to the "editorial board" class session, students should have read and preferably discussed the shared reading or essay so they will be equipped with a solid understanding of it.

Although this flexible exercise could pair well with nearly any reading, I have used it exclusively for a first year writing course with Jon Krakauer's "Death of an Innocent," an article originally written for *Outside* magazine but one that formed the basis for a nonfiction book on the same subject, *Into the Wild*.

Editor's Note: Because the article was republished by *The Independent*, the text of the article is available with a Google search of the author's name and the article title.

Materials: Have students bring printed articles to class as they will need to make notes on them.

Procedure: Separate students into groups (I prefer groups of three to ensure more participation) and share the following prompt with them (either projected or on a handout):

You are an editorial team working for Outside *magazine preparing to produce materials to commemorate the publication of Jon Krakauer's "Death of an Innocent." As a team, you have to revise the essay for the multiple media purposes listed below to promote the article for your magazine's audience. As your team makes decisions about what to revise and highlight be prepared to provide a rationale for decisions, as you will have to discuss your choices with additional editorial teams before you present them to the class.*

1. *Editorial Team Meeting* (20 minutes):

Online Media: Since the publication of "Death of an Innocent" in 1993, *Outside* has developed a creative online presence. Revise the article to create two items: (a) compose three to five tweets of 140 characters or less that are a blend of paraphrase, quote, and your original writing that work to "hook" potential readers to link to the full article; (b) mark a 300 word (about one double-spaced page) selection from the article to feature on the front page of the website with an accompanying image. This selection can come from anywhere in the article and even from more than one place—like the tweets it should work to interest readers to link to the new article.

Print Media: Jon Krakauer has agreed to revisit the article for *Outside* and will meet with *Outside*'s editor to discuss areas for expansion and new interviews he can conduct. The editor wants the team's advice: select the three most significant moments, arguments, or concepts the article explores and mark sections where new content may develop them for even more significance. In addition to marking locations to expand in the article directly, prepare the following for your editor: (a) a brief rationale about *why* the three moments/concepts you have selected are most significant, (b) specific ideas for how these moments can be expanded and, (c) a brief list of people Krakauer might interview (or re-interview) with ideas for questions to ask them.

2. *Joint Editorial Team Meetings* (10 minutes):

You will now pair up with one or two other teams to share your editing selections. Discuss key similarities and differences and select the following to present to the entire class:

    a. three of your favorite tweets,

    b. three of the most significant moments/concepts your teams selected (highlighting shared moments/concepts across teams), and

    c. up to three ideas on how to expand these moments for the updated article Krakauer will write over 20 years after the publication of the original.

3. *Whole Class Presentations + Reflective Discussion* (15 minutes):

Over the class I embody a role as a facilitator, buzzing between groups and occasionally prompting them with instant feedback, questions, or encouragement. During the class presentations I take notes about particular contributions as well as bigger connections to create questions for the final reflective discussion. Towards the end of the discussion, I ask the class to reflect on the editing process and how revision works when you revise for emphasis and priority (over a sense of revising for correctness).

After Class Session:

Optional: If you want to abbreviate the activity or preserve the content the students produce to share across the entire class, consider having students post their group's submissions online if you use an online course content manager such as Moodle or Compass.

Strongly Suggested: This activity works best when it occurs a day or two prior to students coming to class with an essay draft for peer review (especially since the activity relies on a text students have already read). Conduct your peer review session with similarly structured exercises to the editorial activity so that peer reviewers can focus on advising about significance of ideas and meaningful areas for expansion.

Rationale: In considering and being asked to create multiple versions of the "same text," student writers can see how many choices they have for textual representation with the same subject matter (in the case of Krakauer, the subject of Christopher McCandless and "innocent" adventurousness).

The editorial board activity, which promotes critical thinking about revising for purpose and emphasis, works especially well after a class session or sessions focused on discussing the selected reading and immediately prior to class sessions featuring peer review of student writing assignments so students can see the connections between the editorial board revision process and their own.

Potential Problems: In the past I tried to conduct this activity the first day that we discussed a reading but it felt too rushed to ask students to work with the text in this way before having an opportunity to discuss it for one class session prior. Additionally, I have added and subtracted several of the components of the exercise to adjust for particular classes.

—⁓—

Genre Bending
Teaching the Radical Revision/ Multimedia Project
• Alexandra Oxner *and* Geoff Bouvier •

Abstract: Students expand a traditional expository paper into a new hybrid paper by including elements of at least two different genres (numerous web pages used).

Editor's Note: This is the first of three exercises in a series designed to teach revision (see also "Summary vs. Analysis" and "Making Connections" in this book); each exercise can be used as a standalone or as part of the sequence.

Duration: 50 to 60 minutes

Materials: Computer with Internet access and a projector

Preparation: Students often don't understand what the multi-media assignment is meant to accomplish. Instructors must provide them with an example—preferably one that encompasses more than just two genres. I decided to use *The Ride of the Valkyries* because though it is a "text" that most students will recognize, they are probably not intimately familiar with it. The only preparation required will be to compile a list of links to content such as YouTube videos, web pages, and images.

Instructors should be familiar with the following subjects / web pages (links and keywords provided below):

- The *Nibelungenlied* and the mythical creatures "the valkyries"
- Composer Richard Wagner and his famous composition *Ride of the Valkyries.*
- Composer and conductor Leonard Bernstein and his 1973 lecture "The Unanswered Question: 3 Musical Semantics" at Harvard University
- Francis Ford Coppola's 1979 movie *Apocalypse Now.*
- The *Looney Toons* episode "What's Opera, Doc?"

Editor's Note: Most of the episodes and segments for the exercise are available on YouTube and links and keywords appear below.

Author's Note: For this assignment, students are required to choose one of the traditional "papers" they composed earlier in the semester (they are usually choosing from a personal narrative, position shift essay, rhetorical analysis, ad analysis, snapshots paper, or research paper). Their task is to transform this paper into a multi-media/genre-bending project which utilizes at least two different genres. They also compose a presentation which explains and analyzes how their message changes across different genres/mediums/audiences.

Procedure: Introduce the multi-media assignment (see the assignment description, attached below).

Show the first webpage: http://en.wikipedia.org/wiki/Nibelungenlied
(key words "Nibelungenlied wikipedia").
Explain that the Nibelungenlied is a German epic poem.

Introduce students to Richard Wagner: http://en.wikipedia.org/wiki/Richard_Wagner.
(key words "Richard Wagner Wikipedia.")
Explain that Wagner's famous opera was based off of this original text (the Nibelungenlied).

Explain that Leonard Bernstein is a famous composer who is most well-known for his
position as the director of the New York Philharmonic Orchestra.

Show a short clip from Bernstein's lecture at Harvard: http://www.youtube.com/watch
?v=8IxJbc_aMTg. I found it useful to show them the clip from 29:06–31:40. (key words "bernstein the unanswered question 1973 three musical semantics")

- Here, Bernstein discusses the message of music and "interprets" a classical piano song.

Now play an actual music clip of Wagner's *The Ride of the Valkyries* (use title as keywords):
http://www.youtube.com/watch?v=V92OBNsQgxU.

At this point, most of your students will recognize the song. Now, have them do a three-
to five-minute free-write—their goal is to interpret the music, like Bernstein did in the video
example.

Explain what a valkyrie is: http://en.wikipedia.org/wiki/Valkyrie.
Example of a student response (to be read while listening to *Ride of the Valkyries*):

It is a Saturday morning and a brother and sister walk out of their bedrooms, still yawning and half
asleep. Each youngster has the same goal: watching some T.V. before their parents wake up and
start giving out orders. They quickly realize the other's intent and dash towards the living room.
Once there, the remote control can't be found. The brother tears apart the couch as the sister
climbs the cabinets. An intense struggle breaks out—hair flies, nails scratch. All comes to an end
when their mother appears, remote in one hand and a list of chores in the other.

After students have read their examples to the class (ask for volunteers), discuss how their
story/poem/etc. re-interprets the music. How does it change the message?

Show your students a clip from *Apocalypse Now* (this is when they will become very
excited): http://www.youtube.com/watch?v=GKaYOW9zMoY.
(key words "Apocalypse Now—Ride of the Valkyries (1080p)") Discuss.

Show your students a clip from the *Looney Tunes* episode "What's Opera, Doc?": Discuss.

- *Editor's note:* This episode has been removed from YouTube for copyright violation,
  although various segments remain available on YouTube and other video services if
  the title of the episode is used as a set of keywords.

Finally, play Wagner's *The Ride of the Valkyries* one last time: http://www.youtube.com/
watch?v=V92OBNsQgxU.

Ask your students to do another three to five-minute free-write, only this time, ask them
to write a poem, song, short story, narrative, etc. to accompany the music. Their task is to
transform the song (original text) into another genre (like the creators of *Apocalypse Now* and
Looney Tunes did).

Summing Up: When leading discussion between videos, your conversation should center on this: how does the message of the original text (Wagner's piece) change across medium, genre, and audience? For the Radical Revision, the student's original text will be their essay. They will be transforming that essay into two different genres, and they will have to explain how their message changed.

Potential Problems: This lesson plan also falls under the category of "analysis." Your students may not understand how to distinguish between summary versus analysis. Be ready to ask them more probing, analytical questions.

ASSIGNMENT SHEET

I want you to choose something that personally interests you. If you are a music major, make one of your snapshots into song lyrics and record them. If you have always enjoyed reviewing films/books, write as if you are Ebert and Roeper on your rhetorical analysis. I will particularly be looking for you to move beyond the surface of your ideas, use purposeful detail, have an awareness of your voice and language, and connect to your ideas through the lens of your own experiences. Consider (but do not feel limited to) the following alteration possibilities (and feel free to draw upon more than one radical change as you might alter voice, perspective and format):

Turn your research paper into a newspaper article or advertisement, with professional formatting. Analyze the advertisement that you create.

Turn your research paper or rhetorical analysis into a creative piece—a poem, short story, song, etc.

Write an episode/scene/chapter for the piece of rhetoric you chose to analyze. (Example: Writing an additional scene for *O Brother, Where Art Thou?*, which we discussed in class,)

Create a YouTube video to accompany one of your papers—a PSA, commercial, commentary, review, music video, etc.

Make one of your papers into a work of art—cartoon storyboard, series of drawings or paintings, etc.

Conduct a lengthy interview or series of student interviews pertaining to one of your papers and compile your findings.

If you researched the benefits of organic food or vegetarianism, do an experiment. Eat that way for a week, assess your body, and bring us food.

If you researched how music influences mood, or wrote song lyrics for your snapshots paper, bring your band to class and perform for us.

Create an advertisement or viral campaign for the piece of rhetoric you analyzed for paper 2.

Create a movie poster or series of trailers; design a promotional t-shirt to wear during your presentation, etc. Everything is a text!

For our final week of classes, you *all* will be presenting your radical revision project in front of the class. This will complete the oral rhetoric portion of your ENC 1102 course.

Presentation Guidelines: You *must* show us your project. You do not necessarily have to show us the entire project, but we must see parts or excerpts of the project itself.

You *must* change your original paper into *at least two* different genres. (This means you cannot simply make your rhetorical analysis into some song lyrics. You must create song lyrics and a video; or create song lyrics and record yourself singing them; or create song lyrics with a musical accompaniment; etc.)

You should tell me why you chose to do this revision. What makes it radically different from the original paper?

Why did you choose these particular mediums and genres? Why does this revision matter? What did you hope to accomplish through it? How does the message change? Did your audience change?

What did you learn from the project? Walk me through your creative process!

Writing Process and Paraphrase

The Letters to the Editor Exercise

Teaching Aristotle's Rhetorical Triangle

• Leslie Batty •

Abstract: Students evaluate published letters to the editor by using *ethos, pathos,* and *logos* as guideposts.

This exercise also teaches audience.

Duration: The lecture and exercise are designed to fill an entire class period, and can be adapted for either 50- or 75-minute meetings.

Materials: Actual letters to the editor (author suggests at least five different letters for a class of 20 students), enough copies so that students can work in pairs.

- For shorter class periods, example letters should be brief and straightforward and the in-class review of the worksheet perhaps limited to the second and fourth questions. For a longer class period, teachers might choose longer or more complex example letters, conduct more detailed reviews of the worksheet during the discussion section, or end the class with a more expansive discussion of how all three modes of persuasion can be used in academic writing.

Activity worksheets; see example below (designed for groupwork).

Author suggests a diagram of the rhetorical triangle to illustrate the concept to students.

Preparation: Instructors will need to have an understanding of Aristotle's concept of a "rhetorical triangle" and be able to define *logos, pathos,* and *ethos* for students.

1. The first step is to prepare an introductory lecture on the rhetorical triangle.

The best approach is to explain *logos, pathos,* and *ethos* in turn, first by defining each term, then by listing the textual elements that signal each appeal, and finally by supplying an accessible, concrete example of each mode of persuasion.

For example, one would first define an argument by *logos* as an attempt to persuade through the use of logic and reasoning. Next, one would explain that arguments by *logos* are made through the presentation of facts, case studies, statistics, experiments, analogies, etc. Finally, one would point out that a campaign commercial for an incumbent governor citing 200,000 jobs created and a 15 percent increase in educational funding during her tenure is an example of argument by logos.

2. The next step is to scour newspapers for letters to the editor.

These will serve as an additional concrete, real-world example of argument by one or more of Aristotle's three modes of persuasion.

For the purposes of this exercise, it is best to seek out letters that are a bit imbalanced, leaning heavily on one mode of persuasion while neglecting the other two, like blustery or maudlin letters that appeal to emotion while undercutting the ethos of their own writer, or dry letters built on facts and figures that lose the interest of the reader.

For a class of 20, you will need about five different example letters.

3. Prepare an in-class activity worksheet that asks students to read an example letter, analyze the mode(s) of persuasion it utilizes, and brainstorm ways to strengthen the letter's persuasive power by adding other means of rhetorical appeal.

Procedure:

Execution:

1. Deliver the lecture on the rhetorical triangle. It is perhaps helpful to leave a diagram of the triangle itself and a few bullet-point definitions of *logos*, *pathos*, and *ethos* on the blackboard during the exercise. This takes approximately 10 minutes to deliver, including time for questions, if one focuses tightly on the elements of the basic rhetorical triangle.

2. Divide students into pairs and assign two pairs to work on each example letter. (Having two sets of students working on each example ensures that you will have sufficient time to finish the discussion portion of the activity and makes it more likely that each example will receive a thorough analysis.) Distribute one worksheet per pair, but make sure each student has his or her own copy of the letter. Students will need about 15 minutes to read the letters and collaboratively complete the worksheet.

3. Review the students' analyses in a short discussion session. For each letter, start by having the letter read aloud to the rest of the class. Then, briefly review students' answers to some (perhaps questions two and four for a shorter class period) or all the worksheet prompts. Since there are two pairs of students working on each example, allow one pair to briefly explain their answer to a prompt and then have the other pair respond with any contradictory or additional ideas they might have. The most important prompt to focus on is the fourth question; be prepared to help students understand how the introduction of additional modes of persuasion could be accomplished and why such revision would strengthen the persuasive power and legitimacy of the letter. This takes on average five minutes per example letter, or 25 minutes total.

4. Be sure to close the class by tying the principles discussed in this activity to your expectations for your students' own work. This is the time to explain, in clear, concrete terms, how *logos*, *pathos*, and *ethos* can be brought to bear in research-driven, academic writing. For example, mention that *logos* is tied to finding compelling and relevant facts and putting them together logically; *pathos* can come into play when a researcher is explaining the significance of his or her topic in an introduction or when using a poignant case study; finally, an appeal by *ethos* requires responsible acknowledgement of sources and thoughtful discussion of opposing viewpoints. This is a point you may want to reiterate in the next class period—or perhaps even illustrate with specific examples of *logos, pathos,* and *ethos* in academic writing—but it is important to close this exercise by making these connections.

Rationale: Teaching the principles of the rhetorical triangle in an introductory composition class can be more challenging than one might initially think. While most students can quickly grasp the basic theoretical distinctions between appeals to *logos, pathos,* and *ethos,* they are sometimes still unable to identify these appeals when analyzing arguments and are often unsure of how to incorporate them into their own persuasive writing. While many composition courses require students to write a letter-to-the-editor, this in-class exercise instead requires students to consider how the three Aristotelian modes of persuasion are used (or neglected) in an existing letter.

Additional Author's Notes: The rhetorical triangle and Aristotelian appeals are often taught in the early days of an introductory composition course, and this exercise is useful for illustrating the modes of persuasion at any point in the semester.

However, it is sometimes useful to introduce or refresh this information as the end of the semester approaches, particularly if the class culminates in a major research paper. This is especially important in courses that are focused exclusively on academic writing and research, which often require students to write very formulaic assignments like article summaries and reviews. These genres often include rigid content requirements, and elements of *pathos* and *ethos* (while always present) are more difficult to see. In preparing for a capstone research paper, which is longer, more complex, and often less restrictive, it is helpful to push students toward a more rounded approach to persuasion.

This exercise is also useful when introducing a final research project in a class organized around traditional composition genre essays. In this configuration, students are sometimes led to compartmentalize rather than combine modes of persuasion, seeing *pathos* as confined to the narrative essay, *ethos* to the process essay, and *logos* as the only mode of persuasion in a research-based argument.

Potential Problems: The most challenging aspect of preparing for this assignment is finding good example letters. Leave yourself plenty of time to search selectively for letters that make single-appeal arguments. Because students sometimes find it difficult to focus on the rhetorical structure of an argument with which they strongly agree or disagree, some instructors might prefer to search for letters that are less overtly, or at least divisively, political. Letters from out-of-state papers about local political issues, which students are not personally familiar with or polarized by, are a good substitute for those written about national political issues or contentious topics drawn from your own campus community. The initial time investment in searching out the right letters for this activity is considerable, but they can then be filed and reused indefinitely.

– · – · – · – · – · – · – · – · – · – · – · – · – · – · – · –

WORKSHEET

1. After reading the example letter carefully, summarize in one or two sentences the thesis and main supporting point(s) of the letter. (In other words, what does the author want and how does he/she justify it?)

2. Which mode(s) of persuasion do you believe the writer has used? Point to specific elements of the letter that signal the mode of persuasion.

3. How persuasive do you find this letter to be overall? What elements of the letter leave you most convinced or accepting? What elements of the letter leave you most skeptical or resistant?

4. How might you revise this letter to make it more effective? What kind of new infor-

mation might make it more convincing? In other words, what other modes of persuasion might you bring in?

—m—

Creating Tailor-Made Handouts (Homework)

• Laura L. Beadling •

Abstract: Having students turn in homework on paper is the traditional way of testing student comprehension. To make this more interactive and less instructor-intensive, have students complete small exercises on-line and email them to the instructor or upload them to the course management software before the next class so the instructor can create a tailor-made handout to address concrete problems and issues.

Duration: Length of exercise varies. If there are only two or three examples, then the exercise may only take 15 minutes to complete. However, if the homework reveals multiple problem areas or issues, the exercise may take an entire class session.

Time needed often depends on the complexity of the skill and the number of examples the instructor chooses to include on the handout. The instructor can choose to make this a full-class exercise by including more examples and building in small-group or individual in-class work.

Preparation: This exercise works best after some class preparation in the art of paraphrasing. Students will need to be assigned text to paraphrase in the class before this exercise is given (see below)

Procedure: This is applicable to any skill that an instructor wants to have students practice in homework.

For instance, I ask students to complete small exercises on paraphrasing before they begin working on the first larger paper that requires them to appropriately paraphrase. I give students a short paragraph that they must paraphrase. Instead of having them complete this by hand, I ask them to do it in Word and email me their paraphrase no later than three hours before the next class begins.

I create separate folders in my email for each exercise I ask student to email me, so it's easier to see who has completed the homework and who has not. Course management software would also make this process easy to do and track.

Then, before class, I quickly scan through the students' paragraphs and pick several that demonstrate a range of issues and abilities that need to be addressed and paste them into a new Word document, omitting any student names or identifying details.

Then, during class, I either hand out paper copies of the sample student paragraphs or project it using the overhead projector and ask students to read and think about them.

As part of a whole-class discussion, I ask them which paragraphs they think are the most effective at paraphrasing the original paragraph and what specific aspects are particularly strong, and which paraphrases are less successful and what specifically needs to be improved.

If I have an instructor computer and overhead projector, I bold or underline the parts the students identify as problematic and make corrections based on their input.

If there's time or if the exercise has indicated that students are having difficulty with the skill, I will sometimes ask them to work on however many paraphrases we didn't get to discuss in class for homework either individually or in small groups. Other times, I will remind them that it's easier to critique someone else's writing than it is to write well oneself, and I'll ask them to work on paraphrasing another sample paragraph while keeping in mind what they learned in class.

Additional Author's Notes: By making handouts based on the students' own writing, I as the instructor can see what issues need to be addressed or further developed and give students hands-on practice at analyzing the strengths and weaknesses of their writing. In my experience, students are more engaged with the critique if they know the examples are from their peers in class. Likewise, after the first few in-class critiques, students will report that they take homework more seriously because they know there's a possibility that their writing will be showcased in class.

Variations: If your class is in a computer lab, you can start the class with an explanation of a skill and then have them practice it in class and email you their work in class. If there's time, the instructor can scan a few emails and create a handout in class while the last few students are finishing up and then have a whole class discussion of the examples.

Rationale: This is an exercise in one of the fundamental and often most problematic aspects of college writing: paraphrase. In addition, student writing is often helped by having students re-envision their own writing. This exercise asks students to edit and critique as a group, which allows for a more in-depth examination of students' writing and also bolsters the ideal of teamwork.

Potential Problems: Sharing actual student writing in class runs the risk of embarrassing students whose writing is critiqued. If you have two or more sections of the same class, you can use sample passages from a different section. It is also advisable to remind students before discussing the worksheets that these are real writing samples, which makes the practice and critique more immediate and valuable, but that everyone must also take care to be professional and engage in constructive critique while avoiding any derogatory or offensive language or jokes about the samples. You might also choose to conflate, edit, or change the samples and present them as based on student writing rather than verbatim student writing, although the same caveats about professionalism would still apply.

Exhaust All Questions
Interrogating a Topic
• Rita D. Costello *and* William Lusk Coppage •

Abstract: Students practice observation, generating questions, and writing while observing an unusual object provided by the instructor.

Materials: Find an object with which students will not have any prior experience. Something three-dimensional that can be passed through the class by hand is best.

Context of the Exercise: Frequently, beginning writers do not perform adequate critical thinking before selecting or narrowing a research topic. It is important to take time to make sure not only that the topic is interesting, but also that the topic will allow a writer to argue something new about it. This exercise is for more advanced composition students who are at the point of learning that essays should be adding to the body of scholarly research, not simply regurgitating what has already been previously written about the topic.

The goal of the Exhaust All Questions exercise is to exhaust all surface possibilities before developing the topic or research question. Just as a creative writer writes with the *editor* turned off, academic writers engage in a line of questioning in order to discover paths of research that are not immediately visible.

Process:

1. Give the object to the first student and have the student ask a question about the object. Record on the board at least the essence of the question.

2. Have the first student pass the object to the next student who then will ask a question, and so on until the object has been examined by every student once. No repetition of the same question is allowed. No matter the size of the class, the first round is likely to include relatively surface level questions.

3. Repeat the entire process a second time through the entire class; again no repetition of previously asked questions is allowed. Students may take longer to ask their question each time during the second round, but the resulting questions should be delving toward deeper meaning by this point (naturally, without prompting).

4. In most classes, the process can be stopped after the second round, but if the questions are still surface level, repeat the process until they get to substance.

5. When stopping the process, ask for any final questions that have come to mind out of turn.

6. When moving into lecture/discussion, point out the ways in which the questions have become more specific and in-depth through the process.

7. With the help of the class, adapt a few of the last round questions into potential research questions that could lead to viable avenues of research.

8. Point out that the latter, viable, avenues of inquiry would not have been reached without exhausting the earlier more surface levels of inquiry.

Although this method could be used with other situations, it is most valuable near the start of a research-methods based composition class. Here is another version that allows students to practice on their own:

1. Find an object that you have no prior knowledge about. It might be something in a store, a museum, or just an image of the object online.

2. Write down 20 questions about the object. Any question is acceptable, except questions that have been previously used. Do not take too long with this initial step; just write down the first 20 questions you can think of in relation to the object.

3. Take out a new sheet of paper. This time write down an additional 15 questions about the object. Do not reuse any lines of questioning previously used on the first list. The questions may be a little more difficult to come up with because they take more critical thought.

4. Take out a third sheet of paper and write another 15 questions; none of the lines of questioning from the first two lists may be reused. Again, this may take a little more time and thinking, and the questions are probably growing longer and more detailed.

5. Now look at the third set of questions written and cross out any questions that do not merit a line of research.

6. Organize questions that contain similar patterns and themes into at least four different categories. The same question may cross over and be used in multiple categories.

7. Focus on only one of the four categories you constructed. These questions serve as a stepping-stone for research. By answering the questions in this category, the writer should have an original idea that can be defended through future research on the topic.

If a research methods course includes a prospectus or research plan for the semester, this exercise would fit with that; however, it is also useful at the beginning of the first paper in a research-based composition course.

Rationale: Students should learn to move past the surface level when developing research questions and viable avenues of inquiry. Depending on how it is presented, it is also useful for pointing out how questions allow us to begin researching without a solid stance in mind and how questions help to develop our critical thinking.

Potential Problems: Students may need prodding after the first round of questions; the more intriguing the object and energetic the class, the more likely things are to run smoothly.

—⅏—

Show, Don't Tell
A Description Exercise
• Rita D. Costello •

Abstract: Half the class writes descriptions of an unfamiliar object (provided by the instructor) while the other half of the class waits outside in the hallway. The students in the hallway then return to the classroom and draw the object based on their classmates' descriptions.

Duration: I do both parts of the exercise together in a single class and compress or expand it to fit 50 to 75 minutes; in a three hour course, I would take about 60 minutes.

Materials: Part 1 requires an object (or the like) which students can describe and are not likely to find familiar. Part 2 requires a collection of images that do not already incorporate a description or a purpose in words.

Preparation: This exercise can accompany almost any paper assignment and works at all composition levels; I always use it with early levels, but not necessarily with research levels. I tend to use this early in the semester, around the second or third week of class.

Procedure:

Part 1: The basis for Part 1 is something physical that most students have not seen before. In fact, the origin of this exercise—more than a decade ago—may have been based on my love for juggling sticks (also known as rhythm sticks). However, anything physical should do the trick—a souvenir from another culture, an obsolete or rare kitchen implement, an obscure musical instrument, and so on. I suspect this part of the exercise might also work with unfamiliar music or food, but I have not tried it that way. Keep the object out of view when arriving for class.

Step 1: Divide the class in half by any means desired and send half of the students into the hall (or some other place they cannot observe).

Step 2: Demonstrate or share the object in question (for example, I juggle sticks for the class and then pass them around).

Step 3: Have the people in the classroom write a description of what they have observed. (A few sentences should suffice.) In some less interactive groups, I clarify this as explaining in words what you see for someone who is blind. Most groups, however, do not require this or any additional clarification.

Step 4: Collect the descriptions, put the object away, and invite the rest of the students to return to the room.

Step 5: Either read the descriptions aloud to the whole class or pass them out among the students who have just returned. Ask the students who have just returned to draw what they see based on the description.

Step 6: The penultimate step is to share the drawings and descriptions together and discuss what worked or did not work in the original descriptions. I typically reserve Steps 6 and 7 until after having completed Part 2 (the second exercise).

Step 7: Homework for the next class is to explain what they saw/did in class to at least three people and report back next class on how it went. (Were they able to make the people understand using words alone? Did it require re-telling the information in different words? And so on.)

Part 2: This exercise echoes the first one so closely that I think of them as a single exercise and fuse the two into a single class period. For this exercise, the instructor should bring several visual images (postcards, fashion magazine photos, sports action photos, landscapes, fine art, and so on). It is important that the images do not contain words that explain the image or its purpose. In other words, an advertisement is fine as long as the ad does not include words explaining the product or the way the image is supposed to promote the product. I tend to choose images from several different types of sources but lean toward images that tell some sort of story.

Step 1: Divide the class in half again. It is important that the two halves of the class do not communicate or see what the other half is doing. Some environments may allow this without sending students into the hall, but I typically send half of the students into the hall to work. Place students in groups of two or three students (within each half-class). For example, in a group of 20 students, I might create 10 groups and send five of those groups into the hall.

Step 2: Provide each group with one of the images.

Step 3: As a group, students should discuss the best words to describe the image and write it in a single version for the full group.

Step 4: Collect all of the group descriptions and provide the inside descriptions to the outside groups and vice versa.

Step 5: As a group, students should discuss and agree on what is happening in the written description they received and then draw what they see.

Step 6: Bring all the groups together again in the classroom. Have the first group come to the front of the class with the drawing and the description they had been given.

Step 7: As the description is being read and the drawing displayed, whoever has the original image being described should hold it up to display or pass it through the class.

Step 8: Repeat Steps 6 and 7 with the rest of the groups.

Step 9: Discuss the variations and any suggestions for improving the descriptions.

Additional Notes: This exercise has never hit any unexpected snags for me, and I have used it and adapted it for years. Every once in a while a student/group writes a description that does not provide enough (or any) information, but even those situations do not deter from the exercise or its purpose. In fact, since students tend to react so well to the exercise(s), this can actually make it more interesting as well as provide a self-correcting environment. As mentioned earlier, I have shared this exercise with friends and colleagues throughout the years and many of them have used only the second part of the exercise; separating it out as an independent exercise seems to work just fine.

Rationale: Students primarily learn description skills; this exercise also offers a venue for discussing audience, examples, and precision of language/word choice. A beneficial side-effect is that the importance of language and word choice is elevated while students still feel like they are doing something fun.

Freshman students really benefit from the concept of "show don't tell" in terms of description and example writing; however, the concept itself is not always an easy one for first-year composition students. This exercise is one I've used over and over, sometimes with great variation, but always with great success. I usually do two separate exercises in a row that I think of as a single class/single exercise. When I've shared this exercise with others, very often they use only the second part/exercise, and the results have been successful. Both of these exercises are fun and usually get the students actively excited about what they are writing. Also, both of these exercises are adaptable to surroundings and to other modes that make heavy use of description such as narrative.

—ᴍ—

Cultural Literacy vs. Personal Literacy
Using Lists as Evaluation
• J.D. Isip •

Abstract: In the first class, directed by the instructor, students list the factors that influence their cultural literacy; in the second class, students reevaluate their and their classmates' lists which lead to a cultural literacy essay.

This essay also teaches idea generation.

Duration: One to two 50-minute class periods (an essay can be assigned based upon the exercise)

Preparation: Instructors might consider using one of the numerous videos available on YouTube of Emory University professor Mark Bauerlein talking about his book *The Dumbest Generation*. (Just so they know that there is an idea that "if you only know X, you will be a better person." I find that most students, at least in part, agree with this idea.)

Class Requirements: If you will be showing the Mark Bauerlein video (it's on YouTube, an interview he did with *ReasonTV*), you'll need computer/projector capability. Otherwise, you only need a white board or chalk board.

Instructors may also consider acquainting students with E.D. Hirsch's ideas in his book *Cultural Literacy: What Every American Needs to Know* (New York: Vintage, 1988).

Suggested Reading: This is an entire unit for any of my Freshman Composition classes and I have used the same two readings for a few years: Plato's "The Allegory of the Cave" (which is free online or is in just about any reader);

David Foster Wallace's "This Is Water" Speech to Kenyon. The *Wall Street Journal* has this article up online for free or you can find audio on Audible.com

Author's Note: The goal of this exercise is to give students a solid understanding of the concepts surrounding discussions of literacy. Rather than asking for a "literacy narrative" (e.g., "when I was in sixth grade my teacher assigned a book I hated and I've hated reading since" and its ilk), I show students how a type of literacy is developed—in this case, "cultural literacy."

This exercise is *not* aimed at deconstructing the idea of cultural literacy, but rather to problematize the concept and, more importantly, demonstrate how easily our own literacies are affected by forces around us.

Procedure:

First Class Period

Draw a simple pie chart on the board. This represents our understanding of the world around us. Ask the class, by show of hands, how much of this pie is influenced by

Our close circle of friends	Society
Our family	Ourselves

Start to write random dates, names, and phrases on the board—these are things the "culturally literate" might know like: September 11, JFK, Mickey Mouse, "Just Do It," blogging, Hitler, etc.

Ask each student to make a list of "25 Things You Need to Know." This list is something they might pass on to their child, so personal stuff should be included, too, like "You need to know grandma." Students will complain that 25 is not enough. They're right. This will probably take the rest of the first class. Make sure you give them time (even if they have to work on it as homework) to create a list they are absolutely proud of.

Second Class Period

Each student must look at 12 other students' lists and replace one of their items with an item from the other student's list. They must list the name of the student whose list they took the new item from next to that item (keeps them honest). This becomes absolutely maddening to the students. They cannot believe how many things they must lose from their list.

There is one caveat to this: if a student has an item that is the same as another student, the student can keep the original item and just write the other student's name next to it.

Once everyone has their 12 names/new items, have them write a reflection on this exercise.

Direct them back to the pie chart you began with (you might want to re-draw it on the board).

These questions are helpful:

- What made you decide on the items in your original list? What might this tell you about your values?
- What did you think about having to take items from other classmates' lists? What do you think the purpose of this was?
- Do you think you "pick up" ideas from others in your everyday life? Do we have infinite capacity for ideas or do some ideas push others aside?
- What do you think this has to do with your literacy?

My students love this exercise. I admit, it is a sort of "get to know you" exercise where my students get to interact and talk with one another about ideas that *seemingly* have nothing to do with writing. It's a good exercise for the middle of the semester when energy is waning because it is very active and it sort of blows their minds.

Literacy Essay: How We Construct Meaning

The essay that comes out of this exercise is a definition essay if we have to give it a name, but it can also be a research or narrative depending on what you want to emphasize. I ask my students to consider the idea that literacy is *how we read and interpret a text*, but where or by whom did we learn how to "read" (e.g., understand)? Where and by whom did we learn how to "interpret" (e.g., construct meaning)?

These are big concepts, so I ask them to write specifically about their experience in the exercise.

What did the exercise reveal to them about influences? About values? About the amount of control we have over our literacies?

To add a bit of research, simply have them look up "cultural literacy" online and see what they get. Ask them what they agree with and what they disagree with after the exercise.

Potential Problems: The in-class exercise has been rather smooth for me. I would only suggest that you take at least two class periods to really let this exercise "sink in" with students. The first portion can just feel like a game, but splitting the lesson between two days allows students a chance to think about what is happening. Three days is even better.

The readings are difficult. I have absolutely no problem with students going to something like Wikipedia for a synopsis of "The Allegory of the Cave." I've created my own handout for it. "This is Water" is just a tad long, so I offer my students the choice to simply purchase the speech online and listen to it.

—◦◦◦—

Direct, Indirect and Impressionistic

Crafting Good Essay Openers

• Debra Rudder Lohe •

Abstract: This exercise leads students through several types of introductions: direct, indirect, and impressionistic.
This exercise also teaches idea generation.
Duration: 30 to 40 minutes in class, the meeting prior to the first essay's due date. (This could take a whole class period, though; students really loved it and made some great discoveries, and they were wishing we'd had more time.)

Author's Note: This exercise was connected to the first essay of the semester. In the class period before the first draft was due, students were asked to bring their notes and any plans they already had for the essay. During class time, we examined how a few other writers did their openings, then we spent about 30 to 40 minutes in class doing this exercise.

Suggested Readings: As mentioned above and in the essay assignment, students had already read the following essays, so we were able to examine their particular openings: Anne Lamott, "Polaroids," *Bird by Bird: Some Instructions on Writing and Life* (Random House, 1995); Maxine Hong Kingston, "Tongue Tied" *The Woman Warrior: Memories of a Girlhood Among Ghosts* (Vintage, 1975); Nancy Mairs, "On Being a Cripple" *Real Essays with Readings*, 4th ed. (Macmillan, 2012); David Sedaris, "Old Faithful," *The New Yorker* online (free text; use title as keywords); Sarah Vowell, "Shooting Dad," *Take the Cannoli: Stories from the New World* (Simon and Schuster, 2001). However, this exercise could work with all sorts of readings.

Procedure: The exercise itself is done using a worksheet (attached). I provide a very short summary of some of the essays/openers we've examined together, then ask students to do a kind of focused free-write, using three different prompts:

- a "Direct Opener,"
- an "Indirect Opener,"
- and an "Impressionistic Opener."

After they've written for about seven to 10 minutes for each type, we discuss, as a group, what discoveries they have made. Much of the class time, then, involves quiet, reflective space for writing; I sit quietly, insisting that they write, write, write.

Then, the last 10 minutes or so is a full-class discussion.

The exercise involves working with the first essay of the semester, which asks students either to use a simile or metaphor to describe their writing process or to write an essay that uses a simile or metaphor to convey something about the sound of their own voices (whether spoken or written). (Specific assignment sheet attached.)

Rationale: The purpose of this exercise is to get student writers thinking in new ways about how to open their essays. In particular, I was interested in re-directing the tendency to start with more automatic kinds of introductions, to get them experimenting a bit with other ways to draw in readers. The course was a junior-senior level composition course called

Exposition; in it, students were to become more intentional about the choices they made as writers, and to think in new ways about how to sharpen their writerly "eye" and to bring new consciousness to all the writing they did, including their disciplinary work. One important element of the course was an insistence that all writing has "voice," even if that voice is cultivated to seem voice-less.

The exercise should help students to see try multiple ways of saying the same things, to experience the differences in different kinds of essay openings, and to think more creatively about how they engage readers from the outset. It should also help them to narrow down and focus on what really matters in the essay they're working on.

Potential Problems: None, really. Students seemed to benefit from the exercise, and at the end of the semester, they were still talking about it. Several admitted they'd done the same exercise, on their own, for different papers (not just the ones written for my class).

— ·· — · — ·· — · — ·· — · — ·· — · — ·· — · — ·· — · — ·· — · — ·· — · —

WORKSHEET

Openers: A good opening is essential to setting the tone of your essay, establishing the persona you'll use, and setting your readers' expectations. The essays we've looked at already have fairly enticing openings—Lamott declares outright that writing is like watching polaroids develop; Kingston begins by setting out the tension between silence and speech that will permeate her essay; Sedaris begins with the troll-like boil. The writing prompts below ask you to experiment with possible openers for Essay 1. Try your hand at more than one kind of starting point. See what comes of the experiment.

Direct Opener: try writing the beginning of your essay using a very direct opening line, like "My voice is ____" or "Writing, for me, is _____." Several of the essayists we've looked at have these straightforward openings. They use direct statements to frame the essay, to declare something about themselves, or to draw us in.

Indirect Opener: now, try writing an opener that leads us to your declaration in an indirect way. Maybe begin with an anecdote, or a description, maybe a series of fragments that attempts to create a particular kind of impression. If you're writing about voice, try starting with a quote, maybe something someone has said to you.

Impressionistic Opener: try an opening series of impressions, maybe using free association to list out the words that come to mind when you think about your writing process or your voice. Once you have a list of words / images you might use, think about the order in which they might come—what makes sense, given the overall point you want to make in your essay?

— ·· — · — ·· — · — ·· — · — ·· — · — ·· — · — ·· — · — ·· — · — ·· — · —

ASSIGNMENT SHEET

Length: four pages
Texts:
   Lamott, "Polaroids"
   Kingston, "Tongue Tied"
   Mairs, "On Being a Cripple"
   Sedaris, "Old Faithful"
   Vowell, "Shooting Dad" (as useful)

Assignment: In this first essay, you will build on preliminary work we've already done to further explore either your writing process or your voice. Listening more closely to your own voice—both in speech and in writing—can help you to better understand your relationship to writing and to more consciously craft the writing you do. Understanding your writing process—both in theory and in specific situations—can help you to better determine what works for you and what doesn't.

For this assignment, select one of the two prompts below and write a short essay that helps us to experience either your writing process or your voice. Include narration/description, and consider the persona you want to communicate. Above all, produce an essay that accomplishes the goals spelled out below and that does so in a voice/style that feels authentic for you.

Option 1. Anne Lamott describes writing as a process of watching polaroid photographs develop, and she uses several linked anecdotes to help make her point. In this essay, you should explore your own writing process—how you first begin working out an idea, how that idea makes its way into print, how you deal with frustrations along the way. Using a metaphor or simile, develop an essay in which you explain your writing process and what it says about you. Draw on a particular writing occasion, using at least one anecdote to help us experience the process you're describing.

Option 2. Maxine Hong Kingston describes the sounds of Chinese (women's) voices in American classrooms. Her own voice, she writes, was more than dissatisfying to her; it was the product of a pained and painful effort to produce sound in a terrifying setting. The terror she experienced, she makes clear, was linked not only to her personal shyness, but also to her cultural situation. In this essay, you should explore the sound of your own voice—dealing with either / both your spoken voice and/or your written voice. Using a metaphor or simile, develop an essay in which you describe your voice and how it came to be the way it is. Draw on a particular speaking situation, using at least one anecdote to help us experience what you're describing.

Assessment Criteria: Essay 1 should cohere around a main idea, employ an extended simile/metaphor, include anecdote/narration, have paragraphs with transitions between ideas, draw on evidence from personal experience (and the readings), and demonstrate evidence of revision.

—∞—

Summary the Second
Time Around
Forging the Reading-Writing Connection
• Joseph McCarty •

Abstract: Using reading strategies as a spring-board, students highlight and annotate assigned readings; students are then graded on how well they use their own highlights and annotations to create paraphrase.

Duration: Two days (first day is not an entire class period), and homework on the second day

Preparation: Students will need to bring paraphrases of the reading below to class.

Suggested Reading: "Chapter Three: Listening to a Text" and "Chapter Seven: Making Knowledge: Incorporating Reading into Writing," both from *Reading Rhetorically*, 2d ed. (John C. Bean, et al.).

Procedure: This assignment for the composition classroom is designed to help students understand the connection between reading academic material and integrating that material into their own writing.

Following classroom discussion and take-home reading geared toward understanding and making use of reading strategies, students implement those reading strategies in class on a second assigned reading.

The instructor then asks students, as homework, to summarize the second assignment.

Students are informed they will be graded primarily on how well their annotations and other markings to the second reading match up with their summaries.

I have found this method to be incredibly useful in promoting the use of academic reading strategies.

Rationale: This assignment for the composition classroom is designed to help students understand the connection between reading academic material and integrating that material into their own writing.

Ultimately, this technique is designed to improve a student's ability to integrate sources into his or her own research essays. Having students write a summary where the main requirement is a demonstrated connection with their own notes on the reading helps fit together important concepts about reading and writing.

Potential Problems: Please remember to ask students to turn in their annotated photocopies of the summarized reading. Otherwise, we would find drawing comparisons difficult.

Occasionally, students may have fun with this assignment's condition that accurate reading and sentence-level writing play only supportive roles in grade calculation. During my more recent implementations, I have admonished students about drastic inconsistencies between the reading and submitted summaries. (One student, as an annotation to a section about asking questions of the text, made a note that the author was clearly afraid of horses.) Similar problems can arise when students hear their spelling will not severely affect their grades. A simple blanket statement explaining any summaries not composed in earnest will not be accepted will usually minimize tomfoolery.

Additional Author's Notes: I grade these summaries with a heavy emphasis on the connections: 20 percent on accurate annotations, 20 percent on writing (structure, local fluidity), and the remaining 60 percent on how well the student's annotations and highlighting from the reading appear in his or her summary. This means a student could conceivably misinterpret the reading, write poorly, and still earn a passing grade on the assignment. By lowering affective filters related to reading complex material and composing academic writing, we can encourage students to hone in on the connections between what they read and what they write.

The grading structure for this summary is the key element in this technique. But students must be made aware of it. I typically explain to the class that they can misread the material, can misspell words and punctuate awfully, and can still do just fine on this assignment. Overlooking sentence structure on one assignment is a small concession to make if, by doing so, we can teach students to write in ways that continue academic conversations.

—∿—

Interactive Lecture/Practice
Sentence Cohesion and Paragraph Development
• Maria L. Soriano •

Abstract: Instructor assembles random student sentences into a single paragraph and projects it for the whole class to critique; students then select a topic sentence from the assembled paragraph and rewrite by expanding on its ideas.

Duration: 50 minutes

Author's Note: The lesson and its practice component are extremely flexible, depending on class meeting time. Ideally, however, the entire lesson should be incorporated into one class session to allow students to learn, discuss, and practice right away (though the practice could begin in class and end as homework, if necessary).

Materials: Overhead projection

Projection speeds up the composing process, allows the teacher to hide the initial text, and then allows everyone to view the final text.

Procedure:

1. Begin by asking students to open their notebooks to a blank sheet (you'll collect this and their practice work later). Pose a simple question that evokes a one-sentence response—something that every student would have an answer for quickly.

My prompt, for example, is as follows: "Imagine that you have been asked to share with students from your high school one positive aspect of this university. Write that answer in one sentence."

2. While they write, open a blank Microsoft Word document on the front computer that you control and turn on the overhead projector, but blank (or "mute") the screen so that the students cannot see the document or what you type.

3. Ask for five or six volunteers to share the sentences they wrote with the rest of the class. Type their sentences in succession, formulating them into one paragraph. Do not change or edit anything, as this is supposed to be detached and messy. After typing all of the sentences, turn on the projector screen and read the resulting paragraph to students.

Though the resulting paragraph is an extremely exaggerated example, I likened the detachment and wide jumps in subject between each sentences to many of the paragraphs I read in their papers. As many teachers can attest, First-Year Writing students have many ideas and want to write down everything they can—which ends up proving detrimental to point development.

We then critique and discuss the example paragraph, and students identify the weaknesses:

the sentences each express a completely different idea, the subjects jump around too much, and the reader is left questioning both the point and the central focus of the paragraph.

Now that we have discussed the problems as a class, we can move on to the solutions. Here is where I introduce students to the pivotal "so what?" question—a poignant writing lesson I learned from my American Literature professor as a junior English major, and one that transformed my writing.

4. As a class, select one of the sentences that a student offered in the first paragraph to make as the "topic sentence." On the Word document, hit "Enter" until the old paragraph is out of sight, and then type the selected sentence into the document. After doing so, stop and ask students, "so what?"

Challenge them to think about why that sentence is important, what it means, and its significance to the prompt at hand. Encourage them to answer the question, and in doing so, turn that "answer" into the next sentence into the paragraph—that sentence *should* be a connection and answer to the previous sentence.

Repeat the verbal prompt after every sentence until a new paragraph is developed. This step will take the most time in the lesson, since students are being asked to compose aloud and on the spot.

5. Upon completion, re-read aloud the original paragraph, and then read the new paragraph. As a class, explore the reasons why the new paragraph is stronger and more reader-friendly.

I explicitly asked students to explain in detail *how* and *why* each sentence is connected to the previous one, incorporating practical concision strategies like repeating key words at the beginning of a new sentence or introducing explanations or definitions.

6. To complete the lesson and challenge students to apply the discussion, have each student implement this thinking and writing process onto their notebook paper, beginning with the sentence they wrote at the beginning of class and using the "so what?" question to develop it fully.

This will take time, since they have to stop and think after each sentence, so the practice may be extended into homework if necessary.

Rationale: I collected the work of the students who finished the Interactive Lecture in class and read them shortly after, and I could already notice a difference. Many of the students were using the word repetition and explanatory phrase techniques we had talked about, and I could see evidence of a shift in their thinking and writing strategies based on the lesson. Furthermore, in end-of-semester reflections and portfolios, many of my students noted the significance and usefulness of this particular lesson in influencing their writing. Since I incorporated it before the third essay of the semester was due, students then had two major assignments left in the semester where they could practice thinking and writing in this manner, and could then evaluate their concision and development in the first two essays while revising at the end of the semester. During the revision period, many students diagnosed their own weaknesses in these areas and decided to revise paragraphs for their final portfolios, sometimes eliminating large chunks of text in favor of rewriting with more focus and forward development. I was pleased to see how well the lesson worked, and that so many of them noticed a difference in their writing and worked to apply it right away.

Potential Problems: The only limitations arise during the verbal composition step, when First-Year Writing students may still be too timid to share aloud. Timing, however, makes a difference—halfway through the semester, students have settled into the class community and know each other well. As with any group, of course, there will always be leaders and learners; some students will be eager to share sentence ideas, and others may simply want to learn from watching and listening. Composition takes time, and we want to honor and encourage that thoughtfulness. This is one reason why I suggest choosing an "easy" or "general" topic where everyone would have an opinion to contribute. The prompt could easily adapt to a course theme, reading, or assignment, if necessary. Encouraging students to compose and revise aloud in the classroom setting also prompts creativity and fosters an environment of learning through collaboration—even if that means that one student suggests a sentence topic and another picks up that idea and contributes to its articulation.

Additional Author's Notes: Above all, I found this interactive process to be effective in demonstrating to students an issue that I often identified and commented on repeatedly in many individual essays. Beginning with an exaggerated example allows teachers to prompt students to locate and discuss writing weaknesses and the negative impact that sentences lacking cohesion and development have on readers. By challenging students to reflect on and prove the significance of each idea they write, they will train their minds to fully develop their ideas and explanations, resulting in cohesive paragraphs that are well-composed.

Throughout my semesters of teaching First-Year Writing, I consistently struggled to find a meaningful, poignant way to show students how to connect sentences and ideas within their paragraphs as a way to push and fully develop their thoughts. After reading and individually commenting on this issue in essay after essay, and assigning textbook readings and writing lectures on the topic for half the semester with lackluster results, I finally devised an interactive plan that would clearly illustrate to students how the disconnect between sentences and ideas that are simply composed and divided into paragraphs does not aid the audience's reading and comprehension of the student's writing.

—∞—

Paraphrase to Avoid Plagiarism
Diagnostic and Assessment
• Rick Williams •

Abstract: Students paraphrase a section of a reading they have already completed and then assess paraphrases written by fictitious students of the same passage. The instructor leads a discussion of student responses about the quality of each paraphrase. Finally, the students write an assessment of their own attempts.

Resources/Methods: Atwan, Robert, ed. *America Now*, 10th ed. Boston: Bedford/St. Martin's, 2013.

Lunsford, Andrea A. *Easy Writer*, 4th ed. Boston: Bedford/St. Martin's, 2010.

Procedure: The students had been assigned a critical reading of an article in the Atwan text about modern marriage by Aja Gabel (71–76) and subsequently discussed it in the previous class session. Prior to the present session, the students were assigned reading in the Lunsford handbook which includes working with sources, paraphrasing, quoting, summarizing, and avoiding plagiarism (192–202).

At the start of the session, students are told, "Paraphrase with documentation paragraphs 24 and 25 on pages 74–75 of the Gabel article. You may use your handbook to assist you, especially pages 193 and 194. This is a diagnostic piece of writing; it is not a test. I want to assess what you know about working with sources."

The students are given 10 to 15 minutes to complete this stage of the task. As each student finishes, I collect the paraphrase and give a copy of the handout containing samples of five incorrect and one correct paraphrase of the same passage, written by the instructor. (See attached worksheet.) When all students are engaged in this portion of the task, I instruct them that this is not a multiple choice assessment; there could be more than one item correct or no items correct. They are to assess each one on its own merits.

When all students finish the second stage of the task, we discuss the effectiveness of each of the choices. I then ask the students to assess the paraphrase, which they had done at the start of the session. I tell them that I will assess them, and then return them at the next class session.

Results: Most students are very accurate in their own assessment, pointing out a lack of understanding, or a failure to document, and even admitting to unintentional plagiarism. Most students also gain another insight into the precision of college writing.

Rationale: Students arrive in college-level composition classes with a range of skills regarding ability to work with sources correctly. This series of tasks allows me to diagnose each student's ability to paraphrase and document a passage of a college-level text. The tasks also engage the student's attention in such a way that most students assess their own paraphrase accurately.

WORKSHEET

On one sheet of paper, write a paraphrase of paragraphs 24–25 of Aja Gabel's article on pages 74–75 of the Atwan text. Use easyWriter pages 192–202 to assist you. Include documentation.

Then, imagine that six other students performed the same task that you did earlier in class. Using the original quote from Gabel pages 74–75 of Atwan and your handbook pages 192–202, assess how well each of these students paraphrased the passage. In your assessment, determine that the attempt contains no type or amount of plagiarism; conveys only the opinions/ideas of the source (not the student writer); displays that the student writer understood the source; uses Standard English with correct documentation; and includes all the ideas of the original.

DOUG: I agree with both of them. My parents have been married for over 30 years, and they seem happy with the marriage and with each other. And they were both twins.

SHELBY: According to Emery, who is a professor of psychology at Virginia, early research suggests that marriage has evidence of happiness in marriage as both a cause and an effect (74–75).

HOPE: In a happy marriage, you are less depressed, less anxious, less likely to have legal problems, less likely to drink or use drugs, and more likely to live longer.

JEFFREY: Emery is using twins to do research about happiness in marriage, and there are some early results (Gabel 74–75).

MALIKA: Emery's study of happiness in marriage uses twins as an experimental control. The findings are early ones, but there seems to be a relationship between successful marriages and happy people. Depression, anxiety, addictions, and criminal activity seem to decrease in a happy marriage, and longevity seems to increase. This psychologist suggests a cause/effect relationship between happiness and marriage (Gabel 74–75).

PEYTON: Emery is in the middle of a study that has the following focus: Does marriage make couples content or do contented couples marry more than discontented couples? He is studying the marriages of siblings who are twins to control for flexible data based on genes. He is finding, initially, that marriage does make people content and content people more often marry. A happy marriage has many mental positives; a married person might be less down, less tense, less in jail, less drunk or high, and live longer (Atwan 74–75).

You have just completed a paraphrase of a passage from our text. Now, imagine that six other students performed the same task. Using the original quote from Gabel, pages 74–75, of Atwan and your handbook pages 192–202, assess how well each of these students paraphrased the passage. In your assessment, determine that the attempt contains no type or amount of plagiarism; conveys only the opinions/ideas of the source (not the student writer); displays that the student writer understood the source; uses Standard English with correct documentation; and includes all the ideas of the original.

DOUG: I agree with both of them. My parents have been married for over 30 years, and they seem happy with the marriage and with each other. And they were both twins.

SHELBY: According to Emery, who is a professor of psychology at Virginia, initial results suggest that marriage has evidence of happiness in marriage as both a cause and an effect (74–75).

HOPE: In a happy marriage, you are less depressed, less anxious, less likely to have legal problems, less likely to drink or use drugs, and more likely to live longer.

JEFFREY: Emery is using twins to do research about happiness in marriage, and there are some early results (Gabel 74–75).

MALIKA: Emery's study of happiness in marriage uses twins as an experimental control. The findings are early ones, but there seems to be a relationship between successful marriages and happy people. Depression, anxiety, addictions, and criminal activity seem to decrease in a happy marriage, and longevity seems to increase. This psychologist suggests a cause/effect relationship between happiness and marriage (Gabel 74–75).

PEYTON: Emery is in the middle of a study that has the following focus: Does marriage make couples content or do contented couples marry more that discontented couples? He is studying the marriages of siblings who are twins to control for flexible data based on genes. He is finding, initially, that marriage does make people content and content people more often marry. A happy marriage has many mental positives; a married person might be less down, less tense, less in jail, less drunk or high, and live longer (Atwan 74–75).

Finally, assess your own attempt at paraphrasing in light of what you have learned.

Composing Comics
Writing Description and Dialogue
• Dennis A. Yommer, Jr. •

Abstract: During group work, students compose a written description of a page of comic panels, focusing particularly on environment, character, and expression. Next, students work to construct a dialogue that pairs with the previous descriptions.

This assignment teaches techniques of creative writing.

Duration: 50 to 70 minutes, depending on class size and length of in-class discussion

Preparation: Prior to giving this lesson, instructors will need to find and prepare (or design) a single page digital version of a graphic novel or comic book. The selection should include multiple characters, a vivid environment, and three or more speech/thought bubbles.

Once a page is chosen, it must be edited (in "Paint," or another program) to remove all text. Save a copy of each file, one with and one without text.

Materials: Students will need a black and white full page copy of the non-text version of the selected comic, a scrap sheet of paper, and a pen or pencil for writing.

The instructor should also print a full page color copy of the original (full text) version of the comic/graphic novel.

Procedure: To begin the lesson, give students a few basic sentences to work with. For example, "There is a cat over there" and "That was very good." Work with students to modify each sentence so that it is a more concrete sentence (add adjectives, replace pronouns, etc.). Discuss why these seemingly simple options are often overlooked, how they can be incorporated into a larger work, and how they enhance a narrative/fictional story.

Once discussion settles, have students organize into groups of three (there may be a group of four, or two, depending on your class size). Distribute the text-free black-and-white print of the selected comic/graphic novel to each group. Instruct groups to work together and compose a very primitive, basic overview of what they see. Limit groups to no more than three or four sentences.

When groups complete the basic sentence summary, ask a group to read their work aloud. Discuss how this resembles the sentences first written at the start of class. Illustrate the problem of bland writing by comparing the basic summary to the entire detailed scene before them.

Have groups revisit the scene, asking them to more descriptively illustrate everything they see. Instruct them to give color to the images, depth/emotion to the characters and their interactions with one another, meaning/background to the flat setting, and progression to the brief storyboard. Remind students not to use any form of dialogue as of yet. Allow students up to three paragraphs for this portion of the assignment.

Direct a basic discussion of how this section better represents the comic by "painting a picture" for the reader. Touching on the idea of how a single visual page can evolve into an entire textual chapter can also factor into this discussion.

Transition by reminding students that descriptive writing does not always mean lengthy writing. Use dialogue as an example; as in this occasion, often less is more. As a final task, have groups fill in the blank bubbles on their comic/graphic novel worksheet, and then incorporate these selections into their text description of the scene. Add that in a work such as this, these minuscule text (dialogue) elements can ultimately define the characters, plot, setting, etc.

To conclude, have groups read their dialogues aloud, explain how they decided what each character would say, and discuss why these selections enhance the overall storyboard in both all text, and all image, form. During this discussion, pass around the original full text color print of chosen comic/graphic novel for students to view and compare to their own work. After the groups conclude, sum up the lesson by reminding students how small elements such as description and dialogue can dynamically improve a narrative or fictional work.

Rationale: By composing a number of descriptive sentences, and comparing those sentences to basic level writing in context, this exercise is designed to enable students to construct more descriptive sentences that can be incorporated into their work throughout the semester. In addition, it introduces students to the use of dialogue in narrative and fictional pieces of writing.

Author's Notes: One of the most common issues among early college writers is incorporating vivid descriptions in their work. In addition to this, most have little to no experience in using dialogue within a story. For teachers who wish to incorporate a narrative or fiction assignment into their course, this lesson helps bridge the gap between description and dialogue.

This exercise is designed (in most instances) to be given early in the semester, as many other writing skills build off of these basic concepts. In some cases, a more expansive lesson on dialogue can be given as a follow up to this session. A creative writing essay assignment (narrative, fiction, etc.) generally follows this lesson within a reasonable amount of time, enabling students to put these skills to use in a constructive work of their own. For a sample essay assignment, see "A Picture Is Worth 1,000 Words: A Descriptive Essay" on page 213.

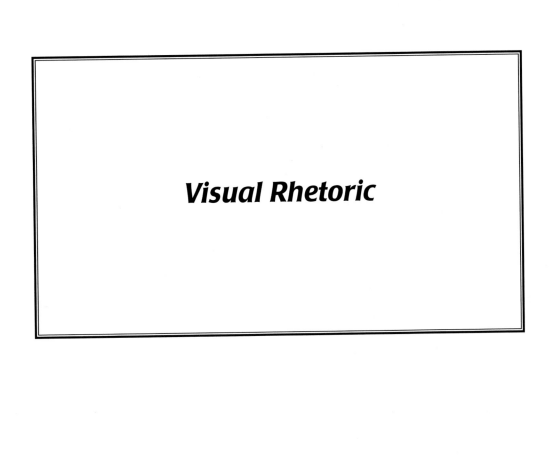

Visual Rhetoric

A Picture Is Worth
a Thousand Words

Arguing from Close Observation
of a Photograph

• Catherine Gubernatis Dannen •

Abstract: Students construct arguments based upon close observation of photographs; students then pair up and draw pictures based on the arguments their classmates have written.

Duration: 50 minutes

Materials: Overhead projection

In addition, this exercise requires a variety of printed images, enough so that each student should get her or his own individual picture to write about during class—the author suggests black and white photographs. I also make sure I have found a very diverse set of pictures to work with in class.

Preparation: I have used a variety of photographs for this assignment, ranging from landscapes and cityscapes, to close-ups of nature, to crowd shots, to sports action photos. Some of these photographs have come from the Internet, some I have shot myself. I rarely use portraits of individuals because they are very intimating to draw and to describe. I also always use black-and-white photos because they are easier to print out en masse and easier for students to draw with pens and pencils.

Before this exercise, I usually assign a short reading for homework that provides students with the vocabulary needed for discussing visual images in detail, such as point of view, arrangement, pattern, color, foreground/background, etc.

Suggested Reading: Most recently I have used a short selection from Toby Fulwiler and Alan Hayakawa's *Pocket Reference for Writers* (Longman, 2007) titled "Reading Images Critically," which contains much of the above terminology.

Procedure: In order both to help students construct arguments about visual texts and to encourage them to make their writing more detailed, I have created an hour-long exercise based on the idea that "a picture is worth a thousand words." This old adage argues that visual images can convey complex ideas, and using it as the foundation for this exercise allows me to demonstrate that visual texts, just like written ones, make claims that need details to support them.

1. Show the class a photograph.

2. Ask the class to construct an argument about the photograph, asking "What is this photograph about?"

3. Discuss student answers and emphasize the importance of detail in supporting arguments about images.

4. Distribute the printed images to students. Students are instructed not to show their pictures to others.

5. Students are given 15 minutes to write a paragraph that (a) constructs an argument about their image (perhaps answering the question, "what is this picture about?") and that (b) supports the above argument by discussing the details of the image.

6. Put students into pairs and have them *draw* pictures based *solely* on their partner's original paragraph.

7. Have students look at the original photographs and compare them to their drawings in order to assess how accurate their arguments and descriptions are.

8. Have students change their original paragraph based on their partner's picture and revise what they've originally written to include those additions.

Rationale: My composition classes are driven by the idea that "Everything's an Argument," thus we spend time thinking about how visual texts as well as written ones make claims, persuade viewers, or send messages. Students are exposed to hundreds of images everyday and it is important for them to learn why a picture is a powerful rhetorical tool.

This activity can be used with any assignment that requires students to make claims about visual texts, whether they are analyzing ads, thinking about why certain photographs accompany magazine articles, or even discussing what pictures are used to grace the covers of novels. Most recently I have used it as part of a rhetorical analysis assignment where students are asked to identify and evaluate an author's/editor's use of *ethos, pathos, logos,* style, and visuals in an argumentative magazine article.

Overall, this activity works well with writers of all skill levels; it provides an accessible lesson about the importance of detail and the newness of the activity pushes both experienced and more inexperienced writers out of their comfort zone.

Potential Problems: Because image analysis can take place on a more unconscious level, students sometimes have a hard time articulating succinctly what argument a particular image is making. Asking the question, "What is this picture about?" helps students overcome this obstacle. Students also struggle with the amount of detail they need to provide in their paragraph. Comparing their drawing to the original photograph often gets a good laugh, but it also immediately allows students to see how accurate their description of the photograph was and how descriptive their paragraph actually was. Lastly, drawing usually sees the most student resistance. Many students don't like to draw, don't think they draw very well, or don't feel comfortable showing their artwork to others. In order to qualm their anxieties, I remind them that this is just for fun and that they are not being graded on their drawing skills. I also encourage them to complete the assignment using whatever artistic means necessary, even stick figures.

—m—

Reading the Magazine Ad
Ethos, Pathos *and* Logos *Group Activity*
• Martin J. Fashbaugh •

Abstract: In group work, students analyze magazine advertisements for elements of *ethos*, *pathos*, and *logos*.

This exercise can also be used to teach the elements of argumentation.

Duration: Approximately 15 minutes

Preparation: Magazine ads, enough for each group of students

Procedure: The purpose of this activity is to help students obtain a more thorough understanding of Aristotle's three rhetorical appeals: *ethos*, *pathos*, and *logos*.

Following a brief presentation (usually a handout and PowerPoint), I hand each group (consisting of three or four people) either an essay or magazine ad, asking them to find evidence of all three rhetorical appeals.

They are given approximately 15 minutes to find at least two pieces of evidence for each of the appeals.

Students must write down their responses, and, to ensure that every student is participating, groups must delegate responsibilities:

- one student will do the writing;
- another student will present their responses;
- and the remaining students will engage actively in the discussion.

To help ensure engagement, I monitor the discussions.

I have found that group work is especially helpful in assisting students in identifying each of the appeals and understanding how they work together to produce a desired effect.

Purpose: In either Composition I or Composition II, I frequently give a major essay assignment, which asks students to analyze and evaluate the use of ethos, pathos, and logos in a piece of visual or written rhetoric. This exercise better familiarizes them with these rhetorical terms so that they have a better idea of what I expect of them when they write their analytical/evaluative essays.

—⚭—

Visual Analysis Warm-Up
Learning Cultural Influences Through Imaginary Advertisement
• Becky Adnot-Haynes •

Abstract: Students create an imaginary product, develop a print ad for the product using drawing materials and magazine clippings, and as a class discuss the cultural influences that shaped their choices as an introduction to visual rhetoric.

This exercise also teaches cultural critique and deals with the nature of media.
Duration: 40 to 50 minutes
Materials: Instructors will need to bring to class magazine scraps, colored pencils, markers, etc., for the students to create their collages.

A document camera or overhead projector may be helpful for large classes where it might be hard to see students' final products, but isn't necessary.

Preparation: A discussion of visual rhetoric with examples of advertisements might be advisable.

Author's Notes: The following procedure generally breaks into five minutes to explain, 20 to complete the exercise in groups, and 15 minutes for discussion and sharing afterward.

This exercise best accompanies a visual analysis or advertisement analysis, but may also be used in discussions of cultural values.

Procedure:

Instructions to the Class (first five minutes): In small groups, task students with creating a fictional product and provide a very brief history.

- What does this product do? What company or what person produces it?

Then task students with creating an idea for a print ad that would sell this product.

Students Work in Groups: (This exercise generally takes about 20 minutes from this point onward.)

First, students should decide what value or values they will use to market their product; how will they make it appealing?

- Romance? Individualism? Patriotism? Family values? Tradition? Reliability?

Tell students to create a rough sketch using the materials provided, including text if applicable.

Also tell students not to worry about the artfulness of their drawings—stick figures are fine!

Students should have a specific demographic in mind for their product

- Are you trying to appeal to young people? Men? Working moms?

Inform students that they should be prepared to share their ideas with the class. This exercise is meant to be fun for students.

Follow-Up Discussion (15 minutes): As each group presents their advertisement, ask students questions about specific choices they made in creating their advertisements (scale of figures, placement of figures, representation of people, color, content of text, etc.).

Try to get students to identify the cultural values that they either purposely or unconsciously included in their advertisement (for example, did they assume that a vacuum cleaner would appeal to women?)

After they have completed the activity, ask students to share their creation with the class, as a way of beginning a discussion about visual rhetoric and the way that images impact consumers.

Rationale: This exercise also helps foster discussion about cultural values and gets students to begin to examine the choices made by the producers of images as a way of achieving a desired effect.

Potential Problems: Students who feel they have no artistic ability often feel self-conscious, but most students have fun with the activity once they're reassured that their drawing ability isn't what counts.

—ᴍ—

Their Own Visual Rhetoric
Using Student Photographs to Teach Ethos, Pathos, Logos
• Courtney Hitson •

Abstract: Students take or bring in photographs taken on their digital devices and present these to their fellow students in small groups; students are to determine if the photographer is using *ethos, pathos,* or *logos*.

Instructors have the option of assigning homework as either essays describing the experience or as blog postings in which students discuss their findings.

Duration: Generally one 45-minute exercise in the classroom, although two class periods can be used if, for one class period, students are sent outside the classroom to gather photographs.

Materials: Students will need digital cameras or electronic devices (such as iPhones or Androids) with which to take photographs.

The exercise requires a computer classroom so that students will be able to share digital photographs.

It is also helpful for instructors to locate an environment which would provide multiple opportunities for photography.

Preparation: Before starting the exercise, make sure that your students have a basic understanding of *ethos*, *pathos*, and *logos*.

Students should also have registered themselves on a blog-site, which they can use to post digital photographs.

Suggested Pre-Reading: "Reading Images Critically," in *Pocket Reference for Writers* by Toby Fulwiler and Alan R. Hayakawa.

Procedure:

First Class

I assigned students to groups of three to travel the city and snap photos. If you teach at a traditional university (outside of an urban area), have your students take their photos outside of class.

Second Class

During the next class period, I had my students reconvene into new groups and present their photos.

Fellow group members were then prompted to try and guess what sort of rhetorical device was being used—*ethos*, *pathos*, *logos*, or a combination of some sort.

Homework

Following this, the students were instructed to post the photos to their blogs and write on the rhetorical devices being used and justify the ad's use of *ethos, pathos,* or *logos*.

If you don't use blogs in the classroom, simply have your students turn in a short paper that discusses the same idea.

Rationale: Students are allowed to indulge their creativity, while familiarizing themselves with devices of rhetoric. In confronting rhetorical devices through a medium other than language, students are better able to identify and utilize rhetoric in texts. This exercise builds on the digital world contemporary students are already very familiar with.

Additional Author's Notes: This activity can be used with any assignment that requires students to make claims about visual texts, whether they are analyzing ads, thinking about why certain photographs accompany magazine articles, or even discussing what pictures are used to grace the covers of novels. Most recently I have used it as part of a rhetorical analysis assignment where students are asked to identify and evaluate an author's/editor's use of *ethos, pathos, logos*, style, and visuals in an argumentative magazine article.

—⚏—

Assignment
Photo Essay
• Fred Johnson •

Abstract: Students construct arguments out of photographs that they gather from Flicker websites.

Discussion: The photo essay explicitly reverses the formula from my freshman writing course's first assignment. In the first assignment, students create a list of observations, then analyze them in order to make generalizations about what they have observed. In the photo essay assignment, my students begin with a point they would like to make about a person, place, or thing, and they develop a series of photos designed to make that case—moving from generalization to backing for the generalization. In both assignments they must break down a whole thing into parts in order to make and defend a generalization about it, but I give them different starting points.

For my course, there are three major benefits to the photo essay format. The first benefit is that the assignment introduces visual evidence and visual rhetoric, which are integral to other assignments throughout the course. The second benefit, which is relevant even for courses where visual rhetoric is not a major component, is that the photo essay format pushes the idea that arrangement of evidence in a compelling way is crucial to an argument's success. The simplicity with which photos can be arranged and rearranged makes it easy for students to try several arrangements or to experiment with rhetorical tropes like comparison/contrast or metaphor, and this kind of thinking can be helpful to them as they develop evidence and structure for future essays. (A teacher might even require multiple versions of the photo essay, where students make the same point in different ways via different photo arrangements, or where they make different points by arranging the photos in different ways.) The third benefit is that the exercise emphasizes choosing compelling concrete details to make a case; my students have to ask what elements they can put into their pictures to help them make their cases as powerfully as possible.

Class preparation for the photo essay includes consideration of how photographers can use a few basic guidelines (like the rule of thirds) to improve their compositions; how the visual details in an image can communicate; how photographers can manipulate the visual details in images (honestly and dishonestly); how a caption or accompanying text can affect a viewer's perception of an image; how juxtaposing one image with another can almost compel viewers to draw conclusions about what the images mean; and how basic rhetorical moves (like comparison/contrast, illustration, and so on) can be made with visuals. Depending on your course's goals for teaching and working with visual rhetoric, you might do only some, or all, or more than all of these things. Certainly consideration of a few rhetorically powerful images can prepare students for making their own rhetorically powerful images. Errol Morris's "Liar, Liar Pants on Fire," an essay/blog post at the *New York Times* website makes a nice introduction to the ways captions and context affect image reception. Scott McCloud's *Understanding Comics*, particularly its chapter on "closure" in comics, provides some excellent ways to talk about what happens when images are juxtaposed with one another; especially helpful is McCloud's series of six typical comics transitions, explained with illustrations. And a basic understanding of shot angles and distances from film/cinematography can be learned and taught quickly; these tend to add a lot of visual power to my students' sequences.

The explanatory introduction is crucial, for them and for me. It is a place where they can make clear what they meant to do, in case they have not been 100 percent successful with their visual rhetoric. That makes it a useful reflective exercise for them and a helpful clarification for me, as I grade. It has become much easier to do an assignment like this since digital cameras, laptops, and high speed wireless Internet became the norm on campus. Still, I warn my students at the start of the course about the technical requirements of this assignment, so that they can make arrangements to borrow equipment, if needed. I continue to use the online photo sharing site Flickr.com for this assignment, in part because its photo sorting application makes it easy for my students to arrange and rearrange photos visually. That capability helps bring home lessons about arrangement and rhetoric. Other tools besides Flickr could be used, however, including desktop slideware applications like PowerPoint, so long as they allow students to easily sort and view and caption their visual sequences. I require 16 photos in my current version of this assignment, but most students exceed that number, sometimes by a lot, because of the requirement that they use McCloud's comics transitions and another rhetorical strategy from my rhetorical strategies handout. This means you may want to put a top limit on the number of photos included, though I have not found that to be necessary. On the technical end, I do not give a great deal of class time to learning the software. Instead, I point my students toward basic tutorials and encourage them to help one another, and that is enough for the student population at my institution. Other contexts might require more class time given over to technical skill building.

Included: Assignment sheet (two pages), a "simple rhetorical strategies" sheet referenced in the assignment, and workshop instructions. (Because my Flickr help sheet goes out-of-date frequently, as the software changes, I have not included it.)

— · — · — · — · — · — · — · — · — · — · — · — · — · — · —

ASSIGNMENT SHEET

Flickr's In-House Guided Tour: http://www.flickr.com/tour/

Three Due Dates: Sun. 9/26, before midnight: Flickr Site created, link posted to wiki ("Photo Essay Links" page)

Mon. 9/27, at class time: photos shot, uploaded to Flickr, and ready for you to work with in class

Fri. 10/1, at 5:00 p.m.: photo "sets" in final form for grading, with captions and opening essay

Requirements

- 20 to 30 interesting photos (at least), shot digitally and ready to be loaded onto a computer. (Shoot a lot of digital photos to give yourself plenty of options.)
- At least 16 shots (but likely more) posted to (and later arranged on) your own Flickr account.
- Explanatory introduction (300 to 500 words) on Flickr, arranged photo "set" on Flickr, and captions on Flickr.
- Use of at least two of Scott McCloud's transitions, *not including the "non-sequitur" transition* and at least one other rhetorical strategy from the "Simple Rhetorical Strategies" sheet.

Your Mission

For this project, you'll use visual rhetoric—in the form of a series of photos—to represent something: maybe a person, maybe a place or event, maybe even an interesting object. The choice is yours. Whatever *subject* you choose, you will want to take a lot of pictures so that, as you *arrange your photos in a meaningful order*, you'll have many options to choose from. You will make your photos available to the world using the online photo sharing site Flickr.com. (See "Presenting Your Photos" on page two of the assignment sheet for further info about how you need to set up your photo set.)

Equipment

You'll need a *digital* camera, or a *friend* with a digital camera. (If you have a cell phone camera, that will work, too, *if*, and *only if*, you can get the photos from your camera onto a flash drive or onto your computer. Please let me know right away if you have trouble finding a camera to use.)

Comics Transitions + "Simple Rhetorical Strategies"

Scott McCloud suggests that there are six different kinds of transitions that a comics artist might use to organize images. You need to take advantage of at least two different kinds of comics transition in your final photo essay. You should also make good use of at least one of the strategies on the separate "Simple Rhetorical Strategies" handout. To get the most from

McCloud's transitions and/or from those "Simple Rhetorical Strategies," get familiar with them before you shoot photos, and shoot some photos that will fit the patterns they suggest.

Gathering Data: Photos with a Purpose

You should shoot at least 20 to 30 (and maybe many more) interesting photos that can visually communicate something about your subject. Using the camera tricks and tips we discuss in class, try to go beyond simple snapshots. Choose moments that are meaningful. Grab some close-up shots of details that are significant in some way. Try to combine pictures of objects and pictures of people. If possible, do both—some action shots and some still shots. And always keep in mind the possible ways one of your captured images can communicate something crucial about your subject. That is, try to shoot pictures that will show, visually, the *character* and *qualities* of your subject.

Taken together, the 16 (or more) photos you choose to include in your photo essay should be able to make some kind of statement about your subject. As with the observation-to-analysis exercise, your job here is to look for patterns, this time in your photos. Look for repeated themes or ideas, and then decide on a generalization you can make and support about your subject using your photos. You should look to make a *true* generalization, of course. Your goal should be to find a specific, interesting, unique-to-you generalization, then to arrange and caption your photos in a way that supports your generalization. (Important Note: Carefully read the Flickr help sheet's section on uploading photos to Flickr, which can be really easy or really hard, depending on how you do it.)

Presenting Your Photos, Making Your Argument

We will begin work together on this portion of the project during our in-class workshop (see project dates, above). If you would like to start earlier, you're welcome to do so, of course, but you may need to come to me for some technical help with Flickr's organization tools.

Once you've uploaded your photos to your Flickr site, you should create a "Photo Set" for them. Essentially, Flickr lets you group selected photos together, and it automatically turns them into a little photo essay. (There's even a slide show version.)

To complete this portion of the assignment, you need to do three things with your photo set: put your photos in a purposeful order, caption them, and add a short, explanatory introduction.

Purposeful Order: This step is the hardest, and it is crucial to your success. Give it substantial time and creative energy. Flickr's photo organization tools (which are built into the site online) make it easy to arrange and rearrange your photos within a "set." You should arrange your photos in a way that helps them to *make a point* of some kind about your subject, as explained above. To create the best possible photo essay, you should put some *serious thought* into the way you organize your photos. What patterns do you see in the photos you're using? Can you arrange them based on categories? Can you build a case? Find the order that best *leads* people, step by purposeful step, to understand and accept the generalization you want to make—that conveys the message you want to send and will show people the most about your subject. Ask yourself how you can take advantage of the organizing principles on the

"Simple Rhetorical Strategies" handout. *Don't forget to incorporate at least two of Scott McCloud's comics transitions and one other "simple rhetorical strategy."*

Captions: Caption at least 10 of your images. As Errol Morris explains in his "Liar, Liar" essay, captions are an important part of the rhetoric of photos, directing our attention to certain aspects of photos and suggesting how we should understand them. *You'll use captions as a powerful tool to guide your readers,* step by step, in their experience and understanding of your photo essay. (Please use formal writing conventions in your captions—proper grammar and spelling, etc. You may do okay on a photo essay with poorly written captions, but you won't receive an "A" on it.) The best captions will add something to your reader's understanding of your photo essay's subject. You might use descriptive captions, but you could also choose to use captions that are poetic in some way.

Introduction: The introduction goes on the main page of your Flickr "Photo Set," just below the image on that page. The introduction should be a fairly brief, fairly technical discussion (probably 300 to 500 words) identifying the subject of your photo essay, clarifying what you are trying to say about the subject (your basic argument), and reflecting on how you selected and arranged your images to help you make your point. This can (and maybe *should*) be a fairly technical discussion of choices you made about angles, shot distances, subjects of shots, organizational strategies, use of captions, and so on. It should reveal how your growing understanding of the rhetoric of images helped you to create a stronger photo essay. *Be sure your introduction points to the places where you've taken advantage of Scott McCloud's comics transitions and strategies from the "simple rhetorical strategies" sheet.*

Scoring Rubric

10—Introduction is present, formally written, and meets the technical requirements explained on the assignment sheet.

10—Captions are present, grammatically correct, and make a substantial contribution to the photo essay's argument/meaning.

20—Subject is clear and the photo essay says something substantial about the subject.

30—Purposeful Arrangement: Each photo advances the photo essay's argument in some way; you have included at least two "McCloud" transitions and one additional "simple rhetorical strategy."

30—Verve, energy, and variety of photos (including use of multiple appropriate shot angles and shot distances, and use of the rule of thirds).

- -

SIMPLE RHETORICAL STRATEGIES TO ORGANIZE & ENHANCE YOUR CASE

These rhetorical strategies work well with *both images and words.* When you're stuck for a way to make your case, one of the strategies here might help you find a way forward.

"What Is It?" Strategies | Focused on the qualities of the subject.

Description. As you begin to make a case about a subject (person, place, thing, or idea), describe the subject honestly in the clearest way possible, *highlighting the details that will best help you prove your claim* or make your point about the subject. Visually, this might be done with a series of photographs pointing to different important details.

Definition. Clarify the meaning of the subject or idea. While description focuses on concrete details, definition (which may still use concrete details) tries to explain the more abstract meaning of a thing.

Illustration. Give an example. If you say something is interesting, exciting, worthwhile, or likely to destroy the world, provide an example of your subject doing or being what you say it is.

Spatial Order. Useful for description of a space or of a series of things that often occur together. Move through the space in a logical way that helps your readers to understand it. Or describe a thing systematically (head to foot, for example, or front to back) in a way that makes it easy to envision.

"This Is Like That" Strategies | Focused on things similar to (or different than) the subject.

Classification. Fit your subject into understandable categories. How does this thing you're talking about fit in with things we might already understand in some way? What is it *like*? Classifications can be basic, like showing that an athlete (big category) can be classified as a soccer player (smaller category). You could go farther by classifying the player in terms of her playing position (even smaller category).

Comparison or Contrast. Clarify your description of a thing by comparing it to another thing or by showing how it is different from another thing. Here you may be focused not on large categories so much as on making an illuminating pairing of your subject with something else. A football player compared to a soccer player, for example. Or two football players with different kinds of skills, compared and contrasted. Or texting contrasted to making a phone call. Imagine how a music writer argues for the uniqueness of a musician among other musicians—telling who he's like, but also telling how he is distinct from others similar to him. Or imagine a sportscaster talking about what makes a team stand out this season from similar teams. Visually, you could do this with two images—the subject followed by the thing you are comparing or contrasting to the subject. With some staging (or photoshopping) you could create one image that contains a comparison or contrast inside itself.

Metaphor or Analogy. Another comparison strategy, but with more poetic license. You should remember this from high school English classes. If you argue that some athlete who is *not* a boxer is "the Mohammed Ali of his sport," you're deep into analogy/metaphor territory. If you say that a businessman approaches his work like a gladiator, you're doing analogy/metaphor. Comparisons of two seemingly un-like things can be great for getting at the hard-to-explain qualities of a thing.

"How It Works" Strategies | Focused on describing a process.

Process. Break down a process into significant pieces to show what is important about each piece.

Chronological Order. This is a process or event explained in the order it happened, again highlighting the most important moments in the process and explaining what makes those moments significant.

Cause/Effect. A cause/effect argument can be a kind of process argument, obviously, but it is particularly focused on the consequences of an action or attitude.

Narration/Story. Stories contain a lot of complex information, and the best of them can contain all of the above rhetorical strategies, from every category. Consider whether a good, specific story can help you make your case.

—··—·—··—·—··—·—··—·—··—·—··—·—··—·—··—·—··—·—·

PHOTO ESSAY ASSIGNMENT: IN-CLASS WORKSHOP

Workshop Instructions

Part I: In Class, with a Partner:

1. Open your photos in the Flickr Organizer, create your set, and put them in the order that makes sense to you. Don't spend too much time on this, at this point. It's just a "rough draft" of your order.

2. Explain your set to your partner: Why have you sequenced the photos this way? What sorts of photography techniques (like angles, shot lengths, rule of thirds, framing, "McCloud" transitions, and so on) are you using to make your photos more vivid, interesting, and memorable? What other simple rhetorical moves are you making?

3. Work with your partner to come up with alternate ways to arrange the set, and be sure to consider photos that you might add or subtract to make the set more effective.

Part II: After Class. Email Your Partner (and Me) Responses to the Following:

1. In your opening, talk about how the set makes use of an interesting array of photographic techniques, or talk about how your partner might make better use of photographic techniques like framing, shot angles, shot distances, and the rule of thirds.

2. Talk about how the set already makes good use of sequencing.

3. Make some suggestions about ways to improve (or completely change) the sequence and offer some ideas about images to add to or remove from the set to help it communicate more vividly and completely.

—·m·—

Assignment
Critical Analysis of a Documentary Film
• Fred Johnson •

Abstract: In this essay, the author explains how he uses documentary films to demonstrate that communication is comprised of multiple messages, to task students with making a systematic argument, and then to write an analytical essay based upon this skill-set (worksheets are included).

The second essay explains how students expand on the film essay in an assignment that joins observation to analysis.

Essay: Critical Analysis: The first major writing assignment in my freshman writing course is an analytical essay.

In that assignment, students are required to closely observe two documentary films and then choose one to analyze formally. I ask my students to make a case about how the filmmaker has made some point with his or her documentary, and I discourage them from trying to identify *the* point of the film.

The idea is that they will see their chosen film as a complex rhetorical object; I hope they will begin to see how the filmmaker, like any sophisticated communicator, is making a lot of different points, some explicit and some less explicit, some intended and some perhaps incidental to the central narrative.

I have (for example) used Alexandra Pelosi's 2002 documentary *Journeys with George* as an option for this assignment. The film nicely resists being boiled down to a point or two about its apparent subject (George W. Bush during his first presidential campaign), and it allows engaged students to discover subtle narrative threads about things like the lives of reporters, the shaping of political narratives, and even the nature of friendship.

For their analytical essays, I ask my students to avoid (please!) retelling the movie in order and to draw together evidence of all kinds (including visual, cinematic, and aural) from throughout the film, to show how the filmmaker has made a case systematically. So I ask my students to make a systematic case about an argument made systematically by the content of the film, whether or not that argument seems to lead to the "main" point (or even an intended point) of the film.

By the time my students write this analytical essay, they need to have a sense of what it means to do an analysis, they need to have begun thinking about what it means to build a case (rather than just make a series of loosely related points), and they need to have begun to think about how evidence and examples can be used to build a case. To that end, the semester actually begins with two preliminary, relatively low-stakes analysis assignments. In the first of those two assignments, my students gather observational data by observing a slice of day-to-day campus life, then look for patterns in the data, and finally create a document that makes sense of the data. In the second assignment, my students choose a point that they would like to make about something—person, place, or thing. They then take a series of photographs that they hope will help them make that point, and they arrange and caption those photographs carefully to communicate the point.

Discussion: Observation-to-Analysis: In the data-gathering assignment (which I explicitly call an "observation-to-analysis" assignment) my students collect data and then make sense of it; in the photo essay assignment they choose a point to make and then gather and arrange the evidence needed to make that point visually. Both assignments demand a movement from pieces of evidence to a whole message, and so both require engagement with analysis as a process: breaking the whole into parts, closely observing the parts, defending conclusions about the whole based on what they have concluded about the parts. In that context, I present the films to them as complex rhetorical objects ripe for close observation and analysis.

Important class discussions leading up to this assignment introduce the notion of rhetoric, the whole-parts-whole analytical process, making and defending generalizations, the merits of close observation, the demerits of five-paragraph essays, and the ways concrete language can add power and clarity to communication.

Because my students complete a photo essay, and because film analysis requires that they be attuned to visual argument, we spend considerable class time thinking about visual rhetoric, too: basic photography tips, basic cinematography (shot angles and distances, as used to create emphasis), the rhetoric of images, the power of adding captions to photos, and the uses of sequence to communicate (aided by some basic comics and film theory). The film analysis assignment could be done, in some form, and quite successfully, without all of this, however.

What is most necessary is that class discussions following the films focuses on the ways that the filmmaker gets his or her messages across to the audience, rather than on the messages themselves. That is, reflecting on the meanings of the films should be a secondary goal, at best. Choosing films that are *interesting*—rhetorically and topically—rather than deliberately tendentious helps with this goal. To that end, I require my students to take thorough notes during the screenings and to talk as a class about the kinds of messages being sent, the kinds of evidence presented, the camera work used, and so on. I cue them to focus on the filmmakers behind the films before they watch the films. In an out-of-class prewriting exercise, I ask them to begin informally drawing together their thoughts about one filmmaker's messages and message-sending techniques, and during an in-class workshop day I guide them through refining their major claims and gathering evidence of all kinds, and then I have them talk with a small group of classmates about their developing papers, asking their peers for advice about additional evidence in support of their claims.

Included Below: The assignment sheet (two pages) and prewriting instructions.

--·--·--·--·--·--·--·--·--·--·--·--·--·--·--·--·--·--·--·--

CRITICAL ANALYSIS ESSAY (ANALYSIS OF A FILM)

Length: 5–9 pages

The Assignment

For this essay, you will choose to write about either *Journeys with George* or *It Might Get Loud*. This is the major question you'll answer with your essay:

How does the filmmaker systematically use a technique, or a set of techniques, to make a point of some kind?

How will you do this? You will begin as soon as you begin viewing these films, by watching actively and taking good notes about what you're seeing. That's how you'll start to collect great raw data for your essay. In class, we'll talk about what you saw and begin to draw some conclusions about how the films work—how they try to suggest conclusions about characters, events, and ideas. That's the next big step. Finally, based on your careful viewing, our in-class discussions, and your own reflections on the films, you'll write your critical analysis, offering and defending your answer to the question above.

Beginning (Claim), Middle (Evidence), End (So What?)

As we've discussed in class, most good essays have clear beginnings, middles, and ends.

Beginning

In the *beginning* of your essay, you ought to be letting us know about the claim you're going to make and hinting at how you'll be proving it. Recommendation: If the introduction is giving you trouble, *write it later* in the process. If you know what claim you're going to make, you can skip ahead and start writing your evidence paragraphs, which are often easier to construct.

Your paper should have a *major claim, established somewhere in the first paragraph.* The claim should tell us that the filmmaker wants us to draw a certain kind of conclusion, see some sort of reality, or understand some person, place, or thing differently than we otherwise might. Remember that in the rest of the paper you will be laying out the evidence: talking about the sorts of moves the filmmaker makes throughout his or her film, explaining how those moves are used and how they convey messages, considering what has been included and how it affects the film's messages.

Middle

In the *middle*, you should be presenting and evaluating evidence. Rather than retelling the film (book-report style), you should be grouping together bits of evidence from all over the film in logical ways. (E.g., from *It Might Get Loud,* you could gather moments when Jack White appears and explain how the filmmaker, Davis Guggenheim, creates a "Jack White" character. From *Journeys*, you could gather together moments where Bush is funny and explain how Alexandra Pelosi systematically reveals his humor.) Your evidence can include many things, including, but not limited to, points about techniques chosen by the filmmakers, moments of dialogue, images or imagery used consistently throughout the film, single images or moments that are telling.

You'll want to find a purposeful, rhetorically effective way to group and arrange your evidence. Your paragraphs should lead us naturally, step by step, to your conclusion, and there should be a clear reason why one paragraph follows the next as you develop your argument and convince us to agree with your claim. (The "Simple Rhetorical Strategies" handout might be helpful to you.)

Also, remember this: You're not just listing evidence. You're explaining how it all works together. Don't just drop in a quote. Introduce the quote, give the quote, then explain what it tells us and why you're pointing it out to us. Don't just list a series of moments. Introduce them, and then explain what they reveal to us, considered together.

End

And the end is your "So What?" So what has all this well-presented evidence shown us about the film? How can we now appreciate the artistry of the filmmaker and the complexity of the film in ways we might not have appreciated those things before? Why is this essay a worthwhile one for people who are interested in this film, this topic, or this filmmaker?

A Note: We're Building On...

This essay builds on both the observation-to-analysis exercises (which led to the writing of your letters, business proposals, and short essays) and the photo assignment (where you thought hard about visual rhetoric and about evidence arrangement). Here, you'll closely observe a film, noticing its use of rhetoric to say what it says, and then you'll analyze what you've seen. As with the observations and the photo essay, you'll then arrange your observations so as to make a clear, interesting point.

Advice: Talk About One Point or Idea, Not THE Point or THE Idea

I'm not interested here in seeing you tell me *the* point or *the* major idea of the film. Both of the films we're watching are so complex that there isn't just one major point or one theme or one idea expressed in the whole film. (That's true of most interesting things in the world, from books and movies to national elections to good conversations with friends.) Instead of identifying *the* major point, you're going to reveal how the filmmaker expresses and defends *one* idea (or set of ideas) among many.

This doesn't mean that you're looking for a moment in the film when the filmmaker says something like, "This is an idea I want you to understand: George W. Bush is kind of a goofy, funny, likeable guy when you strip away the politics." What it means is that you're looking to see the filmmaker expressing ideas craftily, through smart, rhetorical use of stories, images, dialogue, and other tools.

Advice: Group, Don't Summarize

This is a big deal: Don't retell the movie. If you find your paper is organized according to the order of the movie—as a summary or condensation of the story—you probably need to improve the rhetorical strategy behind your organization. Summary-style papers that primarily retell a story in condensed form tend to end up repeating themselves *a lot*. By the third time Bush reappears on the plane, the summarizer would be saying something like, "And, once again, Pelosi shows Bush's funny side." And your audience/readers will be exasperated with you: "Yes, you've said that. So what? Move on, please. Get to a point." So a better strategy for you might be to (for example) group Bush's different airplane visits together in a paragraph about Bush's appearances on the plane. Or maybe to write a paragraph about all the funny Bush moments in the film. Bottom line: As you did in your observation-to-analysis writing, *you need to group your major points together, not retell everything that happened.*

If you wanted to look at Alexandra Pelosi's portrayal of Bush as a nicer guy than many people believe him to be, you would want to observe and analyze the moments when Bush appears in the film. You might talk about what those moments have in common. You might do a paragraph on the development of the George-and-Alexandra relationship. You might talk about the contrast Pelosi establishes between Bush in the press and Bush as the guy who shows up on the plane now and then.

If you wanted to talk about how Davis Guggenheim delivers the idea that a musician's personal history affects the way he plays his instrument, you could talk about Guggenheim's overall strategy of giving insight into the non-musical backgrounds of the guitarists he features. You could look at how the music of each guitarist is presented in the context of his life. But you might also look (for contrast) at how the musicians share and get along and have a lot in common when they talk together about playing guitar.

Any of those strategies require you to leave behind plain old summary and start analyzing evidence from across the film, grouping it so you can comment on what the filmmaker has accomplished *systematically* through the film.

About Scoring

This is a more traditional essay, so there is no formal rubric for it. "A" papers will likely feature a clearly articulated major claim; very strong organization, leading to a strong, earned conclusion that explains "So what?"; a substantial amount of specific evidence from the film, artfully presented in defense of the major claim; and excellent grammar and mechanics.

CRITICAL ANALYSIS WORKSHOP, PART 1

Before you get going, remember the central question for the Critical Analysis essay:

How does the filmmaker systematically use a technique, or a set of techniques, to make a point of some kind?

Step One: State your claim.

Though neither filmmaker comes right out and says, "Hey, *this* is my major point," both filmmakers make several points about several different things. Some points are very big (like Alexandra Pelosi's major point about how much the process of reporting on a presidential candidate distorts our view of the candidate), and some are smaller (like Pelosi's point about how being in the travelling press corps is hard on the personal lives of reporters). You'll want to choose one point that one of the filmmakers is making. (I hope you'll choose the point that you, personally, find the most interesting.) Your initial claim will run something like this: [This filmmaker] uses [these interesting visual and verbal techniques] to argue that [a particular point is true].

You can change your claim as you write later this week and next (and until the essay is due), but take a shot, right now, at putting your claim into words, just as a starting point.

Step Two: 20 minutes of focused writing

Option 1: **Outline** an argument for a critical analysis of your film's smart use of a technique or a set of techniques to make a rhetorical point. You may choose to outline in any way that makes sense to you, but you should do so with the goal of creating a thorough outline that someone else could understand. You should aim to show the step-by-step process you'll use to make a claim about how the film works, show evidence that your claim is valid, and explain how you have shown us something interesting and worthwhile about how the film works. Spend a minimum of 20 minutes (though, depending on your personality, outlining might take much longer).

Option 2: **Freewriting**. If you choose this option, you will write steadily for 20 minutes about the techniques your chosen filmmaker uses in his or her film to make his or her case. This is unedited writing, so don't worry about spelling and grammar and that sort of thing. Do worry about putting down a lot of ideas. "Freewriting" means writing freely on a subject, without worries about whether what you're saying is good, bad, right, wrong, or anything else. You're just dumping out lots of ideas. The only guidelines is this: stay focused on the ways that the film works. Don't wander into irrelevant material unrelated to the film.

Step Three: We'll do much more with these materials in class.

Note: Hold onto the work you do for all three steps. You'll turn it in along with your final essay, as a record of your process, evidence of your work, and proof of active participation.

Reading the Opening Credit Sequence
Visual Analysis Assignment Sheet
• Tessa Mellas •

Abstract: In this assignment, students "analyze the cultural values, attitudes, desires, and concerns conveyed" through the opening credit sequence of a movie or TV show.

The assignment sheet provides a script, suggests approaches, and poses questions to lead students through the assignment.

Duration: 50 minutes

Materials: Overhead projection, Internet access or DVD player

Preparation: Instructors will need to practice analysis with students by projecting credit sequences from YouTube onto a projection screen.

Some credit sequences that work well in class discussions are those from *Full House, Saved by the Bell,* and *Fraggle Rock.*

When I analyzed these sequences with my students, they came up with interpretations about how *Full House*'s sequence juxtaposes images of San Francisco with images of three men raising daughters in order to prepare America for same-sex parenting. They talked about how *Saved by the Bell* portrays and encourages anti-intellectualism. And they talked about how the power structure between the giants and the Fraggles is indicative of race issues in America.

Other programs mentioned on the assignment sheet include *M. *A. *S. *H., Gilmore Girls, The Brady Bunch,* and *Gossip Girls.*

Procedure: See the following assignment sheet.

Rationale: This assignment targets the following skills: *visual analysis, critical thinking, visual rhetoric, description, use of evidence to back up an interpretation.*

The essay teaches students to interpret visual images by looking at a video sequence and analyzing the rhetorical moves, symbols, messages, and values conveyed by the creators. Visual interpretation is an important skill in our increasingly media-based culture. The strength of this assignment is that students will find the topic fun. They love television, so this essay won't feel like a chore, and they will be enthusiastic when the assignment is introduced. Also, working through the essay in steps is fun in class (though you might have the *Fraggle Rock* theme song stuck in your head for a week).

Potential Problems: Although students are accustomed to seeing credit sequences of television shows, they have likely never analyzed them closely. Students quickly find that they don't have much experience in picking apart visual images, though they see them every day. It will take practice and time to get them to dig deep in their interpretations rather than just giving surface level reads.

ASSIGNMENT SHEET

The Assignment

Most of us have memorized the theme song and sequence of images that accompany the credits at the opening of our favorite TV show. But how much attention do we pay to what these images are actually saying?

In a three to five page essay, you will discuss how the credit sequence from a television show (of your choice) comments on an aspect of American culture. You will analyze the cultural values, attitudes, desires, and concerns conveyed through the sequence. You will explain what the sequence reveals about American culture at the time the television show aired. You will discuss how the design choices in the television sequence help to communicate certain conscious or unconscious messages about American culture.

Your Argument

In an essay that asks you do interpretive work, you will be arguing for your interpretation. You *won't* be deciding if the images are good or bad, or whether you like or dislike them. Your argument will be that you believe the video sequence is sending *this* particular message about American culture, and you will use evidence from the video sequence to support your interpretation.

Research

Research isn't required for this paper, but it is likely that you will use it. Any information that you take from online or print sources must be cited. Use your best judgment to determine whether the source is reliable or not. We will discuss how to cite media sources in class and will look at how to use the library's resources to your advantage.

Getting Started

To start organizing your thoughts, analyzing the video sequence, and figuring out what cultural messages are embedded in the credit sequence you've chosen, answer these questions in as much detail as possible. We will do freewrites to answer these questions in class and for homework. Some of these answers might end up in the paper. Some may not.

What do you see in the opening shots or in the credit sequence?

(a) What do the characters look like?
(b) What are the characters doing?
(c) What does the setting look like?
(d) What colors are used?
(e) What types of shots are used—long shots, close shots, action shots?
(f) What type of lighting is used?
(g) What type of mood is established? How?

How do the images in the credit sequence establish what the show is about? How do the images introduce the characters, setting, and plot of the show? What can you tell about the characters, setting, and plot just from the opening shots or the credit sequence?

What audience do you think this show is targeted towards? Be as specific as possible.
Identify the specific age group this show is aimed at? How do you know?
Is this show aimed at one gender more than another? How do you know?
Is this show aimed at a particular class or race? How do you know?
What time is or was this show on? What day of the week? What does this say about the audience that is being targeted?
Examine the time period during which this show aired.

What was happening in the United States at this time? Look at the major historical events of that time (wars, cultural movements, elections, famous figures). What was the general condition of the country at the time (economic prosperity or decline, major concerns, fears, lifestyles)? Was this pilot episode aired post or pre–9/11?

Is the show set in the same time period or a different time period than the air date? What might this say about what American audiences are looking for at the time?

Note: Any information that you gather about the time period of the show or about the show itself must be cited. Write down relevant information needed for citations. We will use MLA style.

- How do the images persuade the audience to tune in every week? What in the opening shots or credit sequence will appeal to Americans? Consider these aspects.
- What do the characters look like? Why do the characters' looks appeal to Americans?
- What key themes are introduced in the sequence? Why might these themes appeal to Americans?
- Why might the setting, the time period and the place appeal to Americans?
- What type of show is it? Detective show? Doctor drama? Sit-com/Comedy? Family show? Why might this type of show appeal to Americans at this time period?
- Now identify the key messages about American culture that are embedded in the television sequence. Here are some sample theses:

The credit sequence of *M*A*S*H* highlights America's concern in 1972 with the Vietnam War, their fears for the safety of family and friends, and their concerns about the foolishness of the U.S. government's involvement.

Fraggle Rock's theme song sequence introduces the show's themes of racial diversity and the interconnectivity of different societal groups; this speaks directly to the movement in the 1980s to become aware of and combat racial prejudices and social conflicts.

The opening shots of *Gilmore Girls* shows the main character Lorelei walking through an idyllic New England small town. These shots show America's yearning for safety, security and small town values in the year 2000, when *Gilmore Girls* first aired.

The credit sequence from *The Brady Bunch* shows that though Americans were increasingly divorcing and remarrying in the late 1960's, it was still important to present a pristine familial image to the public.

The opening shots of the *Gossip Girl* pilot episode emphasize contemporary teens' obsession with wealth, technology, and drama.

Last Word

Have fun with this assignment! Dig deep! Come see me if you need help!

About the Contributors

Becky **Adnot-Haynes** is a Ph.D. candidate in English at the University of Cincinnati.

Leslie **Batty** is a professor of English at Purdue University.

Laura L. **Beadling** is a professor of English at Youngstown State University.

DeMisty **Bellinger-Delfeld** is a professor of English at Fitchburg State University.

Svetlana **Bochman** is director of the Writing Center at the City College of New York.

Geoff **Bouvier** is a Ph.D. candidate in poetry at Florida State University.

Christina **Boyles** is a professor of English at Baylor University.

Russell **Brickey** is an independent writer.

William Lusk **Coppage** is a poet and writer for the *Delta Democrat-Times*.

Rita D. **Costello** is director of freshman and sophomore English at McNeese State University.

Francesco **Crocco** is an associate professor of English at Borough of Manhattan Community College.

Christine **Cucciarre** is a professor of English at the University of Delaware.

Catherine Gubernatis **Dannen** is an assistant professor of English at Alabama State University.

Gerardo **Del Guercio** teaches at Group SLC and the Shakespeare Language School.

Melissa **Dennihy** is an English instructor at Queensborough Community College, City University of New York.

Chad **Engbers** is an associate professor of English at Calvin College.

Mike **Farmer** teaches at Gaston College and Cleveland Community College.

Martin J. **Fashbaugh** is an assistant professor of English at Black Hills State University.

Roslyn Reso **Foy** is an adjunct professor of English at Tulane University.

Priscilla **Glanville** is an associate professor of English at State College of Florida, Sarasota-Manatee.

John P. **Hazen** is an English lecturer at Youngstown State University.

Josh **Herron** is an English lecturer at Anderson University.

Mary Lynne Gasaway **Hill** is an associate professor of English at St. Mary's University.

Courtney **Hitson** teaches at Columbia College Chicago.

Brianne **Howard** teaches at Youngstown State University.

J.D. **Isip** is an English instructor at Texas A&M University–Commerce.

Fred **Johnson** is an associate professor of English at Whitworth University.

Afaf (Effat) Jamil **Khogeer** teaches at Umm Al-Qura University, Saudi Arabia.

Denise **Landrum-Geyer** is an assistant professor of English at Southwestern Oklahoma State University.

Debra Rudder **Lohe** is director of the Reinert Center for Transformative Teaching at Saint Louis University.

Kathleen **Maloney** is an associate professor of English at St. Mary's University.

Lauren **Matus** is a visiting assistant professor at Miami University, Middleton, Ohio.

Joseph **McCarty** teaches at California State University, Stanislaus.

Mary Jo **McCloskey** is a writing lecturer at Manhattanville College.

Tessa **Mellas** teaches at Bowling Green State University.

Kristin **Mock** teaches at the University of Arizona.

Lori **Mumpower** is associate director of the Center for Teaching and Learning Excellence at Embry-Riddle Aeronautical University.

Alexandra **Oxner** is an English instructor at Florida State University.

Christine **Photinos** is an associate professor of English at National University, San Diego.

Ben P. **Robertson** is an associate professor of English at Troy University.

Abigail G. **Scheg** is an assistant professor of English at Elizabeth City State University.

Maria L. **Soriano** is director of the Writing Center at John Carroll University.

Nichole E. **Stanford** teaches at City University of New York Graduate Center.

Chelsea R. **Swick** is a Ph.D. candidate in English at Kent State University.

Virginia **Tucker** is coordinator of interdisciplinary programs at Old Dominion University.

Gary **Vaughn** is an associate professor of English at the University of Cincinnati.

Beth **Walker** teaches at the University of Tennessee at Martin.

Dana **Washington** teaches at Lock Haven University.

Martha A. **Webber** is a professor of English at California State University Fullerton.

Rick **Williams** is an English instructor at Youngstown State University.

Dennis A. **Yommer, Jr.,** is an English instructor at Youngstown State University.

Index